# Talking About Crime and Criminals

## PROBLEMS AND ISSUES IN THEORY DEVELOPMENT IN CRIMINOLOGY

**Don C. Gibbons**

*Seaview University*

PRENTICE HALL, *Englewood Cliffs, New Jersey 07632*

*Library of Congress Cataloging-in-Publication Data*

GIBBONS, DON C.
    Talking about crime and criminals : problems and issues in theory
development in criminology / Don C. Gibbons.
        p.   cm.
    Includes bibliographical references and index.
    ISBN   0-13-669137-4
    1. Criminology.   2. Criminal behavior.   3. Crime.   I. Title.
HV6025.G47   1994
364—dc20                                                          93-11980
                                                                        CIP

Acquisitions editor: Nancy Roberts
Interior design: Joan Stone
Editorial/production supervision: Merrill Peterson
Copy editor: Jan McDearmon
Cover designer: Carol Ceraldi
Production coordinatior: Mary Ann Gloriande
Editorial assistant: Pat Naturale

©1994 by Prentice-Hall, Inc.
A Paramount Communications Company
Englewood Cliffs, New Jersey 07632

Printed in the United States of America

10   9   8   7   6   5   4   3   2   1

ISBN   0-13-669137-4

PRENTICE-HALL INTERNATIONAL (UK) LIMITED, *London*
PRENTICE-HALL OF AUSTRALIA PTY. LIMITED, *Sydney*
PRENTICE-HALL CANADA INC., *Toronto*
PRENTICE-HALL HISPANOAMERICANA, S.A., *Mexico*
PRENTICE-HALL OF INDIA PRIVATE LIMITED, *New Delhi*
PRENTICE-HALL OF JAPAN, INC., *Tokyo*
SIMON & SCHUSTER ASIA PTE. LTD., *Singapore*
EDITORA PRENTICE-HALL DO BRASIL, LTDA., *Rio de Janeiro*

# Contents

**CHAPTER 11**

# The Future of Criminological Theory, 199

# Preface

In a recent essay, John Braithwaite (1989a: 133), one of the new stars of criminology, offered these pessimistic comments about the state of the field:

> The present state of criminology is one of abject failure in its own terms. We cannot say anything convincing to the community about crime; we cannot prescribe policies that will work to reduce crime; we cannot in all honesty say that societies spending more on criminological research get better criminal justice policies than those that spend little or nothing on criminology.

Braithwaite's negative remarks centered on the failure of criminologists to develop valid theories which explain crime and which might also inform public policy. He is one of a number of critics who have complained that little theoretical progress has been made in criminology in recent years.

I do not argue that all is well with criminology and that we currently have a wealth of clearly articulated theories which have been subjected to research scrutiny and have been found to be largely if not wholly accurate. At the same time, when compared to earlier decades, criminology has grown markedly, both in the number of theoretical formulations and in the sophistication of many of them.

I have examined the origins and growth of sociological criminology in the United States in an earlier book (Gibbons, 1979), and I provide an abbreviated version of this developmental history in the present work. Both of these sources indicate that American criminology arose in the early

1900s. However, it was not until the 1930s that a truly sociological version of criminological analysis began to take shape, largely through the pioneering efforts of Shaw and McKay, Sutherland, Sellin, and a few other scholars.

In the early 1950s, three undergraduate textbooks captured most of the market: Barnes and Teeters's *New Horizons in Criminology* (1951), Reckless's *The Crime Problem* (1955), and Sutherland and Cressey's *Principles of Criminology* (1955). The first contained indignant remarks about the crimes of the powerful, along with a vigorous argument in favor of treatment of offenders in place of punitive policies, but it had relatively little to say about crime causation. The second book also was largely devoid of causal theory, for Reckless argued that about the best we could do would be to identify "categoric risks," that is, social variables such as race and sex that are statistically associated with lawbreaking. The Sutherland and Cressey volume was the only one that contained a coherent perspective on the causes of criminality, and it was also distinguished by the depth of its coverage of the research evidence that had accumulated up to the 1950s. The book was highly regarded and monopolized the textbook market for many years.

However, some indication of the expansion of criminological theorizing and research activities can be seen in a comparison of the 1955 Sutherland and Cressey text with more recent books, such as my own *Society, Crime, and Criminal Behavior* (1992a). There are a large number of theoretical perspectives in the latter which have developed only in the last two or three decades. Additionally, it is clear from my text and other recent ones that the research evidence has been growing at an exponential rate.

This book is focused largely upon contemporary criminological arguments about the causes of crime and criminality. Although it outlines the claims that are advanced in a large number of theories, its central purpose goes beyond that of simply providing an inventory of current perspectives and viewpoints. My aim is to identify a number of unresolved problems of criminological theorizing and to examine some of the structural defects that plague many of our efforts to identify causal problems.

One major unresolved problem of criminological theory has to do with the dependent variable, that is, the question of whether crime is a homogeneous phenomenon, and if it is not, how we are to come to grips with the variability that exists among forms of crime and kinds of lawbreakers. Chapter 4 is concerned with these matters.

Another criminological problem that cries out for attention is that of social-structural processes in criminality. Although considerable progress has been made in recent years in the way of crime-specific accounts of causal relationships, more effort is in order, spelling out how various social and economic factors have a causal impact on criminality.

Why do specific persons engage in or refrain from lawbreaking? Although criminologists have made substantial gains in the direction of answering that question, more work surely is required. Chapters 7 and 8 take stock of what has been learned to date and involve commentary regarding the unresolved question of whether biosocial factors must be incorporated into our explanatory formulations. Chapter 8 also has much to say about psychological influences in lawbreaking and the challenge that psychological explanations pose for sociological versions of criminological thought.

In recent years, much has been heard about the alleged defects of "mainstream" criminological thought and the need for alternative forms of theorizing, such as "feminist criminology" and "realist criminology." Chapter 9 deals with these proposed alternatives to more established thoughtways and identifies those features of the "new criminologies" that are truly new, as contrasted with those elements that are merely recycled forms of earlier viewpoints, or "old wine in new bottles."

Finally, a number of criminologists have recently been arguing for integrated and/or general theories of crime and delinquency. The arguments for theoretical integration and for general theories are clear: Integrated theories will give us a "bigger bang for the buck" in the way of explanatory prowess, and general theories promise the parsimonious explanation of criminality by a single theory. But, as we will see in Chapter 10, it may be considerably easier to state the case for integrated or general theories than to actually develop them.

Many contemporary criminological theories not only fail to deal adequately with these issues, but they are also open to another criticism as well. The title of this book speaks of "talking about crime" and is intended to draw attention to the fact that much of the time criminologists literally don't know quite what they are talking about. Much of what passes for theorizing in criminology involves fuzzy or undefined concepts, propositions that are implicit rather than explicit and/or that are internally inconsistent, and kindred other problems of exposition or logical structure. I argue that criminologists need to put more of their energy into the task of speaking more clearly, that is, into the development of more rigorous versions of criminological argumentation; indeed, I contend that theoretical flabbiness is the most serious problem which criminologists must confront.

I received a good deal of helpful commentary and criticism from a number of colleagues as I went about writing and revising this manuscript. Ken Polk, University of Melbourne, and Joseph F. Jones, Kathryn Ann Farr, and Annette I. Jolin, Portland State University, deserve particular mention. Also, Prentice Hall reviewers Lee Ellis, Minot State University, Marylee Reynolds, Caldwell College, and M. Joan McDermott, Southern Illinois University offered some helpful criticisms and suggestions about the manuscript, and I have endeavored to respond to most of them. I also want to acknowledge the considerable support and encouragement I received for this project while I served as George Beto Chair Professor at Sam Houston State University. A number of students and faculty members at Sam Houston State made important contributions to this book. Of course, the defects that turn up in it are solely my responsibility.

*Don C. Gibbons*
Seaview University

# CHAPTER 1

# Introduction

## THE CRIMINOLOGICAL ENTERPRISE

**INTRODUCTION**

This chapter begins with some basic questions: "What is criminology?" and "What is a criminologist?" As we shall see, the answers are not as straightforward as one might suppose. Individual scholars differ in their views as to the proper subject matter of criminology, and they also offer varied opinions about whether criminology is best defined as an academic discipline, a multidisciplinary field of study, or something else. Then, too, while it might seem that a criminologist is someone who "does criminology," that definition is less clear in practice than on paper. Although these matters are of some significance, they are only touched upon in the following section because the major concern of the chapter and the book as a whole is with a detailed examination of the major activities that constitute the criminological enterprise, that is, the study of crime and its control.

**WHAT IS CRIMINOLOGY?**

What is criminology? One widely cited definition is that of Sutherland and Cressey (1978: 3), who declared: "Criminology is the body of knowledge regarding juvenile delinquency and crime. It includes within its scope the process of making laws, of breaking laws, and of reacting to the breaking of laws." I expanded their definition in my criminology text (Gibbons, 1992a: 32–39) to involve the following matters: the nature of crime and criminal behavior, the origins of criminal laws, the extent and distribution of criminality, social structure and criminality, the origins and development of criminal acts and criminal careers, and social reactions to crime. Another way of expressing the fourth and fifth of these entries would be to speak of "the rates question" and the "Why do they do it?" question, in that the first centers on explanations of crime rates or crime in the aggregate, while the second zeroes in on factors that account for lawbreaking or conforming conduct on the part of specific individuals. I will return to these distinctions later in this chapter.

Note that my definition of criminology and the Sutherland and Cressey one both speak about the topics with which it deals, rather than the kinds of individuals who carry on criminological work. However, some persons define criminology in the latter way, arguing, with considerable justification, that criminology is principally a subfield of the discipline of sociology. Those who define criminology in this way point out that a large share of the theorizing and research work on criminality (and juvenile delinquency) has been carried on by persons trained in sociology, and moreover, most of the formal training in criminological inquiry has traditionally taken place within graduate programs in sociology (Akers, 1992).

This sociology-linked definition is not universally accepted, largely because persons from a variety of scholarly disciplines have made and continue to make contributions to criminological understanding. The list includes geographers who have examined various spatial and physical factors in crime; economists, including both advocates of Marxist or radical economic perspectives on crime and economic modeling–rational choice investigators who have zeroed in on decision-making processes said to characterize offenders; psychologists and psychiatrists, some of whom have examined the proposition that many offenders exhibit pathological personality patterns which have impelled them into crime and others who have explored the role of normal personality variations in lawbreaking; as well as political scientists, historians, and representatives of most of the other social sciences. Finally, there is one other group of contributors, namely, persons of a biosocial persuasion, some of whom are physical scientists and others who are social scientists. Sociobiological hypotheses about lawbreaking are given short shrift by many sociological criminologists, but as I will argue in Chapter 8, the evidence regarding possible biosocial links to criminality is growing, making it increasingly difficult to deny that "there may be something there."

Most of these persons in fields outside of sociology do not identify themselves as professional criminologists. Moreover, criminological analysis is not a special field within the disciplines represented by these investigators. But even so, the contributions to criminological knowledge that come from these directions must be acknowledged.

Because criminology is not a wholly owned subsidiary of sociology, some persons have argued that it is a multidisciplinary field of study in its own right, or in other words, criminology is a distinct discipline that synthesizes the work of contributors from various component disciplines.

Is criminology a distinct discipline? The question to be raised first has to do with the nature of scholarly disciplines. What do we mean when we identify some line of activity as a "discipline"? My view is that the hallmarks of a scholarly discipline are a set of distinctive questions which are asked by a group of scholars, along with a distinctive set of concepts which they employ in addressing those questions.[1] Sociology is a discipline because it is concerned with questions about the relatively enduring effects of social structure upon human actions and also because it has a body of sociological concepts, that is, concepts that are not also common to another scholarly discipline. Economics, political science, and other established fields qualify as disciplines for the same reasons.

From this perspective, criminology is *not* a discipline. There are no distinctively criminological questions; instead, we pose sociological, psychological, economic, or other queries about crime and criminal behavior. Similarly, few if any concepts are unique to criminological inquiry; instead, propositions about lawbreaking and lawbreakers are posed in the conceptual language of the established disciplines, or put another way, sociological, psychological, or economic concepts and propositions are brought to bear upon lawbreaking in the effort to explain it. Accordingly, it seems most sensible to identify criminology as a multidisciplinary field of study.

In *The Criminological Enterprise* (Gibbons, 1979), I noted that criminological work began in Europe in the nineteenth century and emerged in the United States in the early 1900s. Also, that book indicated that modern criminology grew up in this country largely as a new creation, rather than as a continuation of the European efforts of the 1800s. Criminology in the United States was much more closely tied to sociology departments and sociological perspectives than it was to its European roots. Finally, that earlier book noted that modern criminological work is more prominent in this nation than anywhere else in the world. Chapters 2 and 3 take up the developmental history of criminology in more detail, but it should be noted at this point that the contemporary criminological enterprise is worldwide in scope. Relatively large numbers of persons are doing criminology in England, Germany, and a number of other European countries. Criminology is also flourishing in Australia (although with more emphasis upon legal studies than in the United States). There is also a substantial group of criminological investigators in Canada, Japan, and some other countries, as well as pockets of them in China, Pakistan, and various other countries around the world.

Another matter needs some mention. The preceding definitions of criminology by Sutherland and Cressey and by myself include reactions to lawbreaking as one component. "Reactions to criminality" is a broad term which encompasses informal responses such as neighborhood gossip and other kinds of social control, along with all of those activities of formal agencies of social control that have become prominent in modern societies. The formal social control machinery includes the police, courts, jails, probation organizations, prisons and other institutions, parole agencies, and some other components as well.

Until the late 1960s, university courses dealing with the criminal justice system, and particularly with the treatment and/or punishment of offenders, were offered principally within sociology departments. Some sociological criminologists specialized in these topics; they identified themselves as "penologists" and were referred to by others as "penologists." However, in the late 1960s, in considerable part as the result of rising fears of crime in the United States and of federal funding for a "War on Crime," we began to hear a good bit about "the criminal justice system" and its problems. One of these problems was identified as the lack of trained workers to carry out the myriad tasks of fighting crime. A major response to this newly emphasized need was the creation of undergraduate programs in Administration of Justice or Criminal Justice in colleges and universities throughout the United States. Considerable encouragement for this development came from federal funding, which was made available to academic institutions in order to support these new programs.

Initially, the staffing of these undergraduate programs included a diverse collection of persons: "retreaded" ex-police officers, lawyers, sociological criminologists, and individuals with other backgrounds as well. However, graduate training in criminal justice ultimately began to be offered at a number of universities. Doctoral degrees in criminal justice have now become fairly common. Finally, criminal justice has been identified by a number of persons as a new, multidisciplinary discipline.

Although questions similar to those posed about criminology might also be addressed to those who assert that criminal justice is a bona fide discipline, the fact is that it is a robust field of study, at least in terms of student enrollments.

Are criminal justice and criminology related, and if so, what is the nature of the relationship? Some have likened criminal justice to "applied criminology," but that view has "gone down lumpy" with representatives of the first-named field. Perhaps a more reasonable answer is that criminology gives prominence to questions about the *causes of criminality*, while the *control of lawbreaking* is at the heart of criminal justice.[2] Some indication of this division of labor can be seen in textbooks in the two fields. Most contemporary criminology textbooks are weighted heavily in the direction of etiological materials, while criminal justice textbooks give less attention to causation.

This causation-control distinction is useful in identifying the parameters of these two fields. However, there is an additional comment to be made before we move on, to wit, those who seek to identify effective ways of controlling or preventing crime or delinquency surely ought to know a good bit about criminological theory and evidence. Consider one illustration of this point. There is currently a good deal of interest in "community policing" in the United States. Advocates of community policing as a new style of law enforcement are not all on the same wavelength regarding what they mean by these terms, but the effectiveness of community policing, whatever brand is implemented, depends in considerable part upon how it meshes with other, informal measures of social control that characterize urban communities in varying degrees. The criminological literature indicates that some urban neighborhoods are "social jungles" in which new styles of policing may have little impact, while other neighborhoods are characterized by informal ties among citizens and other features which augur well for community-oriented policing (Reiss and Tonry, 1986). The thrust of this and of similar illustrations that could be offered is that the relationship between criminology and criminal justice ought to be complementary, not adversarial or hostile.

## DOING CRIMINOLOGY: TALKING ABOUT CRIME AND CRIMINALS

The cover of *The Criminological Enterprise* included the title and my name, printed against a background consisting of the names of a number of other criminologists, both living and dead. This cover drew attention to the fact that criminology is an activity that is carried on by persons with names such as John Hagan, Joan McCord, Travis Hirschi, Margaret Farnworth, John Irwin, Freda Adler, Terence Thornberry, Sally Simpson, and Austin Turk and whose work is influenced in important ways by their personal experiences as well as by their professional training. A striking case in point is Irwin, who served four and one-half years in a California prison prior to becoming a professional criminologist. His widely praised book, *The Felon* (1970), was a notable contribution to our understanding of criminal pathways and the impact of prison experiences upon lawbreakers, in part because of the evidence that Irwin gathered from offenders but also in part because it was informed by his own experiences in custody.

Unfortunately, we know relatively little about the biographies of most criminologists, although the publication of the American Society of Criminology, *The Criminologist*, has from time to time included personal accounts of a few contemporary criminologists, in which these persons have pinpointed some of the experiences that have influenced their criminological thinking and their scholarly activities. Additionally, a few fairly detailed efforts have been made by others to draw portraits of the intellectual histories and work styles of some criminologists. My report (Gibbons, 1974) regarding Maurice Parmelee, a lesser-known pioneer of American criminology is one, as is Paul Colomy's (1988) account of the personal and professional development of Donald R. Cressey, who was probably the most prominent American criminologist in the period since the 1950s.[3] Also, *The Criminological Enterprise* contains a good many biographical bits and pieces about a number of earlier and contemporary criminologists. However, the most useful and detailed collection of this kind of material is John Laub's (1983) oral history volume, in which the detailed interviews that he conducted with nine contemporary criminological "heavyweights" are presented. Laub interviewed Hans Mattick, Leslie Wilkins, Solomon Kobrin, Daniel Glaser, Edwin Lemert, Donald Cressey, Thorsten Sellin, Albert Cohen, and Lloyd Ohlin, asking them questions about their social backgrounds, academic experiences, the nature of their criminological work, and their views regarding a number of contemporary issues in criminology. This book is an extremely valuable source of information regarding criminology as it was lived and experienced by a group of persons who made major contributions to the field, particularly in the period from the end of World War II up to the 1980s.

Let us zero in more closely upon the activities of criminologists. My guess is that if some of my neighbors were asked to indicate what criminologists *do*, some of them would answer "Not much!" Unlike many occupations, that of criminologist is a low-visibility one.

The majority of professional criminologists are faculty employees of colleges or universities. Much of what they do on a day-to-day basis is mundane stuff, involving the delivery of lectures to undergraduates regarding the theories and findings of criminology. Some of those criminologists, myself included (Gibbons, 1992a; Gibbons and Krohn, 1991), also write textbooks, in which they attempt to assemble and make sense out of the collective wisdom of the field. Both of these activities are forms of "talking about crime," which is one reason for the title of this book.

However, "talking about crime" refers to other, more important matters as well. As I have already indicated, criminology is the body of knowledge regarding crime and delinquency and it differs from criminal justice in terms of its emphasis upon causal or etiological questions. How do we go about our efforts to identify causal factors in lawbreaking? The answer is that we engage in inquiry, a process which has two interrelated parts: the creation of theories and the empirical scrutiny of those formulations.

For the moment, a workable definition of theory would be that it consists of symbolic accounts, either verbal or written, which are representations of reality which purport to capture the nature of criminality and its causes. Put another way, a theory is a symbolic picture of "how things work." In a sense, theories are literary creations, but the ultimate test of them goes beyond literary criteria. It is not enough to pronounce a theory to be "elegant," plausible, or personally pleasing; rather, it ought to also be congruent with the empirical evidence. In some instances, we render tentative judgments about the adequacy of theoretical accounts by scrutinizing the body of existing evidence that can be brought to bear upon them, while in other cases, we engage in new research that specifically addresses the propositions or contentions within the theory. This description of commentary on criminological inquiry captures the broader meaning of "talking about crime."

Let me emphasize another point regarding inquiry in the social and behavioral sciences generally and in criminology specifically, namely its *interactive* nature in which the development of theories and research examination of them go hand in hand.[4] Unfortunately, the bifurcation of "theory" and "methodology" is entirely too common in sociology and other social sciences.[5] In this view of things, "theory" is frequently identified as abstract and speculative thinking, divorced from factual evidence, and often resulting in arcane terms and discursive presentations in which the structure of the basic argument is obscure. Additionally, "methodology" is frequently disparaged as atheoretical "mindless number crunching" and downplayed in other ways.

This division of work into separate spheres of "theory" and "methodology" (or "research") is a serious misrepresentation of the nature of scientific (and criminological) inquiry. Theorizing and research are interrelated parts of the process of inquiry. The reader who proceeds further in this book will discover that it is unabashedly neopositivist in nature. Among other things, neopositivism involves emphasis upon the need for clearly stated theoretical arguments which are amenable to research scrutiny.

The chapters to follow have much to say about the activities that go into the construction of theories, but a few words are in order here.

Textbook discussions sometimes draw a contrast between two seemingly distinct approaches to theory development, often referred to as *inductive* and *deductive* forms of theorizing. Inductive theory construction refers to a process in which an explanatory formulation is developed *after* the researcher has engaged in observations of the phenomenon of interest, while a deductive theory is stated *in advance* of research on the topic about which the theory speaks. One illustration of an inductively derived explanation is Cressey's (1953) account of how financial trust violation (embezzlement) arises. He studied a sample of trust violators and concluded that all of them had gone through a process in which they had developed nonshareable problems, had identified theft from their employers as a way of solving these problems, and had developed rationalizations or excuses for their unlawful behavior *in advance* of the act of stealing. A contrasting example of a more deductively derived theory is Baron and Straus's (1990) formulation regarding state-by-state variations in rates of forcible rape. They conjectured that these rates are influenced by the extent of gender inequality in individual states and also by variations in pornography readership. They also theorized that "cultural spillover," by which they meant variations in socially approved forms of violence across individual states, is a factor in rape, as is social disorganization, by which they meant loose social ties among residents, indexed by such measures as divorce rates and church membership figures for states.

Although it might be said that a deductive theory precedes research while an inductive one flows out of or follows research, matters are not this simple in real life. Deductive theories do not simply emerge from the fertile minds of theorists; rather, they usually are developed in response to puzzles that are posed by an existing body of research evidence or other unexplained facts. Baron and Straus, for example, wove some lines of theorizing already in existence together with some existing evidence on rape in order to produce their own formulation.

Turning to inductive arguments, or what some have called "grounded theories" (Glazer and Strauss, 1967), it would be a mistake to assume that these arise solely out of research observations or that "the facts speak for themselves." In Cressey's case, for example, he began by quizzing trust violators about financial problems which might account for their criminal actions. He did *not* ask them whether they had been abused as children or whether they had fantasized about engaging in incest with their mothers, nor did he explore myriad other questions. Put another way, Cressey's data gathering was guided by some kind of implicit theoretical or explanatory framework.

Which of these forms of theorizing should we favor in criminology? It should be obvious that this is the wrong question, for both have a place in criminological inquiry. The question then becomes, under what circumstances should we adopt one approach or the other? And the answer to this query is pretty clear. When we are faced with some crime-related phenomenon about which little is now known, inductive and oftentimes exploratory research is in order, but when we have already identified major parameters of some phenomenon, along with having produced research evidence on some of the explanatory variables that account for the behavior in question, it may be time to move another step further in the direction of a deductive and formalized theory.


## KEY QUESTIONS IN CAUSAL ANALYSIS

The opening remarks regarding the nature of criminology identified "the rates question" and the "Why do they do it?" query as two related but separate causal questions posed by criminologists. Let us examine these distinctions a bit more closely.

### Social Structure and Criminality ("The Rates Question")

Probing the causes of crime and delinquency is a principal task of the criminologist. His or her major goal is to develop generalized and valid propositions accounting for criminality. One of the two main components of causal inquiry involves developing explanations for the *kinds and degrees of criminality* observed in a society or across societies, while the other centers on discovering the *processes involved in the acquisition of criminal behavior patterns by specific individuals* (Cohen, 1959, 1985). Regarding these two problems, Donald Cressey (1960: 47) commented:

> A theory explaining social behavior in general, or any specific kind of social behavior, should have two distinct but consistent parts. First, there must be a statement that explains the statistical distribution of the behavior in time and space (epidemiology) and from which predictive statements about unknown statistical distributions can be derived. Second, there must be a statement that identifies, at least by implication, the process by which individuals come to exhibit the behavior in question, and from which can be derived predictive statements about the behavior of individuals.

Throughout this book, I shall refer to the first concern as *social structure and criminality*, or "the rates question," and to the second as *the origins and development of criminal acts and careers*, or the "Why do they do it?" query.

What would a theory directed at social structure and crime look like? Consider some examples. National statistics on crimes reported to the police, compiled by the Federal Bureau of Investigation, indicate that predatory property crime rates vary significantly from one state to another and from one city to another in the United States. What might account for these differences? One possibility would be variations in levels of income inequality across states or cities, such that those states and urban communities marked by the most pronounced disparity in incomes between the very rich and the poorest citizens are the ones with the highest rates of predatory lawbreaking. Research efforts to verify this contention would center upon correlational analyses of income levels and crime rates for the various states or cities.

Social-structural analyses are pitched at various levels; that is, some of them examine rate variations across nations, others across states, and still others zero in upon smaller population aggregates. Suppose we next focus on lawbreaking within particular cities and discover that certain forms of adult property crime and certain kinds of juvenile misbehavior are concentrated in lower-income areas but are less common elsewhere. We might then probe such questions as "Why are crime and delinquency common in some areas and virtually nonexistent in others?" and "Does something within a community's social organization, such as different social class patterns or variations in the quality of the high schools in different areas, partially explain these patterns of crime and delinquency?"

Perhaps variations in neighborhood social structure that reflect income inequality are, at least in part, responsible for widely divergent rates of lawbreaking. To examine this claim, data would be needed to provide indices of neighborhood social organization, differential social class values, and so on. In turn, the hypothesis would be supported to the degree that correlations were observed between crime rates and the measures of social organization. Insofar as those areas with high crime rates are also the most disorganized, and to the degree that low-crime neighborhoods are the most cohesive, the hypothesis would be verified (for relevant evidence, see Reiss and Tonry, 1986).

Still another kind of social-structural analysis would address data indicating that American society is more plagued with lawbreaking than most European countries. According to a common sociological hypothesis, American society is more *criminogenic* than other societies because of the inordinate emphasis on material success and the disrespct for law and order that is endemic in the United States. These claims have not been adequately tested, and such research would be costly and time-consuming, but the kinds of evidence called for are clear. Crime rates would have to be obtained so that we could rank nations in terms of criminality, and data on cultural values, attitudes toward materialism, law enforcement, and so on, would have to be gathered so that we could scrutinize causal propositions through research evidence.

Other illustrations of theorizing and research directed at social-structural facts in lawbreaking could easily be offered. For one, the Baron and Straus (1990) study of state-by-state variations in rates of forcible rape is an example of "the rates question." We will examine a number of other instances of theorizing at the social-structural level in the rest of this book.

### The Origins and Development of Criminal Acts

Social-structural explanations make no mention of specific individuals, nor do they involve efforts to account for lawbreaking by some of them and conformity by others. Discovery of the processes by which individuals acquire criminal attitudes and/or behavior patterns is an analytically separate endeavor (although a researcher may address both of these questions within a specific study).

At the same time, these are not entirely distinct questions. After all, crime rates are aggregate or summary measures of criminality which results from the actions of individual lawbreakers (even though we may not be able to identify precisely how many persons were involved in the number of criminal events or occurrences that make up the numerator of the crime rate). The burglary rate in a community expresses the frequency with which a collection of persons goes about doing burglaries (and the extent to which other persons refrain from such activities). In the same way, the forcible rape rate summarizes the activities of specific sexual assaulters. No wonder, then, that many criminologists exhibit a good deal of curiosity about the processes that account for lawbreaking by some individuals and desistance by others.

Because crime rates reflect the behavior of individuals, explanations of those rates and accounts of how persons become involved in the acts reflected in those rates ought to be related to and consistent with each other. For example, if income inequality explains variations in rates of predatory crime, some manifestations of income disparity ought to be observed "inside the heads" of real-life predators, although additional factors may also contribute to their lawbreaking. For example, perhaps predatory offenders are often particularly poor and frequently verbalize strong feelings of economic deprivation. Similarly, if high rates of forcible rape are related to sexual inequality and if rape is employed by males in sexually unequal societies in order to maintain this state of affairs, we might anticipate that many forcible rapists would be particularly concerned about preserving the sexual status quo. But again, other factors may also be implicated in the behavior of individual rapists. Also, we might discover that some sexual assaultists are involved in sexual misbehavior due to motives other than an interest in maintenance of gender discrimination.

Let us pursue the distinction between the "rates" and "Why do they do it?" questions through the previous example of variations in crime and delinquency rates across neighborhoods in an urban community. Suppose that male juveniles in high-delinquency areas exhibit various patterns of behavior. Some have high occupational aspirations, are motivated to do well in school, and are nondelinquent. Other juveniles are "corner boys," not heavily involved in delinquency but also not caught up in patterns of mobility striving (achievement). They are unmotivated conformists whose actions reflect short-run hedonism. A third group is heavily involved in delinquent activities; its members view themselves as "tough kids" and "delinquents." One concern in this case would be to uncover the factors that led the youths into these different pathways. One hypothesis might be that delinquents feel the "sting of relative deprivation" most strongly; another would be that these boys are from more lax or criminalistic homes. Or perhaps association in conformist or delinquent peer groups is important.

As Cressey argued in the passage quoted earlier, causal analysis should explain both variations in rates of crime and involvement in criminality or law-abiding conduct in particular neighborhoods, social classes, or other settings thought to be conducive to criminality. Indeed, some instances of criminological theory or research have been jointly concerned with these two problems. Nevertheless, it makes sense to keep these matters analytically separate, particularly because criminological theorists or researchers have often concentrated on one or the other.

### Concluding Comments

This chapter began with the question "What is criminology?" A definition was offered which identified the basic questions or topics that are addressed by persons who study crime, whatever their educational backgrounds or professional affiliations. And we saw that representatives of a variety of disciplines are involved in the study of lawbreaking. At the same time, the largest share of criminological work has been and is being carried on by persons who have been trained in the discipline of sociology.

We also observed that a good deal of discussion in the past few decades has revolved around the question of whether criminology is a field of specialization within sociology or a discipline in its own right. Also, the rise of criminal justice has led to questions about the relationship between criminology and this newer field. The view put forth in this book is that criminology is a multidisciplinary field that is heavily concerned with causal analysis, while criminal justice concentrates upon the control side of things.

Another matter dealt with in this chapter was that of social inquiry generally, as well as the more specific topic of inquiry in criminology. The chapter argued that both inductive and deductive forms of theorizing and research are required.

This chapter concluded with an examination of the two major questions posed about causation: "the rates question" and the "Why do they do it?" query. Most theorizing in criminology is organized around one or the other of these analytically separate concerns.

Attention turns in Chapters 2 and 3 to a brief account of the development of criminology, beginning with events in Europe in the mid-1800s and ending with contemporary directions in criminological analysis. Those two chapters are followed by one dealing with the need for classification systems that make sense of the myriad forms of criminality. Chapter 5 takes up the forms of theory in criminology, concentrating upon the logical structure of many of the major explanatory frameworks in the field. Chapter 6 examines a number of social-structural theories, while Chapters 7 and 8 examine psychological, biological, and sociological answers to the "Why do they do it?" question. Chapter 9 turns attention to certain "new criminologies," including realist criminology, feminist perspectives, and constitutive criminology. Chapter 10 explores the prospects for integrated and/or general theories, and the concluding chapter discusses the prospects for progress in criminological theorizing in the decades ahead.

## NOTES

[1]The distinctiveness of concepts in individual disciplines is, of course, a matter of degree. For example, sociologists are not the only persons to employ such terms as "social stratification," "role," "status," or "cognitive dissonance," nor are economic terms confined entirely to economists. Additionally, many of the terms employed in the social sciences are found in the everyday language of laypersons, albeit sometimes with different meanings. Even so, the case can be made that different disciplines employ conceptual systems that are relatively unique to them.

[2]One indication of the overlapping nature of criminology and criminal justice can be seen in the membership rolls of the American Society of Criminology and the Academy of Criminal

Justice Sciences. A substantial number of persons belong to both of these professional associations.

[3]The entire issue of *Crime and Delinquency* in which Colomy's essay appeared is devoted to papers which take stock of Cressey's numerous contributions to criminology.

[4]In the day-to-day work of social scientists, a number of variants of the theory-research process of inquiry occur. Investigators sometimes begin with an unfocused curiosity about some form of behavior and with few clues as to how that behavior might be accounted for; thus they engage in inductive research procedures that are intended to result in the production of hypotheses and theorizing that can guide additional research. At other times, investigators assess a body of existing evidence concerning some phenomenon, construct a theory tying the information together and identifying gaps in the data, and then go about testing hypotheses derived from the theory.

For another statement regarding sociological theorizing, the interplay of theory and research, and kindred matters, see Lieberson (1992). Lieberson has articulated a position that is, in a number of respects, a more fully developed version of the views I offer in this chapter, although he puts less emphasis upon the formal properties of theories.

[5]A particularly striking illustration comes from the graduate bulletin of the New School for Social Research in New York, which identified the graduate courses in the Ph.D. program in Sociology as falling into three groups: theory, methodology, and "substance"!

# CHAPTER 2

# The Development of Criminology, I

## INTRODUCTION

Chapter 1 indicated that the focus of this book is upon the contemporary criminological enterprise. In particular, it presents a critique of modern versions of causal theory and examines both the content and the structure of various formulations. But before we begin the principal business of the book, we need to get some sense of the major developmental stages through which the field has gone. We need to ask (a) where has criminology as an organized field of study come from, (b) what is its current status, and (c) where does it appear to be going, in terms of theoretical developments?

Chapters 2 and 3 provide an abridged version of *The Criminological Enterprise* (Gibbons, 1979), which traced the growth of contemporary criminology, beginning with the work of Lombroso and various other European scholars in the nineteenth century. Although these premodern figures received some attention, most of the book was devoted to the rise of sociological criminology in the United States, beginning with the writings of Parmelee and some other pioneers, followed by detailed attention to the contributions of Shaw and McKay and Sutherland, who laid out many of the conceptual boundaries that still define the field. Finally, *The Criminological Enterprise* commented upon criminological developments in the post–World War II period, ending with the rise of radical-Marxist versions of theorizing in the 1970s.

Chapters 2 and 3 present a shortened account of these developments and also touch upon contributions that have been made to criminological knowledge from sources outside of sociology, including work of biologists, economists, geographers, and representatives of a number of other disciplines.

The task I have set for these two chapters is fairly daunting. *The Criminological Enterprise*, restricted largely to modern sociological criminology, ran to over 200 pages. Obviously, the summary account here can only touch upon some of the most significant developments in what has been a complex set of events which have transpired as the criminological enterprise has evolved.

## THE ORIGINS OF MODERN CRIMINOLOGY

Who created criminology and when did they do it? This question has frequently been asked about modern sociology, but the answer is less than clear. Some have nominated Comte while others have opted for Durkheim, Simmel, or some other nineteenth-century European scholar as the discipline's creator. Clearly, these varied answers indicate that a number of persons contributed in one way or another to the gradual emergence of sociology over a period of decades. Much the same can be said about criminology. Drapkin (1983) has reached back into prehistoric times and identified the Code of Hammurabi as a precursor of modern criminology, while Schafer (1969: 113) has suggested that J. Baptiste della Porte (1535–1615) was a major figure in the creation of the field, on the basis of the latter's efforts to find links between forms and types of lawbreakers by studying the cadavers of criminals. Finally, Reid (1976: 21) noted that Topinard, an early anthropologist, should be given some credit for coining the term "criminology."

However, most criminology textbooks agree that the more important names in European, premodern criminology included Cesare Beccaria (1735–1795) and Jeremy Bentham (1748–1832), major figures in the classical school of thought; along with Cesare Lombroso (1853–1909), Enrico Ferri (1856–1928), and Rafaelle Garafolo (1852–1934), central contributors to Italian biological positivism (Gibbons, 1992a: 14-27; Vold and Bernard, 1986).

Persons who aspire to become knowledgeable about modern criminological thought can ignore the writings of these premodern figures only at their own peril. I have noted some places where a good share of their writings have been presented in detail. Let me conclude the brief presentation here by repeating some comments I have made in another book (Gibbons, 1992a: 15):

What can be learned from the pioneers in criminology? On one hand, perhaps not a great deal. These initial probers explored many blind alleys. Their efforts to account for criminality were all too often fruitless meanderings into theoretical terrain. Thus inquiry on lawbreaking in the last century or so has not been cumulative. Instead, many of the contemporary explanatory viewpoints are relatively unrelated to earlier theorizing about crime.[1]

## AMERICAN CRIMINOLOGY: THE EARLY YEARS

### The Rise of American Sociology

Because criminology in this country is a progeny of the discipline of sociology, a few words are required regarding the geneology of the parent field.[2] Examination of the history of sociology in America fails to turn up a birth certificate indicating that it sprung up at some precise moment in the past; instead, its origins are somewhat murky. Publications dealing with sociological topics began to appear in number in the United States in the 1880s, while courses labeled as sociological offerings began to be included in college curricula in the 1890s. The American Sociological Society was founded in 1905.[3]

Whether the birth of American sociology is located in the 1880s, 1890s, or early 1900s, the infant discipline showed little resemblance to the field as it developed in the second half of the twentieth century. As Oberschall (1972: 189) remarked, "a striking feature of U.S. sociology was that it was institutionalized before it had a distinctive intellectual content, a distinctive method, or even a point of view."

The rise of sociology was part of a broader historical sweep of events during the first two decades of the twentieth century, which historians have identified as the Progressive Era. Progressives voiced reformist concerns about the harsh social consequences of industrialization and urbanization which were overtaking the nation. In particular, they were appalled by the stark contrasts between the unbridled power and immense wealth of industrial plutocrats such as Morgan, Carnegie, and Harriman, on the one hand, and the abject misery of the great mass of workers, on the other.

Who were the advocates of Progressivism? They were principally middle-class citizens, including prohibitionists, women's rights advocates, small businesspersons, and an assortment of other concerned individuals. They advocated conservation of the nation's resources, regulation of the activities of rapacious corporations, honest government, and other changes in American life. They also spoke out for rehabilitation of criminals, assistance to the poor, and humane treatment of the insane. The spirit of Progressivism centered on the proposition that common citizens could solve problems through reason and sincere effort. The rise of American sociology should be located against this background of Progressive thought.

Hinkle and Hinkle (1954) enumerated four dominant elements in sociology up to the 1930s: belief in natural laws governing social relations, faith in progressive social change, emphasis on social reform, and an individualistic conception of society. Also, they argued that sociology was in considerable part a response to the social dislocations generated by industrialization and urbanization.

There is much more to the story of the formative years of American sociology, including the prominence of persons from rural and religious backgrounds in the ranks of college teachers of sociology in the first three decades of the twentieth century. However, one feature of early sociology stands out, namely that it bore little similarity to the present version of the discipline. Early sociology focused heavily on social problems of one kind or another, often viewing them as individualistic and pathological byproducts of urbanization and industrialization. And, as Oberschall pointed out in the passage cited earlier, much of what passed for sociological theory in the early 1900s bore little similarity to the conceptual structure that eventually emerged, particularly after World War II.

This brief account of the origins of American sociology has set the stage for a discussion of the first gropings toward the development of sociological criminology in the United States. Let us turn attention to the emergence of criminology.

### European Roots of American Criminology

American criminology did not spring up instantaneously as the product of native seeds; rather, it has some tenuous connections to the work of nineteenth-century European scholars (Vold and Bernard, 1986; Quinney, 1975). Quinney (1975) traced the rise of European criminology from the classical school, to the work of Quetelet, Guerry, and others in the so-called cartographic school in the mid-1800s. He also noted the biologically based work of Lombroso and his followers in the late 1800s. According to Quinney, Lombrosian positivism, which emphasized a natural science stance toward the study of crime and deterministic views of crime causation, had considerable influence, albeit indirect, on the writings of many American criminological pioneers.

### The First Stages of American Criminology

Books dealing with crime and delinquency in America began to appear in some number around 1895, including Charles Richmond Henderson's volume on the "defective, dependent, and delinquent classes," as well as exposés of the urban crime problem by Loring, Crapsey, Brace, and others. Other works stressing Lombrosian hypotheses about congenital criminality were also published around the turn of the century.

These emphases on biological and evolutionary theories of criminality continued for a number of years. As Quinney (1975: 7) has said, "the *sociological* study of crime moved very slowly in the United States during the first part of the century. With today's hindsight, we can see that the study of crime by early sociologists was filled with questionable assumptions and was not specifically aimed at social matters."

The eclectic and biological character of early American criminology can be seen in the first criminology text, authored by Parmelee, and published in 1918.[4] His book involved six parts, beginning with a section on the nature of crime. The chapters in this section, which set the tone for the entire book, portrayed criminality as an abnormal and pathological form of behavior. Parmelee also laid out an eclectic orientation to the explanation of lawbreaking, arguing that various perspectives from the biological and social sciences must be brought to bear on the crime problem.

Part II, on criminogenic factors in the environment, included seasonal and climatic variations, urban and rural crime patterns, and economic factors, while Part III discussed criminal types and traits and emphasized the overrepresentation of "aments," "dements," and "psychopaths" in the population of offenders. Parmelee's observations about female criminality reflected the prevailing biases of the day, which held that women are inherently inferior to men.

The remaining sections of Parmelee's book dealt with criminal procedure and allied matters, penology, and crime and social change. Although Quinney (1975: 7) credited Parmelee with initiating the movement of criminology toward sociological analysis and away from eclecticism and biological notions, most commentators have given him little recognition as a founder of the field. On balance, it is fair to say that he became one of the forgotten men of early American criminology.

Other early criminologists faded into obscurity as well, including John Gillin and Philip Parsons. Gillin (1926) authored another of the early criminology texts, as did Parsons (1926). Gillin's treatment of causation paralleled Parmelee's, in that he embraced Lombrosian notions about physical factors in crime and also argued that mental defects are a cause of lawbreaking. His book presented a potpourri of social factors, including the home, playground influences, schools, community factors, customs, beliefs, class hatred, and religion, that were all said to play some role in etiology.

Parsons's book closely paralleled the volumes by Parmelee and Gillin. All three contained few hints about the directions that would ultimately be taken by sociological criminology in the United States. They were relatively nonsociological and eclectic in character and showed little similarity to the criminology textbooks that began to appear in the late 1930s and 1940s.

One other early criminology text should be mentioned. The period in the United States from about 1895 to 1930 was one in which criminology slowly began to move away from the biological and eclectic perspectives favored by European scholars of the nineteenth century and toward a truly sociological form of criminological analysis. Sutherland's *Criminology* (1924) was in some ways similar to the textbooks mentioned above, but in other ways, it represented a significant departure from them. The first edition contained only the faintest hints of what would appear in subsequent editions as the theory of differential association. But what set it apart from the books by Parmelee, Gillin, and Parsons was the well-reasoned and hard-hitting critiques of such arguments as those by Lombroso. Sutherland carefully examined the popular hypotheses of the day, such as those which emphasized alleged physical or mental pathology on the part of lawbreakers, and found them to be unconvincing. Geis (1976: 304) offered the following judgment about the book: "Indeed, if it were used as a text today, the 1924 issue would provide an undergraduate with an excellent understanding of important modes of reasoning about key matters involved in criminal behavior and responses to it."

## CRIMINOLOGY: 1930–1955

Sutherland's textbook helped to turn criminological thought away from eclecticism and biological hypotheses and toward sociological analysis. And, as we shall see, the work of Shaw and McKay in the 1930s represented another signal contribution to the maturation of sociological criminology.

Criminology unfolded in some relatively distinct stages, beginning in the 1930s. Even so, identification of major periods in American criminology requires some relatively arbitrary decisions. The criminological enterprise in the United States can be "periodized" in a number of different ways, but in this book, five stages are identified: the early years from 1900 to 1930; a growth period from 1930 to 1955, in which many of the links in contemporary mainstream criminology were forged; the further development and maturation of the field between 1955 and 1970; the "radicalization" of criminological theory in the 1970s and early 1980s; and the return to conservatism of the last decade or so.[5]

The period from 1930 to 1955 is by no means an entirely arbitrarily chosen one. As Faris (1967) noted, scientific sociology had taken relatively firm root in the United States by 1930, due largely to the efforts of W. I. Thomas, Robert Ezra Park, Elsworth Faris, and Ernest Burgess. The American Sociological Society reached an early membership peak in 1932, with over 1500 persons belonging to it. In short, the sociological fraternity had expanded noticeably by 1930, from the handful of persons who made it up at the beginning of the century. Sociological criminology participated in this growth, particularly through the contributions of Shaw and McKay and Sutherland. It is to these major figures that we now turn.

### Clifford Shaw and Henry D. McKay:
### Delinquency as a Social Phenomenon

It would be difficult to overestimate the significance of the delinquency studies carried on by Shaw and McKay in Chicago and certain other cities from 1929 through the 1930s. Their inquiries provided much of the intellectual capital on which criminologists have continued to draw, even to the present time.

Shaw and McKay were researchers with the Institute for Juvenile Research, a state-supported child guidance clinic, and they also had ties with the University of Chicago sociology department.

Recall the two major questions about the causes of crime and delinquency introduced in Chapter 1, "the rates question" and the "Why do they do it?" query. Both were addressed by Shaw and McKay in their research. In one set of studies (Shaw and McKay, 1931, 1932), they found that juvenile court referral rates were highest in neighborhoods of rapid population change, poor housing, poverty, adult crime, and other social ills. These rates also showed a gradient pattern, being highest in inner-city areas and declining with distance from the city center.

Shaw and McKay also reported that delinquency rates differed markedly within specific neighborhoods. High rates were usually found near industrial areas and deteriorated sections around the city center. These rates had remained stable or consistently high in certain neighborhoods, even though the area populations had changed completely over a 30-year period. This finding led them to conclude that delinquency was a cultural tradition in some urban neighborhoods.[6]

Shaw and McKay also developed an account of the processes through which youths became lawbreakers in delinquency areas, principally through examination of life history documents on youthful offenders (Shaw, 1930, 1931; Shaw, McKay, and McDonald, 1938). They concluded that delinquents were normal youngsters whose involvement in misconduct occurred within a network of interpersonal ties that included family, gang, and neighborhood influences. Offenders became engaged in misconduct as they came under the influence of criminogenic conditions in their communities, that is, the delinquency traditions that existed there.

Shaw and McKay's studies remained influential long after their publication in the 1930s. Their findings were incorporated into the background assumptions on which various sociological theories of crime were subsequently constructed. Many criminologists in the 1940s and 1950s were guided by the premise that crime is often carried on by persons who find themselves in stressful situations, rather than by disturbed individuals acting out their pathology. Shaw and McKay's influence is apparent in the theorizing of a number of criminologists, including Taft, Reckless, and in particular, Edwin H. Sutherland.

### Sutherland's Contributions

*The Theory of Differential Association.*  The author of sociological theories have often presented them in their most favorable light, omitting any mention of their possible gaps or deficiencies. Additionally, they have rarely described the processes involved in the work of converting inchoate ideas into mature theories. However, a detailed account of the genesis of the differential association perspective has been provided by Sutherland (1956). He made it abundantly clear that the formal statement of this viewpoint was preceded by a lengthy gestation period during which his ideas underwent considerable development and revision.

The idea of differential association did not appear in the first edition of *Criminology*. However, the revised, second edition in 1934 did contain an embryonic version of the theory, although that fact was not recognized by Sutherland at the time. The revision of the theory in the 1939 edition was the product of Sutherland's further efforts to develop an abstract explanation of criminal etiology. But that version received a good bit of criticism from other criminologists. Sutherland was aware of many of the problems that were pointed out by others, for he was a severe critic of his own work. The 1939 statement was followed in 1947 by still another version, which continued to appear in all subsequent editions of the book.

The nine propositions or statements which make up the final version of differential association theory are these (Sutherland, Cressey, and Luckenbill, 1992: 88–90):

1. *Criminal behavior is learned. . . .*
2. *Criminal behavior is learned in interaction with other persons in a process of communication. . . .*
3. *The principal part of the learning of criminal behavior occurs within intimate personal groups. . . .*
4. *When criminal behavior is learned, the learning includes (a) techniques of committing the crime, which are sometimes very complicated, sometimes very simple; (b) the specific direction of motives, drives, rationalizations, and attitudes. . . .*
5. *The specific direction of motives and drives is learned from definitions of the legal codes as favorable or unfavorable. . . .*
6. *A person becomes delinquent because of an excess of definitions favorable to violation of law over definitions unfavorable to violation of law. . . .*
7. *Differential associations may vary in frequency, duration, priority, and intensity. . . .*
8. *The process of learning criminal behavior by association with criminal and anti-criminal patterns involves all of the mechanisms that are involved in any other learning. . . .*

9. *While criminal behavior is an expression of general needs and values, it is not explained by those general needs and values since noncriminal behavior is an expression of the same needs and values.* . . . [emphasis in the original][7]

Sutherland's thesis was that criminal behavior occurs when persons have acquired enough sentiments in favor of law violation to outweigh their prosocial or anticriminal conduct definitions. This formulation enjoyed great popularity in American criminology for at least two reasons. First, it was a single, coherent theory that purported to explain the occurrence or nonoccurrence of criminal conduct; thus it represented a giant step away from eclectic, "multiple-factor" orientations which were little more than long lists of specific variables that might play some part in lawbreaking. Second, Sutherland's argument was stated in the language of sociology rather than in some other vocabulary. The sociological perspective argues that individuals are the product of social experiences which provide them with beliefs and standards of conduct that guide their behavior.

However, this theory is not without faults. It contains a number of undefined terms as well as ambiguous propositions, with the result that it is plausible but untestable. It is scrutinized in more detail in Chapter 5, which is concerned with the structural problems of contemporary criminological theories.

**Sutherland's Other Contributions.** Sutherland was a "giant" of modern criminology in considerable part because of differential association theory. However, his stature is attributable to a large number of other contributions as well. Limitations of space prohibit anything more than a few brief comments on these other works.

Sutherland's *The Professional Thief* (1937) was a detailed description and analysis of the criminal profession of theft, particularly skilled forms of swindles. The book grew out of interview information provided to Sutherland by a professional thief, supplemented with interpretive chapters by Sutherland. Even though the book predated the appearance of the theory of differential association, the thief's account which it related did suggest that at least some forms of criminal activity are learned in much the same way as are the elements of skilled, legal professions. Also, it seems reasonable to argue that the book contributed to the elaboration of the theory of differential association, in much the same way that Sutherland was influenced by the findings of Shaw and McKay.

Sutherland, along with his student Donald Cressey (Sutherland, Cressey, and Luckenbill, 1992: 104–18), should also be credited with one version of the "criminogenic culture" perspective, designed to identify broad societal conditions that encourage or discourage criminality. They argued that the social changes of the late nineteenth and early twentieth century, including marked emphasis upon individualism, great stress on the pursuit of monetary wealth, and cultural conflict or normative clashes due to the presence of different cultural groups within the same society, have produced a situation of "differential social organization." They contended that differential social organization should explain the crime rate, while differential association should explain the criminal behavior of a person.

During the developmental decades of criminological thought, most criminologists centered their attention almost exclusively on garden-variety, working-class offenders. Sutherland was almost solely responsible for compelling them to attend to lawbreaking among the privileged and wealthy. Beginning about 1940, he wrote at length about "white-collar crime," which he sometimes defined as behavior that violates laws designed to regulate business and professional activities, including the actions of corporations. At other times, he offered definitions of "white-collar crime" that included embezzlement and other acts that occur outside the framework of regularized business or corporate activity. Moreover, those who have studied "white-collar crime" since Sutherland's time have continued to define the term in varied ways.[8] In his own study, Sutherland (1949a) focused on violations of regulatory statutes such as the Sherman Anti-Trust Act, carried on by the 70 largest manufacturing, mining, and mercantile corporations, which formed his sample.

### Other Contributions

The period from 1930 to 1955 saw a number of other developments in addition to the activities of Shaw, McKay, and Sutherland. One of these was the work of Thorsten Sellin on culture conflict, crime, and conduct norms. In *Culture Conflict and Crime* (Sellin, 1938), he argued that criminal laws change from time to time and vary from place to place, as a result of various other social changes. He concluded that this variability renders legal definitions invalid as the fundamental categories for inquiry. Sellin contended that all individuals are surrounded by social groups and social norms, that cultural complexity leads to a multiplicity of conflicting norms that play upon most individuals, and that criminology should focus on conduct norms and violations of them. This argument seemed appealing at first glance, but there was a fatal flaw in it, namely that conduct norms are no more universal or unchanging than are criminal laws. Even so, Sellin's notions about culture conflict found their way into many of the discussions of crime causation by criminologists in the 1940s and 1950s.

### The Balance Sheet

The contributions surveyed in this section provided the critical mass around which criminology developed in the United States between 1930 and 1950. Shaw and McKay emphasized the acquisition of criminal and delinquent behavior by people who are surrounded by conditions of social disorganization or normative breakdown. Sutherland provided the theory of differential association, which identified processes of cultural transmission that often lead to crime in societies characterized by differential social organization. Although not discussed here, Merton's (1938) influential essay on anomie and deviant behavior had much to say about how variations in access to socially approved avenues to upward mobility and material success are implicated in rates of deviance and the forms of deviant conduct.

However, greater attention was given during this period to how individuals become involved in lawbreaking than to the social-structural "root causes" of criminality. Sutherland's notion of differential social organization was less developed than was differential association theory. Too, Merton's anomie perspective was not pursued through sustained efforts by Merton or others to flesh out, through further theorizing and more research, the 1938 "bare bones" argument.

Critics of the sociological accounts of criminality dealt with in this section have also argued that these theories put forth a view of humans as helpless victims of deleterious circumstances and criminogenic forces that buffet them about and determine their behavior. According to these critics, deterministic views are in error because individuals frequently make rational choices to behave in a conformist or deviant fashion.

Still another charge that has often been leveled is that the criminologists of this period had little to say about lawmaking, and specifically, about "criminalization," or in other words, how and why certain behaviors become identified as criminal in the first place. Insofar as criminologists paid any attention to this issue, they usually offered a consensus view that held that criminal laws reflect broad societal interests and the moral values of societies.

This criticism has merit, for it has only been in the past few decades that criminologists have made sustained efforts to probe the origins of criminal laws, public support for or lack of allegiance to specific laws, and kindred topics (Gibbons, 1992a: 59–69). At the same time, it would be well to acknowledge that Sutherland, Sellin, and other criminologists of this period were not entirely oblivious to the social conflicts that are often played out in lawmaking processes.

## CRIMINOLOGY: 1955–1970

### Introduction

By 1955, the skeletal structure of modern "mainstream" criminology was largely completed. Mainstream criminology can be described in terms of a small number of themes that characterize it. First, it has been dominated by an interest in the behavior of criminals rather than the criminality of behavior. Second, while social-structural defects play the dominant role in causal theorizing, they have been viewed as amenable to social repair. At the same time, the criminogenic influences that produce criminality are pervasive and intimately bound up with the core institutions of modern society, with the result that the task of uncovering them requires a penetrating examination of American society.

Liberalism as a political ideology is usually described as one which assumes that social and economic progress can be made through governmental efforts, that social problems can be remedied through governmental intervention, and that steady progress toward a better world is possible. It is probably true that most criminologists embrace liberal political views and also favor liberal reforms in the criminal justice system, but it can also be argued that mainstream criminology has been and continues to be relatively conservative, because mainstream criminologists have rarely called for wholesale political and economic changes in American society in order to bring about crime control and/or prevention. Rather, they have advocated rehabilitation directed at adjusting offenders to the status quo and other relatively modest or limited approaches to crime prevention and reduction.

Although the major assumptions and perspectives of mainstream criminology have remained largely unchanged since the 1950s, a number of new developments occurred in criminological inquiry during the 1955–1970 period.

One new question that arose had to do with the parameters of criminological study. The investigations of "hidden" or self-reported delinquency produced in this period were linked to this continuing concern (Gibbons and Krohn, 1991: 41–48). These studies resulted in an abundance of data indicating that many youths and adults who had never been apprehended by the police had nonetheless engaged in acts of lawbreaking and forced sociologists to reexamine those theoretical viewpoints that assumed that delinquency and crime were restricted to working-class youths and adults.

A second set of questions also received attention in this period, namely, "How should the heterogeneous mixture of behavior gathered together under the label 'crime' be divided into theoretically meaningful units for study?" and "How can offenders be sorted out into behavioral types, so that the causes of criminality can be more clearly identified?" Advocates of typological approaches argued that theories and hypotheses about specific crime forms or criminal behavior patterns are required if we are to learn more about causation.

Satisfactory answers to these queries have yet to be produced; hence the issue of the "dependent variable(s)" in criminology is still very much alive. Chapter 4 is devoted to a detailed exploration of the dimensions of this problem and of the work that has been accomplished on it to date.

These two directions were tangential to etiological theory in that they did not deal directly with questions of causation. Not so for the very important body of theorizing and research on gang delinquency during this period, beginning with Cohen's *Delinquent Boys* (1955). That book was immediately followed by a number of alternative theories of gang delinquency, but by the latter part of the 1955–1970 period, research on gangs began to catch up with theorizing. As is frequently the case in sociological inquiry, empirical investigations indicated that the real world was a good deal more complex than representations in sociological formulations would have us believe. We will examine these developments in more detail in the following section.

Still another line of work had to do with criminal justice and correctional organizations, and in particular, with studies of prisons, centering most often on the patterns of adjustment to confinement exhibited by inmates. The literature was also enriched by some sociologically sophisticated inquiries on police organizations, as well as research on the workings of the courts. These inquiries were not centrally concerned with causal issues; hence I simply note them in passing.

There was also renewed interest in social control arguments about causation during the 1955–1970 period. Reckless's hypothesis that a positive self-concept insulates youths from involvement in delinquency, which underpinned his writings on "containment theory" (1973), appeared during this period. More important, Hirschi's social control formulation made its appearance in 1969. Hirschi's claims about lack of social bonding and low self-control as major forces in crime and delinquency developed into one of the most dominant etiological perspectives in criminology in the period since 1970, so I want to reserve discussion of it until we turn in Chapter 3 to developments since 1970.

### Subcultural Theory and Research[9]

Although gang delinquency has been a subject of persistent interest since the 1930s, relatively little theoretical or empirical work was carried out on gang misconduct in the period between the investigations by Shaw and McKay and the 1950s. As a consequence, the publication of Cohen's book in 1955 was a major event, for it triggered a resurgence of attention to gang behavior.

Cohen was interested in accounting for the emergence of delinquent subcultures in working-class neighborhoods of American cities. He argued that a delinquent subculture is "a way of life that has somehow become traditional among certain groups in American society. These groups are the boys' gangs that flourish most conspicuously in the 'delinquency neighborhoods' of our large American cities" (p. 13). He also argued that much of the stealing and other behavior of gang offenders is nonutilitarian, malicious, and negativistic and that these boys steal "for the hell of it." He also described subcultural deviance in terms of *short-run hedonism* (lack of long-term goals or planning) and *group autonomy*.

Why did the delinquent subculture develop among lower-class boys? Cohen concluded that it represented a social movement that arose as a solution to shared problems of low status among working-class boys. These shared problems of low esteem stem from the social order. Working-class boys experienced status threats when they were evaluated by a middle-class measuring rod, that is, a set of expectations regarding the characteristics of "good boys." These center on such traits as ambition and individual responsibility. Working-class boys have been inadequately socialized and are deficient in the ability to conform to these standards, and as a result, they find themselves at a disadvantage in classrooms and other social arenas where they compete with middle-class peers for recognition by adults. As a result, they withdraw from situations of social hurt, such as the school, and find their way into the subculture of the gang, which provides them with a shelter against assaults on their self-esteem.

Cohen's portrayal was based on a relatively sparse foundation of solid evidence. Not surprisingly, a number of critics drew attention to errors in his formulation (Gibbons and Krohn, 1991: 122–23).

Cohen's theory eventually provoked some alternative formulations, the most important of which was Cloward and Ohlin's (1960) "opportunity theory." They asserted that delinquent gangs consisted of boys who are concerned about economic injustice rather than middle-class status. According to these theorists, lower-class boys share a common American value commitment to success, measured mainly in economic terms, but they are at a competitive disadvantage compared to their middle-class counterparts. Either they do not have access to legitimate means to reach these goals, or if they do have opportunities for achievement, they perceive their chances of success as limited. As a result, for many of them, a severe disjunction exists between what they want out of life and what they anticipate they will receive. Pressures to engage in delinquency are generated by this goals-means discrepancy.

The particular adaptation assumed by youths is influenced by the opportunity structures for deviant behavior. Some lower-class areas are characterized by integration of criminalistic and conformist patterns of organization while others are lacking in criminal networks. In the former, youths are exposed to older role models who are involved in relatively successful criminal endeavors. In turn, these boys become involved in theft and in careers that often lead them to adult criminality, while in the latter areas, which are lacking in stable criminal traditions and patterns, delinquency takes a conflict-gang warfare form. Finally, boys who are failures in both the legitimate and illegitimate arenas disengage from the competitive struggle and withdraw into drug addiction.

Although initial reactions to this argument were extremely favorable, a number of critical comments were later directed at it (Gibbons and Krohn, 1991: 127–28).

Still another explanation of gang delinquency was advanced by Miller (1958, 1959), who argued that delinquency is the product of lower-class values, or "focal concerns," that is, long-established, durable traditions of lower-class life, rather than the result of responses to conflicts with middle-class values. This argument is a version of the "culture of poverty" thesis, in which the behavior and activities of lower-class citizens are attributed to a distinctive way of life said to characterize them.[10]

Miller contended that gang delinquency was a response to lower-class "focal concerns" (values), including "trouble," "toughness," "excitement," and "autonomy." For example, persons who are motivated to seek out opportunities for risky but exciting activities are often likely to stumble into criminal endeavors.

Critics have pointed to a number of problems with Miller's formulation (Gibbons and Krohn, 1991: 141–42), but a major one centered on its tautological nature. Much of the evidence used to identify focal concerns was drawn from the same behavior that these concerns were supposed to explain, as for example, when assaultive conduct was used to demonstrate that toughness is a lower-class value.

These observations about subcultural theories of delinquency are skimpy ones which do not do full justice to the extensive commentary that was provoked by the three theories I have briefly described. Additionally, there were some other, rival formulations about gangs that have not been mentioned (Gibbons and Krohn, 1991: 141–42).

A considerable body of research which was stimulated by these theories also ought to be noted. By 1970, an extensive but also confusing collection of findings on gang delinquency had accumulated (Gibbons and Krohn, 1991: 128–32). Taken in its entirety, much of it indicated that none of the theoretical perspectives we have looked at were entirely accurate. For example, there was little support for Cloward and Ohlin's contentions about offense specialization on the part of delinquent gangs, nor did the findings lend much support to their argument that delinquent youths come from the ranks of the most talented and most upwardly mobile youngsters in lower-class communities. Finally, the research did not show that gang delinquents were in rebellion against middle-class values.

Even though the major theories regarding gang delinquency did not fare well in the face of the evidence, the basic notion of subcultures as important in accounting for delinquency and criminality has survived and has turned up in such recent ventures as Braithwaite's (1989b) general theory, in which subcultural formation plays an important part. On the other hand, research interest in delinquent gangs waned in the 1970s and 1980s, with only a few studies, such as those of Hagedorn (1988) and Jankowski (1991), appearing in recent years.

## CONCLUDING COMMENTS

This chapter is the first half of a brief account of the development of criminology, particularly within sociology, from about 1900 to the present. This half traced some of the major events up to about 1970. Running through much of the theorizing considered to this point, including both differential association notions and arguments about subcultures, is an underlying theme of essentially "good" persons behaving in "bad" or deviant ways because of economic or other pressures playing upon them. As we move into the 1970s and 1980s in the next chapter, we will see a shift away from this imagery toward the view that delinquents and criminals are "bad" persons, flawed in one way or another.

## NOTES

[1]This is one of those instances where the vessel is half full or half empty. I also noted in the same book (Gibbons, 1992a: 25) that "many of these viewpoints survive in altered form in contemporary efforts to account for criminality." For example, the work of nineteenth-century members of the "cartographic school," involving the study of such matters as regional variations in climate and crime rates, has rough parallels in modern research. Also, the arguments of nineteenth-century classical theorists which stressed hedonism and free will bear some similarity to the claims of rational choice theorists in economics and sociology.

[2]A number of detailed accounts of the rise of American sociology are available. See Barnes, 1948; Hinkle and Hinkle, 1954; Aron, 1965, 1967; Odum, 1951; Bannister, 1987.

[3]For another brief and useful account of the major developments in sociology from around 1985 to the period of the dominance of the University of Chicago from 1920 to 1932, see Faris, 1967.

[4]Parmelee's writings are discussed in more detail in Gibbons, 1979: 28–32. Also see Gibbons, 1974: 405–16. I have pointed out in these lengthier statements that Parmelee's book contained some passages having a more contemporary ring. For example, he suggested that laws often promote religious or class interests to the exclusion of other values; thus it is not always true that criminal laws reflect societal-wide definitions of immoral or undesirable conduct. It would be a serious error to offer a caricature of Parmelee, portraying him as a simpleton espousing silly ideas.

[5]I do not mean to suggest that all individual criminologists can be sorted out in a parallel way; rather, there were important differences among various early criminologists or between specific "mainstream" criminologists in the 1955–1970 period. Then, too, although the "radicalization" of criminology occurred in the 1970s and 1980s, not all criminologists were equally "radicalized." Indeed, the majority of them were not personally influenced in any marked way by radical theorizing. Even so, the emergence of a relatively small and noisy radical-Marxist "school" was a major event in the 1970s. Finally, conservatism is a feature of the 1980s, but there are many criminologists who eschew most of the conservative arguments that appeared in this period.

[6]Finestone (1976a, 1976b) has explicated the structure of the Shaw-McKay argument in detail. He indicated that they were particularly influenced by the views of W. I. Thomas regarding the cyclical processes of social change involving social organization, disorganization, and

reorganization. They viewed the movement of successive waves of immigrants first into inner-city neighborhoods and later to outer-city areas as a case in point of these processes. They initially viewed delinquency as a part of the natural history of the settlement process experienced by newly arrived groups in the urban community.

Shaw and McKay described the process through which youngsters became delinquent in these neighborhoods as growing out of or taking place against the backdrop of social disorganization experienced by immigrants as they and their children encountered the influences of the new culture into which they had moved. Disorganization was manifested through alienation of children from their parents and adult institutions, so that these youths became detached from customary social controls that normally produce conformist conduct. In turn, these detached and alienated juveniles drifted into association with other like-minded youngsters who collectively turned to delinquent acts.

Although this social disorganization-reorganization view made a good deal of sense out of many aspects of delinquency observed by Shaw and McKay, it did not provide an adequate explanation for the persistence of a delinquency tradition in these inner-city neighborhoods, particularly in the 1930s, after immigration had dried up. As a consequence, Shaw and McKay were ultimately driven to develop another argument to account for the relatively stable delinquent value system they observed in delinquency areas. They eventually conceived a functional interpretation that sought to explain the tradition of crime and delinquency as a response of many of the residents to economic pressures. Shaw and McKay came to view crime and delinquency as responses to social strains experienced by economically deprived people in a society that encouraged all citizens to aspire to success goals, which were measured almost entirely in monetary terms. Thus, they ultimately shifted their social change perspective to a viewpoint that anticipated Merton's (1938) anomie theory of deviance.

[7]I have omitted the additional commentary on the Sutherland and Cressey principles or propositions which accompanied the presentation of the theory in their book.

[8]Sutherland's several conceptions of white-collar crime can be found in Sutherland, 1949a, 1949b, 1946, 1945, 1940. There is a case to be made for the argument that the concept of white-collar crime ought to be restricted to violations of laws designed to regulate business affairs and ought to exclude conventional crimes such as assault and homicide committed by persons who incidentally happen to be upper-status persons. Also, embezzlement is not white-collar crime, because it involves surreptitious acts by employees, which are carried on for their own benefit and which are harmful to the interests of the organization. White-collar violations of regulatory provisions, on the other hand, are intended to contribute to the financial success of the organization. Also, certain "fringe" activities of professionals, such as ambulance chasing or subornation by lawyers, should not be defined as white-collar crime. For a detailed discussion of these points, see Gibbons, 1992a: 291–313.

[9]For a more detailed discussion of subcultural theories, critiques of these arguments, and the research bearing upon them, see Gibbons and Krohn, 1991: 121–32.

[10]"Culture of poverty" views are much beloved by conservative Republican politicians such as former Vice-President Quayle. Although many sociologists concede that certain values or interests of lower-class persons operate as barriers to social or economic improvement on the latter's part, many of these observers also argue that the "culture of poverty" is in considerable part the *result* of long-standing patterns of economic and social discrimination directed at marginal and economically deprived segments of the population. Put differently, in this view, the so-called culture of poverty is the product or result of more fundamental influences. By contrast, in the hands of political conservatives, the culture of poverty thesis quickly turns into a form of "blaming the victim," in which the disadvantaged are said to "deserve" to be poorly housed and deprived of adequate medical care, and to live in a situation of economic precariousness.

# CHAPTER 3

# The Development of Criminology, II

## INTRODUCTION

Chapter 2 noted that a number of issues consumed the time and interest of criminologists in the 1955–1970 period. Some of these, such as the study of "hidden delinquency" and unreported crime, as well as typological ventures directed at uncovering offender roles or types, were tangential to theorizing about the causes of delinquent or criminal behavior.[1] Chapter 2 devoted a good deal of attention to the subcultural or gang delinquency theorizing and research of the 1950s and 1960s. It also took note of the resurgence of the topic of social control, which had occupied much of the attention of the pioneers of American sociology but which had fallen out of favor in later decades. However, examination of social control lines of work was deferred to Chapter 3 because social control and social bonding arguments attained greater prominence after 1970.

This chapter begins with social control viewpoints. It also touches upon the growth (and decline) of labeling notions in criminology. We then move on to a number of radical-Marxist challenges to mainstream criminological thought which arose in the 1970s and 1980s. As we shall see, most of the initial ventures into radical-Marxist criminology were instances of "vulgar" or instrumental Marxism, which is another way of saying that they lacked sophistication. These early statements, which were long on hyperbole and bombast, later gave way to more finely grained expositions in the form of structural Marxism. Chapter 3 also touches upon some "new criminologies" of the late 1980s and early 1990s, including "realist criminology," feminist viewpoints, and constitutive criminology. Finally, note is taken of some contemporary instances of narrower theorizing directed at specific forms of crime. We have already encountered one of these in Chapter 1, namely Baron and Straus's (1990) multivariate formulation regarding forcible rape. This discussion of current forms of criminological inquiry also comments on developments in such fields as psychology, economics, and geography, as well as the growing body of sociobiological research on criminality.

I have already alluded in Chapter 2 to the difficulty of compressing the entire twentieth-century development of criminology into two relatively brief chapters. Many topics and issues must be left out of this account, and furthermore, what is included must necessarily be terse, with much detail omitted. Finally, as I indicated with regard to control theory, periodization of these developmental events is to some extent arbitrary. So it is with some other twists and turns in criminological theory identified in this chapter. In short, Chapter 2 and this one provide a more or less accurate account of the development of the criminological enterprise.


## SOCIAL CONTROL–BOND THEORIES

Social control was a prominent area of inquiry in early American sociology, as indicated by the once-numerous textbooks and courses dealing with that topic. However, social control texts and courses all but disappeared in the 1950s and 1960s.

Although the area of specialization withered away, the concept of social control remained alive and is currently one of the major perspectives on criminality and deviance.[2] Also, Gibbs (1989) has recently attempted to resurrect control as sociology's "central notion" or organizing principle.

### Containment Theory

Let us begin with Reckless's (1973) containment theory, which was a case of old wine in a new bottle. Reckless was one of the pioneers of mainstream American criminology, although he ranked a distant second to Sutherland in his impact on the field. In the 1950s, he and his associates conducted a series of studies of "good" boys, nominated by school teachers as unlikely to get into trouble with the law, and "bad" boys, thought to be headed for trouble. Marvin Krohn and I (1991: 107–9) have reviewed these studies, which indicated that considerably more "bad" boys subsequently acquired official records with the police or juvenile court than did "good" boys, leading Reckless to conclude that a positive self-image "insulates" youths from the pull of delinquency, while a deficient self-concept gives

THE DEVELOPMENT OF CRIMINOLOGY, II

slum boys no resistance to deviance. But critics pointed out a number of problems with these data and conclusions, not the least of which is that Reckless failed to show that the nondelinquent "good" boys had actually been exposed to delinquent pressures; thus they may have had nothing to be insulated from.

Reckless ultimately expanded these notions about insulating factors into what he termed "containment theory," which asserts that nearly all individuals encounter, in varying degrees, environmental pressures in the direction of lawbreaking and that nearly all of them encounter biological and psychological pushes toward deviance. Behavior, whether deviant or conforming, is heavily influenced by these external pressures and also by the pushes from within the person. However, much of the time these criminalistic influences are countered by inner or outer containment factors, including a positive self-image.

The critics have not been kind to containment theory (Gibbons and Krohn, 1991: 107–9). In particular, Schrag (1971: 82–89) noted its vague terms and unclear empirical indicators of the major concepts, and the absence of explicit and interconnected propositions in it. While Schrag ably identified a number of serious deficiencies in the argument, he also concluded that with a major overhaul, the theory might hold some promise. But, in fact, containment theory was not overhauled, and it has been supplanted by Hirschi's control theory.

### Hirschi's Social Control Theory

Hirschi's (1969) version of control theory is considerably more detailed and formalized than is containment theory. Its central thesis is that juveniles become free to commit delinquent acts when their ties to the conventional social order are severed. Many delinquent acts are intrinsically attractive or represent the most expedient route to some desirable goal. Consquently, most youths would engage in them if they were not constrained from doing so by their ties to others. No special motivation to engage in lawbreaking is required once these links are broken.

Hirschi identified several dimensions along which the bond to society varies: attachment, commitment, involvement, and belief. *Attachment* has to do with the strength of ties to others such as parents or peers, while *commitment* refers to the person's devotion to conformist lines of conduct. *Involvement* is the degree to which individuals are engaged in activities that restrict the time they have available for deviant behavior, while *belief* refers to the strength of their attitudes toward conformity.

This social control argument provided the framework for a study by Hirschi (1969) in which he gathered self-report data on delinquent involvement and on social control variables from a large sample of juveniles in a California community. The delinquency index consisted for the most part of relatively petty acts of misbehavior. In the main, the findings were consistent with the theory. Delinquent youths showed less attachment to parents, school and school teachers, peers, and conventional activity, and they also exhibited less-positive attitudes toward conformity.

In an earlier comment on Hirschi's theory (Gibbons, 1979: 121), I indicated that "Hirschi's version of social control theory has generated considerable interest on the part of a number of criminologists . . . there are several signs that suggest that Hirschi's theory is likely to be one of the more enduring contributions in criminology."

Since these words were penned, critics have drawn attention to some problems with the theory (Gibbons and Krohn, 1991: 102–5). Some have noted that in practice, commitment and involvement are difficult to distinguish from each other. Put another way, involvement appears to be the behavioral side of commitment; hence these are two aspects of the same thing. However, a number of studies employing bond theory as a framework have been conducted since Hirschi's 1969 study, with results that tend to support the argument. Finally, these research investigations have also indicated that social control or bond factors may account for relatively minor forms of delinquency and for female lawbreaking more satisfactorily than they do for more serious instances of juvenile misconduct.

Hirschi, in collaboration with Gottfredson (1990), has elaborated the initial version of control theory into a general theory of deviance and crime in which they argue that most deviance and criminality is unplanned, trivial, and mundane activity, carried out by persons who are lacking in self-control. I will return to this theory in the pages ahead, and in particular, in Chapter 10 where attention focuses on efforts to develop integrated and/or general theories of crime.[3]

## LABELING THEORY

This account of control theory indicates that some of its basic ideas had origins in early sociological theorizing. Also, variants of the control perspective spanned the period from the early 1900s to the present. In somewhat the same way, elements of what has been called labeling theory have been with us for a long time, but they enjoyed their greatest popularity in the 1970s, which is the warrant for discussing them at this point.

Theorizing about nonconforming behavior has been a part of sociology from its earliest beginnings. At one time, deviants were regarded as persons apart from the majority of conformist citizens. They were seen as carriers of social pathology and the products of various individual peculiarities, biological forces, or temporary social dislocation. Later, norm-violating conduct was attributed to rents and tears in the social fabric caused by urbanization or rapid social change. Also, early theorists embraced an implicit assumption that apprehended or publicly identified norm violators were representative of all nonconformists. Little or no concern was voiced about the role of social audiences in the identification and processing of officially tagged "deviants" and the ways in which these individuals might differ from deviants-at-large, that is, undetected nonconformists.

Labeling arguments arose in response to the shortcomings of these older viewpoints. What are the central arguments of the labeling view? First, deviance is not a property that is inherent in certain acts; rather, social groups and other collectivities create the *social definitions* that lead to certain forms of behavior being singled out as "beyond the pale." Also, the standards or social norms that are transgressed by "deviants" are not universal or unchanging. For example, sexual activity outside of marriage was more widely condemned in the past than it is currently in the United States. Then, too, within a large, complex society such as our own, considerable disagreement exists among various population groups regarding what should or should not be viewed as "deviant." Witness, for example, the current, heated quarrels between "right to life" advocates and those persons who hold that women should have the unfettered right to determine whether or not to carry a pregnancy to term. Finally, some persons who engage in transgressions get identified as deviants while others escape detection and identification (and still other persons are falsely accused of deviant conduct).

Labeling viewpoints also often hold that deviance arises out of diverse sources or circumstances. Theorists of this persuasion deny that some small body of cultural values accounts for the myriad forms of deviance in modern societies; instead, they emphasize *value pluralism*. Deviant acts often occur when persons find themselves pulled and tugged by competing interests and values.

Labeling theorists often distinguish between "nonconformists," that is, persons who have violated a social rule, and "deviants," who are individuals who have become identified through being arrested, committed to a mental hospital, or through some other form of public identification. These theorists also contend that official deviance is the outcome of social processes that involve both the acts of nonconformists and the reactions of others to these violations. They draw attention to "careers," in which individuals who become publicly identified exhibit changes in behavior and self-concept patterns over time. Many of these changes are attributed to social reactions that are directed toward deviant individuals.

Labeling formulations also frequently hypothesize that the organizations and agencies that are designed to bring deviants back into conformity often produce quite contrary results. They stigmatize individuals, seal them off from opportunities to withdraw from deviance, and create other social impediments to rehabilitation. People-changing institutions such as prisons and training schools are suspected of often exacerbating, rather than reducing, the adjustment problems of their charges.

This thumbnail sketch is roughly accurate, but on closer examination, labeling theory turns out to be a loose set of themes, rather than an explicit and coherent theory.

A number of persons have been identified as principal architects of the labeling perspective, but in my opinion, Edwin Lemert was the single most important contributor.[4] His 1951 book, *Social Pathology*, contained virtually all of the concepts and important ideas that were elaborated subsequently by labeling theorists in the 1960s and 1970s. For example, he identified the contexts in which deviance takes place, differentiating between *individual, situational,* and *systematic* deviance. The first refers to nonconformity that arises out of pressures "within the skin," so to speak, of the person. Situational deviance is the result of external stresses and strains, and systematic deviance was Lemert's term for subcultural, organized patterns of nonconformity.

Lemert also introduced the notions of *primary* and *secondary* deviation, the first referring to initial flirtations with nonconformity, and the second, to instances where deviant actors reorganize their self-images and much of their behavior around their status as a "deviant" of one sort or another.

Beginning in the 1960s, a considerable outpouring of essays on deviance centering on labeling themes began to appear in the sociological literature (Gibbons, 1979: 148–52; Gibbons and Jones, 1975). Some of these endeavored to expand upon labeling notions, others were applications of labeling insights to particular forms of deviance or deviant-processing organizations, and still others consisted of critiques directing attention to weak spots in the perspective.

As I indicated, the labeling viewpoint was not restricted to criminality, but many of the illustrative cases invoked to support it had to do with law-breaking. Also, its supporters often applied it to crime and delinquency, arguing that labeling experiences drive offenders further into careers as deviants, rather than drawing them away from criminal pathways.

What can be said about labeling notions in criminology, and in particular, this ironic view of reactions to criminality? Wellford (1975) has reviewed the theoretical and research literature bearing upon the argument. He contended that the assertion that no acts are intrinsically criminal is in error because murder and a number of other acts are consistently prohibited across different societies. He also argued that the claim that the social characteristics of labeled deviants are the major bases on which decisions regarding their fates are made in the correctional machinery lacks empirical support. He contended that most offenders get into the hands of the authorities because of the lawbreaking in which they have engaged and that the major determinant of subsequent decisions about them centers on offense seriousness.

On the whole, the evidence lent relatively little support to the sweeping claims that were made in the 1970s about the deleterious effects of correctional intervention efforts on offenders. Additionally, labeling exponents failed to convert the broad insights with which they began into a fleshed-out theoretical structure that makes sense of causal processes. In short, the early promise of this perspective has been largely unrealized. At the same time, labeling insights were effectively incorporated into such works as Irwin's *The Felon* in 1970, and more recently, into his *The Jail* (Irwin, 1985). On this same point, Braithwaite (1989b) utilized ideas derived from the labeling perspective in his general theory on crime. Then, too, labeling themes can be identified in some of the "new criminologies" (feminist views, realist criminology, and critical approaches) to be examined in Chapter 10. These examples seem to bear out the earlier prediction (Gibbons, 1979: 155): "Certain key insights in labeling perspectives are likely to survive in the criminological formulations of the future."

## CONFLICT AND RADICAL CRIMINOLOGY

### The Development of Conflict and Radical Criminology

The labeling arguments that arose in the 1960s had the effect of compelling criminologists to pay closer attention to the social contingencies that often have much to do with accounting for the fact that some law violators become officially tagged as "criminals" at the same time that others avoid these stigmatizing labels and experiences. However, some more strident and full-blown challenges to mainstream perspectives in criminology arose in the 1970s, in the form of arguments that have been identified variously as conflict, radical, Marxist, or critical criminology (Gibbons, 1992a: 121–33; 1979: 156–94). The dividing point between social conflict arguments and more radical ones is not always clear-cut, but even so, pluralistic conflict viewpoints can be distinguished from more radical, Marxist propositions about criminality.

### Conflict and Interest-Group Theories

The conflict theories which arose in the 1970s were the first major challenge to mainstream views and were followed by more radical viewpoints. Interest-group or conflict arguments attribute lawmaking and criminality to a pluralistic pattern of conflicting interest-group actions and phenomena in American society, rather than to some monolithic political-economic structure.

For example, Turk (1969) has written extensively about conflicts among different groups which all seek to gain social and material advantages over other collectivities. These conflicts are kept under control in part through legal norms and patterns of norm enforcement which the *authorities* (those in dominant positions) impose upon the *subjects* (relatively powerless persons and groups). Turk dealt at length with the conditions under which differences between authorities and subjects are likely to result in conflict and the conditions under which criminalization will probably occur. Crimi-nalization is the assignment of criminal status to people through norm-enforcement mechanisms such as arrest and trial.

Chambliss and Seidman (1971) also put forth a perspective on social conflict, crime, law, and social control, as did Quinney (1970). Some significant insights have come out of these and other writings on the conflict origins of the laws and law-violating behavior. However, the critics have argued that these models favor diffuse, pluralistic conceptions of social conflicts and interest groups and are, as a result, inaccurate. According to the critics, these arguments fail to acknowledge the overpowering significance of class relationships growing out of productive relations in societies, which lead to monopolization of effective power by a ruling class rather than myriad interest groups.

### Radical-Marxist Criminology

*The Origins of Radical Criminology.*   Although conflict-oriented perspectives that stress pluralism in American society existed in rudimentary form for some decades, it was not until the 1970s that a thoroughly radical, Marxist version of criminological thought emerged.

What produced the radicalization of criminologists and the development of radical alternatives to mainstream criminology? Was it because the latter had failed to deal with new empirical facts that emerged in the 1970s? The role of new facts cannot be denied, but those facts arose *outside* of criminology and sociology, not from criminological studies that turned up puzzling results. A 1974 issue of *Crime and Social Justice* put the matter well: "Radical criminology appeared on the crest of the final surges of political protest by women, blacks, the poor, students, and many others whose rage has scoured American institutions through the previous decade."

A number of commentators have pointed to such things as the Vietnam War and the political turmoil that it generated, black militancy, the development of a youth counterculture, widespread brutality and illegality in police responses to political dissidents, and growing evidence of the ubiquity of white-collar crime by upper-class individuals as major forces accounting for the move toward radical views. Interpretations of precisely how these events were tied to radical criminology vary somewhat, but nearly all observers agreed that the role of the state is central in the oppression of the masses of the citizenry through criminal law and a variety of other devices of social control.

*Varieties of Radical-Marxist Theory.* It would be incorrect to claim that a single variety of radical theory monopolized the attention of criminologists in the 1970s. There were a number of variants of this perspective (e.g., Gordon, 1973; Chambliss, 1975; Michalowski and Bohlander, 1976; Quinney, 1974, 1977; Hepburn, 1977; Spitzer, 1975), but, there also were a good many common themes in these essays. Quinney's (1974: 16) set of propositions is representative of this criminological genre:

1. American society is based on an advanced capitalist economy.
2. The state is organized to serve the interests of the dominant economic class, the capitalist ruling class.
3. Criminal law is an instrument of the State and the ruling class to maintain and perpetuate the existing social and economic order.
4. Crime control in capitalistic society is accomplished through a variety of institutions and agencies established and administered by a governmental elite, representing ruling class interests, for the purpose of establishing a domestic order.
5. The contradictions of advanced capitalism—the disjunction between essence and existence—require that the subordinate classes remain oppressed by whatever means necessary, especially through the coercion and violence of the legal system.
6. Only with the collapse of capitalist society and the creation of a new society, based on socialist principles, will there be a solution to the crime problem.

As we can see from Quinney's framework, early radical writings posited the existence of a monolithic ruling class made up of the "shakers and movers" in the worlds of finance and industry, along with powerful political figures. Criminal laws were regarded as consciously created devices through which the ruling class maintains its political and economic domination over the rest of us. Implicit in Quinney's proposition 4 and explicit in much other radical writing is the thesis that the principal role of the police is the protection of ruling class interests, rather than those of ordinary citizens. Finally, many radical theorists additional to Quinney contended that effective crime reduction cannot be obtained from tinkering with the capitalist social order; instead, the only cure lies in a socialist revolution.

The Marxian perspective contained in these six claims was extremely sketchy. As a result, Quinney's book was the target of a number of criticisms. Consider, for example, the argument about the domination exercised by a single ruling class. Some critics charged that this description of a small, monolithic collection of corporate heads who engage in malevolent schemes to oppress the underdogs of American society—blacks, other minorities, women, and working-class groups—was grossly overdrawn.

Quinney followed his 1974 book with another in 1977, *Class, State, and Crime,* which endeavored to expand on Marxist themes and also to deal with some of the criticisms of the earlier work. It included a rudimentary typology of crime forms and it also tried to move beyond gross assertions about the machinations of the ruling class. Then, too, it avoided the romanticizing about garden-variety criminals that was contained in his earlier book and in many of the other early ventures into radical thought by other criminologists.

There are other indications that radical thought grew in sophistication in the first years following its appearance on the scene, including Greenberg's (1977) essay identifying ways in which changes in the extent and nature of youth involvement in crimes have been linked to their historically changing position in industrial societies.

*Responses to Early Versions of Radical Criminology.* Responses to early radical criminology were varied, ranging from mild hostility from some of the leading figures of mainstream criminology to enthusiastic approval by other criminologists (Gibbons, 1979: 186–93). One assessment was expressed by Meier (1976), who declared that there was little that was really new in "the new criminology," as it was sometimes called. He claimed that radical criminologists had taken many established viewpoints from mainstream criminology and rephrased them in more dramatic political terms. Along a different line, Hirst (1972) and Mugford (1974), among others, charged that contemporary Marxist criminological arguments were not truly Marxist, in that Marx said little about crime in his writings. These critics charged that radical criminology presented a distorted version of Marxist thought.

The development of Marxist or radical criminology was similar in some ways to the evolution of labeling theory. Theorists first put forth a sketchy set of claims about the impact of social labeling processes on putative and real deviants, which were then followed by critical essays by others which took a variety of directions. The result was a body of theorizing and counter commentary that cannot easily be summarized in a page or two.

The critical observations about radical-Marxist versions of criminological thought were similarly rich and varied. However, most of them centered on the contention that radical-Marxist thought was in one way or another, "one-dimensional," "vulgar Marxism," or a form of "instrumental Marxism." These were slightly different ways of declaring that radical-Marxist criminology did not reflect the complexities in the arguments of Marx. More specifically, it was said that radical criminology was an instance of instrumental Marxism which asserted that relations of production determine all other social forms in a society and that at any point in time, this economic dominance is readily apparent. Marx actually advanced a "structural" position of much greater complexity, for he contended that "in the long run," social forms would show the influences of economic forces. It was because radical criminology was deemed to have presented an overly simplistic interpretation of Marxist theory that it was also declared to be "one-dimensional" or lacking in sophistication or to be a vulgarized version of Marxist analysis.

This sweeping indictment of radical criminology can be broken down into component claims, such as the charge that much of the early theorizing about the ruling class and its domination of social affairs put forth a picture of the socially powerful and their exercise of social power that did not capture the complexities of the power structures or power relations that actually characterize modern societies. Along the same line, some critics claimed that the ruling-class origins thesis about criminal laws was overly simplified. Then, too, radical theorists tended to express strident and overly simple views of the role of the police in modern societies, ignoring much of the "peace-keeping" activity in which the police are involved. Finally, observations about prisons and other correctional institutions that describe these places as solely engaged in repression of persons who are suspected of being threats to the political domination enjoyed by the ruling class were judged to be wide of the mark.

*Post-Radical Thought.*   I commented briefly in another book (Gibbons, 1992a: 130–33) on developments in radical-Marxist criminology during the period from the 1980s to the present. I noted that it had apparently reached its apogee of influence, judging by such signs as the slowdown in published works on radical criminology and the reduced visibility of radical scholars at meetings of the American Society of Criminology. I also endeavored to identify some of the factors that were responsible for an apparent return to more conservative versions of criminological thought. One obvious candidate is the general drift of American society toward conservative attitudes, growing pessimism about the prospects of social reform, growing fears about "the crime problem," and the spread of "get tough" attitudes and policies toward crime and criminals that marked the Reagan/Bush era.

In this same commentary, I noted that although radical thought had become less prominent, it would be a mistake to announce the death of radicalism. Radical-Marxist criminology moved during the 1980s in the direction of more finely grained structural analyses and away from the simplistic formulations of the 1970s. Two examples of this trend are Colvin and Pauly's (1983) "integrated structural-Marxist theory of delinquency" and Messerschmidt's (1986) socialist-feminist exploration of the linkages between capitalism, patriarchy, sexual discrimination, and crime. Some radical criminologists have been influenced by evidence such as that produced by English social historians regarding changes in criminal laws and procedures in nineteenth-century England and which indicated that lawmaking is an extremely complex phenomenon (Thompson, 1975; Hay, Linebaugh, Rule, Thompson, and Winslow, 1975; Jones, 1982). That evidence influenced some persons to abandon the earlier, gross assertions about ruling class domination of these processes. In short, there are indications that the formerly sharp distinctions between radical and mainstream criminology may become blurred in the decades ahead.

One footnote about post-radical thought is that a very much modified kind of radical argument began to appear in England and the United States in the late 1980s, in the form of "realist criminology." The viewpoint, which emphasizes the serious impact of street crime on its victims, the existence of societal consensus around a core group of social norms, and the need for greater citizen involvement in crime control, was enunciated by persons who had espoused radical-Marxist views in the 1970s. However, as we will see in Chapter 9 when left realist arguments are examined in detail, these are more consistent with traditional, mainstream thoughtways than they are radical in tone.

## OTHER DEVELOPMENTS

Having come this far, we are near the end of our review of major developments in criminology since about 1900. However, some other events require mention.

Contemporary criminology may not be a many-splendored thing, but it would not be inaccurate to assert that the field has expanded dramatically during the past 90 years in terms of the breadth of the theorizing and research that has taken place. Chapters 2 and 3 have given a good deal of attention to the growth in criminological theorizing. In addition, it is clear that the storehouse of empirical facts in criminology has expanded dramatically, particularly since the end of World War II. We now have at hand a very large number of research findings that have come out of specific studies that have been carried out around theoretical notions of a narrower sort than most of the ones considered to this point.

The expansion of knowledge becomes readily apparent when the standard criminology textbooks of the 1950s are compared with a current one, such as my *Society, Crime, and Criminal Behavior* (1992a). In the latter, the chapters dealing with specific forms of criminality (pp. 228–412) are filled with a large collection of specific studies, many of which were completed in the past two decades. Further, the review of evidence in my text is selective and omits mention of a number of other investigations.

Consider a few examples of the theory-informed studies which have been produced. One of these is the Baron and Straus (1990) investigation of gender inequality and other correlates of forcible rape rates, while another would be recent investigations of links between unemployment and criminality, one by Kohfeld and Sprague (1988) and the other by Chiricos (1987). Another indication of the growth of knowledge can be found in the journal *Criminology*, which in recent years has been filled with reports on a number of sophisticated pieces of research. And *Criminology* is only one of a number of criminology and criminal justice journals that have appeared in the past 20 years.

Chapter 1 acknowledged that contributions to criminological knowledge have come from fields additional to sociology. The evidence regarding sociobiological factors in criminality has also grown markedly in the past several decades (Fishbein, 1990; Trasler, 1987; Ellis and Hoffman, 1990). Additionally, there are growing indications that criminologists must come to grips with psychological factors and individual differences if we are to develop adequate causal theories. The challenge of biogenic and psychogenic evidence is discussed in detail in Chapter 8.

Biological and psychological approaches have relevance to "Why do they do it?" queries. Additionally, there have been a number of efforts to attack those questions through social learning arguments, including Akers's (1985) translation of differential association theory into the language of modern behavioral-reinforcement theory. Then, too, social learning formulations have parallels in rational choice arguments (Cornish and Clarke, 1986) that have been developed by economists and some other social scientists. These approaches are discussed at length in Chapter 7.

Finally, as I noted in Chapter 1, modern criminology also includes contributions from a number of other fields, such as political science and geography (Harries, 1974).

## CONCLUDING COMMENTS

Chapters 2 and 3 have provided a selective, chronological account of the development of modern criminology. They have taken note of a number of theoretical directions that have been pursued during the past century, and in addition, a number of unresolved issues in criminological theory have been identified. It is now time to turn to the first of these issues, namely, the nature of the dependent variable in criminological analysis. Criminologists have often observed that criminality comes in a variety of forms; thus murder and murderers have little in common with burglary and burglars, arson and arsonists, or with other forms of crime or types of criminals. In short, many criminologists have concluded that the heterogeneity of their subject matter requires that crime classifications or typological categorizations of offenders must be developed and that causal analysis must be focused on particular types of crime or criminals. However, some criminologists have argued that these classificatory systems are not required. Either way, relatively little progress toward the development of such systems has been made to date.

## NOTES

[1]One reviewer of an earlier version of this book took issue with this description of self-report or "hidden delinquency" studies as tangential to causal theorizing. I described these investigations as tangential because, beginning with the initial study by Porterfield in the 1940s and con-

tinuing with the work of Short and Nye, as well as a number of other researchers, most of the attention was placed upon uncovering "the dark figure of delinquency," that is, the extent of unreported and unrecorded juvenile misbehavior (Gibbons and Krohn, 1991: 41–48). These studies repeatedly turned up evidence that the majority of American juveniles had engaged in petty acts of misconduct during adolescence. At the same time, these investigations also pointed to the existence of a sizable "hard core" of youths who were involved in repetitive, serious forms of misbehavior. These studies ultimately had an indirect but major impact upon causal analysis, for they had the effect of diverting attention away from the kinds of gang delinquents who had been studied by Shaw and McKay and toward juveniles who had been involved in petty acts of misbehavior, for the most part. While these studies did not trivialize the study of delinquency, they did produce a reconceptualization of the subject matter in the form of trivial delinquency. Additionally, a number of investigators, using self-report techniques for identifying "delinquents," or more correctly, variations in degrees of delinquent involvement on the part of youths, ultimately did begin to engage in causal analysis. Nye's (1958) control theory and Hirschi's somewhat parallel argument are cases in point. In this way, self-report investigations did have a roundabout but highly significant impact upon causal analysis.

[2]Some valuable commentary on social control can be found in Davis, 1975; Lemert, 1972.

[3]It might be argued that deterrence should be included in a discussion of social control. As usually defined, deterrence means "to turn aside, discourage, or prevent from acting (as by fear)." The term is usually restricted to tactics of punishment, as opposed to rehabilitative efforts that are designed to replace the antisocial attitudes of persons with prosocial ones. This distinction is easier to make in theory than in practice, for many of the efforts directed at offenders involve both punitive and therapeutic elements. Recent theory and research on deterrence was reviewed in *The Criminological Enterprise* (Gibbons, 1979). However, I have excluded the topic from this book, on the grounds that deterrence refers to actions directed at offenders or potential lawbreakers *after* the major causal events in their lives have already occurred.

[4]Some students of deviance have indicated that they detect the seeds of the labeling orientation in the writings of historian Frank Tannebaum (1938) who over 50 years ago drew attention to "dramatization of evil," which was his term for societal reaction experiences that allegedly drive the deviant further into misconduct. However, his ideas were sketchy at best, confined to two pages in his book, and do not qualify as a developed theory.

# CHAPTER 4

# Defining the Dependent Variable

## PATTERNS OF CRIME
## AND TYPES OF OFFENDERS*

## INTRODUCTION

Chapter 1 probed the question "What is criminology?" and responded that it is a field that deals with the causes and control of crime. A question *not* asked was "What is crime?" but a fair amount of attention has been given to that query by criminologists, with most of them settling for a legalistic definition. Crime is what the criminal law says it is at any point in time. A much smaller number of theorists have opted for a "social definition" of crime, in which acts that are not proscribed or prescribed in the laws but which are viewed by criminologists or some other group as socially harmful are identified as crimes. My own position is a legalistic one—crime is defined by criminal law. "Criminals" are persons who violate criminal laws, whether or not they become detected and identified as lawbreakers.

Adoption of a legalistic definition leads almost immediately to the observation that crime and the criminals who engage in it make up a rich and variegated bundle of activities and persons. In turn, that observation has often led criminologists to the view that the dependent variable of criminology—the thing(s) to be explained—should be specified in such a way as to take this diversity of behavior and actors into account. In this view, classifica-

*This discussion of crime patterns draws heavily upon Farr and Gibbons, 1990. The commentary on offender types is based on Gibbons, 1992a: 193–216; 1985; 1975.

tory systems that make sense out of the forms of crime or types of criminal actors are required as a first step toward explaining these phenomena. Kathryn Farr and I (1990: 223) expressed this theme in the following passage:

> Imagine what entymology might look like if it were composed of two groups of scientists—one engaged in the study of "reddish bugs," "greenish bugs," or "brownish bugs," with the other studying "all bugs, whatever their color." It would represent a field in a primitive stage of development—much like contemporary criminology—since an adequate system for making sense of its subject matter would be lacking. In the case of plants or animals, a taxonomy refers to a classification scheme that sorts these forms into phyla, species, etc. In criminology, taxonomies are classification systems that place crimes or offenders in homogeneous types.

This chapter is concerned with efforts that have been made to develop theoretically meaningful taxonomies of crime forms or offender types. As I noted elsewhere (Gibbons, 1992a: 195–96), two different lines of classificatory activity have been pursued by criminologists, one being *crime-centered* and the other, *criminal-centered*. Crime-centered efforts attempt to identify distinct forms of crime, along with correlates that account for those different patterns. By contrast, criminal-centered endeavors search for relatively distinct patterns or types into which real-life offenders can be sorted, along with exploring the backgrounds that might account for persons following one or another of these criminal patterns.

Crime-centered and criminal-centered efforts are not identical. It may be that distinct patterns of lawbreaking can be identified, but it may be that persons who specialize in those patterns cannot be found. For example, burglary may be a crime form which generally follows an identifiable pattern or set of patterns, but few if any "burglars" who specialize in that kind of criminality may be found in the real world. (Of course, we might find that there are no distinctive patterns, either in the case of crime or in the case of criminal offenders.)

Considerably more effort has been directed in the past at identification of types of delinquents and/or criminals than at uncovering crime types. However, the following discussion begins with the latter and then turns to the results, to date, of efforts to develop offender typologies or taxonomies.

## CRIMINAL LAW AND CRIMINALITY

The reach of the criminal law in modern society is long and wide. When they speak of "crime," ordinary citizens usually have in mind murder, assault, robbery, burglary, and a few other illegal acts, but the scope of the criminal law is much broader. For example, the Oregon criminal code prohibits the "sale of a drugged horse," "failure to maintain a metal purchase record," "unlawful transportation of hay," "transportation of coniferous trees without a bill of sale," and myriad other acts. In all, the Oregon code contains several hundred criminal acts, classified as various kinds and degrees of felonies and misdemeanors. Moreover, there are other bodies of law such as the Fish and Game Code and the Motor Vehicle Code which identify still other forms of criminality, often termed "violations," and which carry lesser penalties than those in the main body of criminal laws in Oregon. These various bodies of law exist in other states as well. Little wonder, then, that criminologists have often argued that crime must be broken down into meaningful categories and separate theories or hypotheses must be developed to account for them.[1] For example, in an essay on criminological theory, Gibbs (1987: 830) argued: "Each theory should be limited to one type of crime if only because it is unlikely that any etiological or reactive variable is relevant for all crimes."

## THE SEARCH FOR CRIMINAL TYPES

### Sutherland's Views

The fact that "crime" is an umbrella term for a large variety of acts of omission or commission has been recognized for many decades. A number of criminologists have asserted that attention should focus on the development of classification systems which sort crime forms or types of criminals into theoretically meaningful types. Even so, we have not progressed very far from the situation described by Sutherland (1924: 22) in the first edition of his textbook: "A great deal of effort has been devoted to the attempt to classify crimes. Most of the results must be regarded as useless. . . ."

In a later edition of his book, Sutherland (1939: 218) wrote:

Most of the scientific work in criminology has been directed at the explanation of crime in general. Crime in general consists of a great variety of criminal acts. These acts have very little in common except that they are all violations of the law. They differ among themselves in the motives and characteristics of the victims, the situations in which they occur, the techniques that are used, the damages which result, and the reactions of the victims and of the public. Consequently it is not likely that a general explanation of all crimes will be sufficiently specific or precise to aid greatly in understanding or controlling crime. In order to make progress in the explanation of crime it is desirable to break crime into more homogeneous units. In this respect crime is like a disease. Some general theories of disease have been stated and are useful. The germ theory of disease is a very useful general theory, but even this theory does not apply to all diseases. Progress in the explanation of disease is being made principally by the studies of specific diseases. Similarly, it is desirable to concentrate research in criminology on specific crimes.

Sutherland and Cressey (1978: 218–22) followed these comments with the suggestion that criminologists turn to the study of "behavior systems," which they said were "sociological units," but without indicating the nature of the latter. According to Sutherland, behavior systems are "integrated units" made up of individual acts, codes, traditions, esprit de corps, social relations among the direct participants, and indirect participation of many other persons. In addition, the behavior is not unique to any individual; rather, "it is common behavior." Unlike psychiatric notions of behavior systems which center on cognitive patterns, Sutherland emphasized behavior shared by group participants. A third characteristic of the behavior system is that it grows out of a unified causal process. Sutherland indicated that kidnapping was not a behavior system, but professional theft qualified as an example. (Kidnapping is a form of crime that is usually carried on by lawbreakers operating alone, while professional thieves make up a criminal network or subculture.)

Even though the concept of behavior systems continued to appear in the text (Sutherland, Cressey, and Luckenbill, 1992: 269–75), it is a conceptual innovation that was stillborn, for it did not provoke attempts at explication by scholars of behavior systems other than professional theft.

### Other Views

Sutherland was not alone, either in (a) his concern about the limitations of taxonomies based *solely* on legal categories, or (b) his efforts to develop theoretically meaningful crime categories. For example, Sellin (1938) argued that the criminal law is an inadequate foundation for criminological work and that attention should focus instead on "conduct norms," but that suggestion did not take hold.

In one ambitious attempt to devise a classificatory scheme, Clinard and Quinney (1973) identified the following types of crime: violent personal, occasional property, public order, conventional, political, occupational, corporate, organized, and professional. This classification was organized around five dimensions: legal aspect of selected offenses, criminal career of the offender, group support for criminal behavior, correspondence between criminal and legitimate behavior, and societal reaction and legal processing.

However, there are problems with this scheme. The notion of "criminal career of the offender," used in an offense-based classification, implies that types of crime and types of offenders are closely related: Burglaries are performed by burglars, auto thefts by car thieves, and so on. But, the evidence does not support this hypothesis about crime specialists (Chaiken and Chaiken, 1982). Behavioral versatility rather than specialization in particular crimes is most common among repeat offenders. Clinard and Quinney also distinguished between such types as "occasional property criminal behavior" and "conventional criminal behavior," but both of these involve larcenies of one kind or another; thus, this is actually a distinction based on the *frequency* of criminal acts on the part of *persons* rather than the identification of distinct kinds of crime.

### Efforts to Identify Specific Crime Types

There are some other, more narrowly focused efforts to identify sociologically meaningful types of crime that are important building blocks upon which the development of crime categories might proceed.

*Folk-Mundane Crime.* Ross (1960–61, 1973) invented the term "folk crime" to designate certain relatively petty, socially invisible, yet frequently encountered forms of crime, such as moving traffic violations, that have often been overlooked by criminologists. Along the same line, I offered "mundane crime" as another type that ought to receive attention (Gibbons, 1983). Mundane crime refers to a collection of criminal activities that includes Ross's folk crimes. However, no one else has apparently been impressed with these categories, for virtually no other work has been done on either folk or mundane crime (although for a review of studies which seem to fit the folk or mundane crime categories, see Gibbons, 1992: 341–61).

*White-Collar Crime.* Sutherland's attempt to limn the contours of "white-collar crime" was a particularly important venture into crime form identification. However, I pointed out in Chapter 2 that his term "white-collar crime" was more colorful than precise and more useful in drawing attention to an overlooked area in criminality than it was a clear conceptual category. Also, Sutherland offered inconsistent observations on what he meant by the term. On some occasions, he focused on white-collar *crime*, and at other times, on white-collar *criminals*; he sometimes suggested that embezzlement falls into this category, but at other times, implied that it did not.

Some criminologists have endeavored to clear up the confusion concerning white-collar crime. Schrager and Short (1978) have suggested that we ought to zero in on "organizational crime," which they believe is also what Sutherland had in mind. Organizational offenses are illegal, serious, and harmful acts of an individual or group of persons in a legitimate, formal organization, carried out in the pursuit of the goals of the organization. In other words, organizational crime is carried on *for* the organization, as contrasted with embezzlement, which involves crimes *against* organizational ends.

A different position was staked out by Coleman (1987), who opted for an omnibus definition of white-collar crime, asserting (p. 407) that "white collar crimes . . . are violations of law committed in the course of a legitimate occupation or financial pursuit by persons who hold respectable positions in their communities" and also that they are crimes "committed for the benefit of the individual criminal without organizational support and organizational crimes committed with support from an organization that is, at least in part, furthering its own ends."

In the opinion of some criminologists, offenses committed to advance organizational ends should be examined separately from offenses by organizational members solely for their own benefit and from "fringe" violations by professionals, such as commingling of funds by lawyers, Medicare fraud by doctors, and the like (Gibbons, 1992a: 284–317; Schrager and Short, 1978). Organizational crime involves law violations to benefit the organization, while embezzlers are "enemies within" whose acts are detrimental to the goals of the firm.

*Political Crime.*   Political crime has sometimes been proposed as another significant category of criminality. In the past several decades, we have been confronted with numerous dramatic instances of hijacking, political coups, assassinations, bombings, and the like; thus the idea of political crime is "in the air." But, how are we to throw a conceptual net around this activity? Turk (1982) has made the most serious effort to bring order to this area, but even so, conceptual ambiguities in the notion of political crime persist (Gibbons, 1992a: 393–98).

Turk's (1982) definition of political crime restricted it to illegal activities on the part of "subjects," reserving the term "political policing" for the criminal acts of the "authorities." By contrast, other criminologists regard illegal acts by the authorities as political crime, particularly since many of these acts are proactive; that is, they are illegal tactics used by governmental agents to prevent persons who are thought to be politically dangerous from acting.

Another difficulty with the political crime category is that it "bleeds into" other kinds of criminality that are not normally viewed as political in nature, such as the bombing of abortion clinics by "Right to Life" zealots. Finally, crimes are usually identified as political or otherwise, not because of distinctive properties of certain illegal acts, but rather on the basis of the motives that are assumed to lie behind the acts. For example, some homicides are "political assassinations," while others are treated as "garden-variety" or routine killings.[2]

### Crime Patterns and Criminological Practice

Although the question of crime forms has been a continuing one, with a number of criminologists attempting to develop crime categories to be used for theorizing purposes, these efforts have not had much impact upon criminological practice or the research efforts of criminologists. The most common crime "type" in research studies is "index offenses," sometimes broken down into "property" and "violent" subcategories, taken from FBI Uniform Crime Reports. Murder and nonnegligent manslaughter, aggravated assault, forcible rape, armed robbery, motor vehicle theft, burglary, theft, and arson are lumped together because these are for the most part serious crimes that are likely to be reported when they occur. However, it would be hard to argue that they "group together" in any other clearly apparent way or that this is a sociologically relevant rubric.

Textbook authors, who have the task of trying to bring order into the welter of criminological "facts," have often found it necessary to adopt classificatory schemes around which to structure their presentations. But these have been *ad hoc* rather than the product of explicit theoretical development. Textbooks have identified as crime "types," commonsense categories that have become conventional among criminologists. These may have some heuristic or pedagogical usefulness, but they are not an adequate foundation on which to build criminological theory.

## A PRELIMINARY CRIME CLASSIFICATION

While the problem of basic crime categories has not been solved, Kathryn A. Farr and I (1990) have tried to identify some major dimensions that ought to be involved in a crime taxonomy and have also sketched out the rough outlines of some of the crime categories which are generated by these basic dimensions.

Because crime is identified by the legal/political community as behavior which produces or results in some societal harm (or conversely, goes against the public good), our starting point for identifying crime forms was to distinguish between the harms to which particular criminal acts are tied. We employed the term "harm" in the legalistic sense, that is, various consequences of behavioral acts that have been defined by lawmaking bodies as having a negative impact upon social interests. For example, burglary is a harm because it is an attempt to deprive owners of their property and it also threatens general social interests.

Harm is a core concept in the legal codes. For example, Oregon statutes identify seven classes of harms: harms against property; harms involving fraud or deception; harms against the person; harms against public order; harms against the state and public justice; harms against public health, decency, and animals; and controlled substance harms. Modifying these somewhat, we identified seven crime categories which are sufficiently broad to accommodate most of the specific felonies, misdemeanors, and violations that appear in federal, state, and local statutes.

Under property harm crimes, we distinguished between (a) *property-*

*predatory crime* (e.g., burglary, robbery, auto theft, and larceny) and (b) *propety-fraudulent crime* (e.g., embezzlement, forgery, fraud, and bribery). Both predatory and fraudulent crimes are generally engaged in for instrumental rather than expressive or ideological gain. In predatory crime, persons are involved in taking or attempting to take directly, without permission, the personal property of others. In fraudulent crimes, the offenders are involved in deceit or manipulation with the purpose of converting property or services (including information) of others to their own use. In fraudulent crimes, unlike the case of predatory offenses, the victim may be unaware that he or she is involved in a fraudulent transaction.

We drew a distinction between two kinds of personal harm. The first, *interpersonal violence—general*, includes such offenses as homicide, assault, and kidnapping, while the second, *interpersonal violence—sexual*, involves rape, sexual abuse, incest, and other crimes which include some form of sexual conduct. This distinction is between violent crimes which do or do not have a sexual dimension—resulting, at least in theory, in different charges leveled at the offenders. It is important to note that rape and sexual abuse often contain elements of criminal assault resulting in physical injury to the victim. Moreover, victims are not infrequently subjected to rape, assault, kidnapping, and even homicide as part of the same basic criminal event. Even so, this distinction serves a theoretical purpose in that there is evidence that the etiology of some sex offenses is different from that of "garden-variety" assaults or homicides.

Farr and I acknowledged in passing that the sexual meaning of behavior is sometimes in the eye of the doer and is often not readily apparent to an outside observer. Put differently, in many sexual assault cases, the sexual nature of the crime is relatively clear, for penis-vaginal contact has been involved. On the other hand, there are other instances of assaultive behavior against females (e.g., vaginal penetration with a foreign object, or the activities of *frotteurs*), in which classification is more problematic.[3]

Farr and I identified three categories of social order–social values harm-related offenses. *Transactional vice* refers to "victimless" offenses involving a willing exchange of goods or services, e.g., prostitution, gambling, and drug sales, while *order disruption* includes escape, resisting arrest, disorderly conduct, riot, loitering, and firearms offenses. While there are no direct victims in these cases, there is public concern about potential victims in some instances (e.g., an offender carrying a concealed weapon eventually harming someone; resisting arrest leading to an assault on a police officer). The final category, *folk/mundane crime*, is a broad rubric which includes relatively minor rule violations (e.g., not purchasing a fishing license, jaywalking), along with more serious ones, such as weight and load regulations concerning commercial trucks. There is considerable public ambivalence about many of these violations. Although such rules have been justified in the name of order, efficiency, or effectiveness, much of the public regards one or another of them as a nuisance or inconvenience, without moral import, and/or as "not really crime."

The identification of these crime forms is only a first step, for they neither constitute crime *patterns* nor inform us theoretically. Standing alone, they are unexceptionable categories. Their value lies in the fact that they are based on a single criterion, rather than a shifting mixture of criteria: characteristics of offenders, organizational context, nature of offender involvement, social stigma, and the like. To illustrate, organized crime is a familiar category which is often defined in terms of the organizational context in which crimes occur, rather than by certain forms of crime, such as fraud or vice. These acts occur both inside and outside of criminal organizations. Differently, conceptions of political crime frequently emphasize the motives of the offender(s), rather than the acts in which they engage. Political crime is often defined in terms of the ends being pursued by offenders, rather than by the nature of the criminal acts in which they engage.

Our classification of crime patterns is not simply a restatement of the criminal laws, for we identified five other theoretically meaningful dimensions of crime additional to the harms they involve. There is considerable criminological agreement on the importance of the first of these, namely the *organizational level* at or around which crime(s) take place. A number of criminologists have argued that it is important to distinguish between offenses carried on within organizational settings and those that are the work of small offender networks or of individuals acting alone and outside of organizational settings. Accordingly, we distinguished between criminal activities carried on by formal or complex organizations (that is, by a substantial number of organizational members), by offender networks (both within and outside of large-scale organizations), and by individuals acting alone (but again, either inside or outside of large organizations). For example, both organizational–white-collar crime and organized crime are engaged in by members of relatively large and/or formal organizations. By contrast, "street hustling" involves small, loosely knit organized networks, as do crime-partner associations among predatory offenders.

Although we took note of crimes occurring both inside and outside of organizations, we refrained from speaking of "criminal organizations." Persons who engage in law violations within complex organizations often believe that their actions are likely to achieve "company goals," and in this sense, these actions qualify as "organizational crime." At the same time, it would be difficult to argue that the organization per se is a criminal organization. For example, in the case of a pharmaceutical company engaged in violating FDA regulations, it might be difficult or impossible to show that all of the employees shared the view that such violations are an acceptable form of conduct.

Our second domain, *legitimacy continuum*, refers to variations in public definitions of the organizational structures in which some crimes occur.

Although there is considerable ambiguity about the "criminal" or "noncriminal" nature of some organizational activities and therefore of the organizations themselves (Gibbons, 1992a: 307), many businesses and corporations are viewed by the general public as being at the legitimate pole on the scale, while the Mafia is assigned to a highly illegitimate point on the legitimacy continuum, as are many (but not all) criminal networks. Car dealerships might qualify as an example of organizations that are at some intermediate point on this scale—since many of them are perceived by the general public to be engaged in illegal or unethical practices.

A number of business firms engage entirely in legitimate business activities, while many others are involved in some blend of legal and illegal endeavors. Drug firms that violate FDA regulations or rental car agencies that charge customers inflated sums for repairs to damaged rental cars are two examples. What is less often recognized is that "organized crime" also often refers to organizations that engage both in such illegal activities as loan sharking and in legal businesses such as dry cleaning. Our legitimacy dimension refers to how organizations are *perceived* by the general public, rather than to the actual balance of legal and illegal activities in which they engage.[4]

The legitimacy/illegitimacy distinction is separate from the issue of the perceived seriousness of specific crimes in the eyes of the general public. There is a modest research literature on public perceptions regarding the "criminal" or "noncriminal" status of various crimes and citizen judgments of the seriousness of these specific acts but relatively little data regarding public evaluations of organizations or the seriousness of offenses attributed to them (Gibbons, 1992a: 69–71). Moreover, the links between public perceptions of the criminality of individuals and of the organizations which they represent require further probing. For example, doctors who engage in Medicare fraud may be held in low regard by citizens, at the same time that the medical organizations within which these persons work are viewed favorably. Citizens may believe that miscreant doctors are "bad apples" in an otherwise legitimate organization.

Since the legitimacy domain refers to the status of organizations or networks, it is not applicable to crime patterns in which individuals act alone.

A third dimension involves the *organizational alignment of offenders*, which includes (a) individuals or networks within an organization who engage in illegal acts while pursuing ends that they perceive to be among the goals of the organization, (b) individuals or networks within an organization who direct illegal acts *at* those organizations (e.g., embezzlers), and (c) offenders who are outside of and thus not aligned with a conventional organization.

A fourth dimension is *range of crime forms*, with specialized patterns at one end and diversified ones at the other. Range of crime forms is a version of the harms we identified earlier, although in Table 4–1, our entries involve more specific forms of the seven harms in a number of instances.

Finally, we took note of the *primary victim(s)*. Victim categories include specific persons, organizations, the general population or subgroups of it, and the "social fabric," which is another way of speaking of diffuse harms with unspecified victims.

We believe that these five contextual domains are useful in the identification of distinct crime patterns. Table 4–1 presents an initial version of a crime classification which employs these five defining dimensions. The first column, labeled "Crime Type," refers to the summarizing label we attached to the various crime patterns that were generated using the variables identified. In most cases, we employed the crime type terminology that has become common in the criminological literature, but in a more precise fashion.

Some subtypes, as well as major forms of criminal activity are identified in the table. We singled out five forms of workplace crime, largely because the criminological evidence suggests that there is considerable variability of criminal conduct within the broad category of workplace crime. Additionally, we separated a pattern of diversified "street crime," in which offenders are involved in a variety of "hustles," as well as some violent criminal activities, from a second form of relatively specialized "street crime," in which offenders are focused primarily on one type of criminal activity, most commonly for instrumental gain.

Table 4–1 represents a beginning venture into crime classification which could profit from a good bit of "fine tuning." In its current form, this scheme serves a heuristic function more than anything else. Put differently, Farr and I hope that others will be stimulated to take up the taxonomic task and to explicate some more satisfactory schemes for identifying crime patterns.

The Farr-Gibbons classification of crime forms is an exercise in conceptualization, involving identification of some dimensions which may be useful in bringing some order to the seeming heterogeneity of lawbreaking. Some indication that we may be on the right track can be found in a recent study of the offenses of a large sample of federal offenders, conducted by Weisburd, Wheeler, Waring, and Bode (1991). These investigators indicated that most of the offenses fell into eight categories: antitrust violations, securities fraud, mail fraud, false claims, bribery, tax fraud, credit fraud, and bank embezzlement. Because these appeared to be a diverse collection of crimes, the researchers were moved to try to find some patterns into which they might be sorted.

Weisburd et al. settled on *organizational complexity* and the *consequences of the crimes to the victims* as dimensions for sorting offenses into groupings. Offenses that are high on organizational complexity are those in which a discernible offense pattern is apparent, organizational resources are employed to commit crimes, and the acts take place over a lengthy time period. The crime consequences variable centered on the number of victims, the size of their losses, and the breadth of the area over which victimization was spread.

**Table 4-1** A Preliminary Classification of Crime Patterns

| CRIME TYPE | ORGANIZATIONAL LEVEL AT WHICH CRIME OCCURS | LEGITIMACY OF ORGANIZATIONAL CONTEXT | ORGANIZATIONAL ALIGNMENT OF OFFENDER | RANGE OF CRIME FORMS | PRIMARY VICTIMS |
|---|---|---|---|---|---|
| Organizational–White-Collar Crime | Formal/complex organization | Legitimate | With organization | Fraudulent (diverse or specialized) | General public, sub-groups, other complex organizations |
| Organized Crime | Formal/complex organization | Illegitimate | With organization | Fradulent, transactional vice, violence—general | General public, sub-groups, social fabric |
| Workplace Crime | Network or individual | Legitimate | Against organization | (a) Fraudulent (e.g., fraud against legal clients) | Specific individuals, sub-groups |
| | | | | (b) Fraudulent (e.g., embezzlement) | Organization |
| | | | | (c) Predatory (e.g., employee theft) | Organization |
| | | | | (d) Transactional vice (e.g., physician drug sales) | Social fabric |
| | | | | (e) Violence—general (e.g., assault by police officers) | Specific individuals, sub-groups |
| "Street" Crime | Network or individual | Illegitimate | Outside conventional organization | (a) Diversified (predatory, fraudulent, violence—general and sexual, transactional vice) | Specific individuals, sub-groups, organizations, social fabric |
| | | | | (b) Specialized (e.g., buying and selling stolen property ring) | Specific individuals, sub-groups, organizations, social fabric |

| | | | | | |
|---|---|---|---|---|---|
| Social Protest (Political Crime) | Network or individual (may be indirect link to organization) | Legitimate or quasi-legitimate | Outside conventional organization or with organization | Order disruption, violence—general | Sub-groups, organizations, social fabric |
| Violent Crime | Individual | NA | Outside conventional organization | (a) Violence—general | Specific individuals, sub-groups |
| | | | | (b) Violence—sexual | Specific individuals, sub-groups |
| Folk/Mundane Crime | Individual | NA | Outside conventional organization | Folk/mundane crimes | Organizations, social fabric |

*Source:* Farr and Gibbons, 1990: 234.

Weisburd et al. indicated that the eight offenses could be combined into three relatively distinct types, forming a rough hierarchy of offense complexity, with antitrust and securities fraud at the top and fraud and embezzlement at the bottom.

The Farr and Gibbons venture into classification was carried on independently of the work of Weisburd et al., but there are some shared notions that are involved in the two classificatory schemes.

## OFFENDER TYPOLOGIES

### Introduction

The thesis that criminals and delinquents can be placed into relatively distinct types dates back to the origins of criminology. For example, Lombroso (1836–1909) argued that there were three kinds of lawbreakers: born criminals, insane criminals, and criminaloids. According to Lombroso, the latter constituted over half of all offenders and were persons of normal physical and psychological makeup who committed crimes because of stressful life experiences.

The proposition that there are a number of distinctive criminal types also surfaced in nineteenth-century England, when many citizens became convinced that they had much to fear from "the dangerous class." For example, Colquhoun, a Scottish social philosopher and police reformer, estimated that there were at least 115,000 members of "the dangerous and criminal class" engaged in full-time crime (Low, 1982: 25–27). He identified twenty-four separate groups of lawbreakers, including "professed and known receivers of stolen goods" and "a class of suspicious characters, who live partly by pilfering and passing base money—ostensibly costard mongers, ass drivers, dustmen, chimney sweepers, rabbit sellers, fish and fruit sellers, flash coachmen, bear baiters, dog keepers (but in fact dog stealers), etc., etc."

A few decades later, social reformer Henry Mayhew listed over 100 criminal types that were said to make up "the criminal class" in late nineteenth-century England. His list included such types as "stook buzzers" (persons who steal handkerchiefs) and "snow gatherers" (individuals who steal clothes off the hedges) (Tobias, 1967: 622–65).

In the 1950s, considerable criminological interest centered on offender typologies, with a number of persons arguing that lawbreakers are so varied that they must be sorted into behavioral types. According to this view, offender typologies are required in order that (1) progress can be made on the explanation of lawbreaking, and (2) effective treatment of offenders can be developed.

The causal argument was that no single theory can account for such diverse types of offenders as embezzlers, rapists, arsonists, or white-collar criminals; rather, separate causal theories must be developed for each of them. The case for typologies and diagnostic classifications in correctional treatment closely paralleled the etiological argument. The basic claim was that "different strokes for different folks" were in order. Specific tactics such as psychotherapy, group counseling, reality therapy, or behavior modification should be matched with particular offender types. Treatment would be tailored to the offender, thereby bringing about more effective rehabilitation (Gibbons, 1965a).

How should we go about classifying offenders? Most sociological classifications of persons or social phenomena are imposed upon the facts of social life rather than being drawn directly from observations. Stated differently, offender "types" such as naïve check forgers or white-collar criminals are identified by criminologists. The real-life offenders who are assigned to these types may very well be unaware that we have categorized them.

One way to sort offenders would be on their specific instant offenses—that is, the crimes for which they were most recently arrested or convicted. However, the practice of "plea-copping," in which many persons plead guilty to reduced charges, means that legal charges often do not accurately mirror the offenses actually committed. Even more important, legal-offense categories often fail to reflect dimensions of lawbreaking behavior that may be of theoretical significance. For example, the legal category of rape includes several patterns of deviant behavior: Some rapes involve extreme violence and the totally unwilling participation of the victim; others involve quite different elements, including a lesser degree of coercion. Another problem with legal-offense categories is that many offenders exhibit versatility over time in the criminal acts they commit. A person who is a burglar today may be a larcenist next week and an assaulter the following week. Given these facts, it is doubtful that theoretically meaningful types of offenders can be identified solely on the basis of legal offenses.

Criminological theorizing requires that we go beyond commonsense observations about the real world. When we sort offenders into behavioral types, we invent conceptual schemes that allow us to see common threads or characteristics that identify groups of similar offenders. Again, these threads may not be apparent at first glance, either to the lawbreakers or to criminologists.

Violators can be classified in many different ways: sex, hair color, race, urban or rural residence, psychological profiles, and so on. When criminologists settle upon one scheme from the many that might be used, they hope they have selected one that will allow them to place offenders into clear-cut categories that are also causally significant. Let us turn to some of the offender typologies that have been put forth, to see how criminologists have approached the taxonomic task.

### Some Typological Examples

One comprehensive typology of adult offenders was created by Glaser (1972: 28–66), who identified ten patterns, including "adolescent recapitulators," "subcultural assaulters," "vocational predators," "crisis-vacillation predators," and "addicted performers."[5] Glaser's scheme was based on what he called "offense-descriptive" and "career-commitment" variables. The former separated predatory from nonpredatory offenses, personal from property crimes, and so forth; career-commitment variables had to do with recidivism, criminal-group contacts maintained by offenders, and related factors. Glaser used these variables to identify *adolescent recapitulators* as "adults who periodically repeat the pattern of delinquency begun in adolescence—or even childhood" (1972: 28), while *subcultural assaulters* were described as persons who "live in a subculture emphasizing violence as a value more than does the rest of our society" (1972: 32).

Doubtless many real-life offenders do resemble the profiles sketched by Glaser. However, he also offered some pithy remarks about the problems with offender classifications, noting that many lawbreakers show diversity rather than specialization in the offenses they commit, making it difficult to sort them into clear-cut types. According to Glaser (1972: 18), "the difficulty arises from the fact that a large variety of offenses are found in most separate criminal careers, and the combinations occur in all possible proportions." We would also do well to keep in mind a related comment by Glaser (1972: 14): "In the real world, the gradations and mixtures of characteristics in people are so extensive that most of our categories must be given very arbitrary boundaries if everyone in a cross section of the population is to be placed in one empirical type or another. Most real people do not fall neatly into uniform patterns."

There is another observation to be made about Glaser's typology. Although his two classificatory dimensions make a good deal of sense, the offender categories that he offered, such as the *adolescent recapitulator*, were not spelled out in sufficient detail to be amenable to research scrutiny. Instead, he endeavored to give some specificity to his types principally through examples of lawbreakers who might be said to exemplify one or other of the types. But absent detailed instructions on how real persons should be sorted into types, it probably would be difficult to carry out research on actual offenders and to assign them to Glaser's types.

Criminologists who have developed typologies of lawbreakers have often pointed to research reports on specific offender types as support for their schemes. For example, in a study of inmates in a District of Columbia reformatory, Roebuck (1966) sorted them into such groups as *Negro armed robbers*, *Negro drug addicts*, and *Negro "short con" men*. His typology was based on the inmates' crime records as revealed in their official records. Thirteen criminal patterns in all were identified.

The list of studies of specific offender patterns or types is fairly large and includes Conklin's (1972: 59–78) research on types of robbers, as well as Lemert's (1953, 1958) studies of naïve check forgers and systematic forgers. These and other studies were of importance in my role-career typologies of delinquents and adult offenders (Gibbons, 1965).

### Gibbons's Role-Career Typologies

I have developed two comprehensive typologies, one dealing with delinquents and the other with adult offenders. The discussion to follow centers on the adult typology.[6]

My typologies were based on some broad sociological assumptions about social roles and statuses.[7] Role and status notions have been applied most often to social positions such as student or teacher, parent or child, and to professions such as school superintendent or physician, but less often to homosexual patterns, drug user behavior, or forms of criminality. Criminal conduct can, nonetheless, be examined within such a perspective. For example, Irwin's (1970) account of the typical careers of felons is a persuasive example of social role analysis in the area of lawbreaking.

In my scheme, offender types were described, in part, in terms of the offenses they commit and the social contexts in which these illegal activities occur. Some criminal acts are carried on in isolation, others take place within a group of participating actors ("fall partners"), and still others occur within a subcultural network of deviant actors.

My typological schemes identified two components of offender roles: *behavioral acts* and *role conceptions* (self-image patterns and role-related attitudes). The distinction between behavior and role conceptions parallels Lemert's (1951: 73–98) notions of *primary* and *secondary* deviance. Some deviants view their misbehavior as atypical of their "real selves" and lack self-images as deviants. Deviance becomes secondary when it becomes a status identified by such self-reference statements as "I am a hype" or "I am a badass."

The two typologies were role-career ones in that they included observations about changes in the activities and/or social-psychological characteristics of offenders over time. As I have indicated, these notions about offender roles and role careers guided, at least in a general way, the development of a typology of adult lawbreakers, in which 20 offender types in all were described:[8]

1. Professional thieves
2. Professional "heavy" criminals
3. Semiprofessional property offenders
4. Naïve check forgers
5. Automobile thieves— "joyriders"

6. Property offenders, "one-time losers"
7. Embezzlers
8. White-collar criminals
9. Professional "fringe" violators
10. Personal offenders, "one-time losers"
11. Psychopathic assaultists
12. Statutory rapists
13. Aggressive rapists
14. Violent sex offenders
15. Nonviolent sex offenders
16. Incest offenders
17. Male homosexuals
18. Opiate addicts
19. Skid Row alcoholics
20. Amateur shoplifters

Detailed descriptions of these 20 alleged types can be found in *Changing the Lawbreaker* (Gibbons, 1965a). However, the description of the semiprofessional property offender is presented in the table that follows (Gibbons, 1965: 104–6).

### Offender Types and Real People

If it were possible to sort lawbreakers into a relatively small number of clear-cut types, we might then be able to throw considerable light upon the causes of criminality. But, how accurate are typological descriptions? How closely do offenders fit the types? How comprehensive are typologies? Do most real-life lawbreakers fit within a typology, or instead, are there large numbers of them who cannot be placed within existing schemes?

Returning to Glaser's typology for a moment, there probably are a number of persons who look more or less similar to his *subcultural assaulters, crisis-vacillation predators, addicted performers,* or other types. But it is also true that we would probably have a good bit of difficulty in reliably sorting offenders into Glaser's types, given the anecdotal nature of his descriptions of them.

Next, consider my role-career description of the semiprofessional property offender. There is a sizable body of evidence on offender behavior that is broadly supportive of this description; indeed, Shover's (1991) review of a variety of data on burglary and burglars contains a portrayal that is similar to this type description.

The question regarding the accuracy of typologies might be referred to as the "isomorphism with reality" issue (*iso-* means equal, *-morph* refers to form). In turn, there are two separate but related aspects to this query: *inclusiveness* and *closeness of fit.* A classification scheme is inclusive insofar as most

The Semiprofessional Property Criminal Role-Career

## DEFINITIONAL DIMENSIONS

*Offense Behavior.* Semiprofessional property offenders engage in strong-arm robberies, holdups, burglaries, larcenies, and similar direct assaults upon personal or private property. They employ crime skills which are relatively simple and uncomplicated. For example, strong-arm robbery does not involve much detailed planning and careful execution of the crime, but rather application of crude physical force in order to relieve a victim of his money. This is referred to as semiprofessional crime, because even though technical skill is not characteristic of these offenders, most of them attempt to carry on crime as an occupation.

*Interactional Setting.* Many of the offenses of the semiprofessional offender are two-person affairs involving an offender and a victim—for example, strong-arm robbery and liquor-store and gas-station stickups. On occasion, semiprofessionals operate in collections of several crime partners, as in instances of burglary and safe-robbery. In either event, the criminal act tends to be direct and unsophisticated, a complex interactional pattern rarely being involved.

*Self-Concept.* Semiprofessional property offenders view themselves as criminals. Additionally, the semiprofessional sees himself as an individual who has few alternatives to criminal behavior and as a victim of a corrupt society in which everyone has a "racket." Thus the semiprofessional is relieved from any sense of guilt regarding his criminality by deflecting blame onto the system.

*Attitudes.* The attitudes of the semiprofessional offender toward the police tend to be hostile. Doubtless, this is in considerable part a function of the large number of contacts with police agents experienced by this offender. Semiprofessionals also look down on conventional occupations as a way of life, holding that "only slobs work." They frequently show a diffuse set of bitter and resentful attitudes toward not only the police and correctional agents, but also their parents, social agencies, and schools.

*Role-Career.* Semiprofessional property offenders represent the more usual outcome of patterns of predatory gang delinquency, in contrast with the professional "heavy" outcome. That is, most adult semiprofessional offenders exhibit backgrounds of predatory gang behavior, and many juvenile-gang offenders continue in criminality as semiprofessionals. As an adult, the semiprofessional rapidly accumulates an extensive "rap sheet," or record of crimes and institutional commitments. Because of the low degree of skill involved in the criminality of semiprofessionals, the risks of apprehension, conviction, and incarceration are high. Many semiprofessionals spend a considerable part of their early adult years in penal institutions, where they are likely to be identified as "right guys," or antiadministration inmates. It does not appear that conventional treatment efforts are successful in deflecting many of these persons away from continuation in crime. On the other hand, many of them ultimately do withdraw from crime careers upon reaching early middle age.

real-life offenders can be placed within its categories, while closeness of fit refers to the degree to which specific persons resemble the descriptions or categories in a typology. Consider a fourfold table of possibilities, the most desirable one being a typology that is both inclusive and characterized by closeness of fit, with every real-life lawbreaker placed precisely in one type or another. By contrast, a typology might be inclusive but not precise, it might be relatively precise but with many individuals falling outside of it, or in the worst case, it might be neither inclusive nor accurate.

Regarding isomorphism with reality, the distinguishing feature of my role-career scheme is that it contains relatively detailed and explicit statements about the identifying characteristics of particular types. For example, we know we are looking at a naïve check forger when we see a person who writes bad checks on his or her own bank account, in certain specified circumstances, and who voices attitudinal or self-reference statements of the sort: "You can't kill anyone with a fountain pen" or "I am not a real criminal like these other people in here (prison)."

There is direct and indirect evidence that bears on the question of the accuracy of my typologies. Let us briefly scrutinize some of it, beginning with reports by Schrag (1961) and Sykes (1958) on inmate types in prison. According to these criminologists, prisoners exhibit social role patterns identified in prison argot (inmate language) by such labels as "Square John," "right guy," "gorilla," "hipster," and "outlaw." These roles are structured around loyalty attachments to other prisoners: the "right guy," for example, is a loyal member of the inmate subculture, while the "Square John" is an outsider who has little or no awareness of the rule-violating activities of the prisoners in the underlife of the institution.

If distinct social roles exist among inmates, this may be an indication of social roles among criminals at large. However, Schrag's and Sykes's observations were relatively impressionistic; hence we might wonder whether these types can be easily and consistently identified. Some indication of the loose fit between typologies and the real world is found in Garabedian's (1964) study, conducted in the same prison studied by Schrag. Garabedian identified social-role incumbents through inmate responses to a series of questionnaire items. While two-thirds of the convicts did fall into types, about one-third were unclassified. Moreover, although various presumed social correlates of the role types were observed (such as long arrest histories on the part of "right guys"), many of the observed associations were weak. This study suggested that social types exist but also that there is less regularity of inmate behavior than implied by Schrag and Sykes.

Even more damaging evidence came from a study by Leger (1979), who employed a number of different techniques in order to uncover inmate social types. He used Garabedian's attitude items, and he also asked inmates to indicate the social type, if any, to which they belonged. Further, he obtained judgments from guards about which convicts were members of particular types. Finally, he sorted inmates in terms of the social backgrounds that are supposed to characterize the different types. There was very little agreement in the findings—very few prisoners were consistently identified as "Square Johns" or some other type.

When investigators begin to examine some specific type of offender in detail, subtypes commonly proliferate, as the researcher attempts to capture the variability of behavior encountered among actual offenders. For example, one project in a federal probation office (Adams, Chandler, and

Neithercutt, 1971) used the present offense of probationers, along with their ages, prior records, and scores on a personality inventory in order to classify them. Fifty-four possible types of offenders were noted and probationers were found in all of these categories.

Somewhat similarly, McCaghy (1967) found it necessary to sort child molesters into six types, and Conklin (1972) contended that there are four types of robbers: professional, opportunist, drug-addicted, and alcoholic. Further complicating matters, it turned out that opportunist robbers also commit other forms of theft, as do addict and alcoholic robbers.

Two studies have been conducted on my role-career scheme. In one of these (Hartjen and Gibbons, 1969), in a California probation department, probation officers attempted to sort probationers into the typology categories, but slightly less than half of the offenders were classifiable, even when relatively relaxed classificatory rules were used. Subsequently, Hartjen sifted through the records of the unassigned cases and managed to place most of them into seven types, such as "nonsupport offenders" or "petty property offenders." However, these ad hoc types did not differ markedly from one another in terms of commitment to deviance, social backgrounds, or other variables.

McKenna (1972) also investigated the role-career typology. Inmates in a state correctional institution were classified into types through examination of their arrest records, and 87 percent were placed in 12 offense types. He then sought to determine whether the combinations of characteristics said to identify particular role-careers actually occurred among offenders, but only in one of the 12 types did the definitional dimension pattern emerge. His findings indicated that many real-life offenders cannot be assigned to the categories of the role-career scheme with much precision.

Finally, a set of studies conducted by the Rand Corporation provided evidence on behavioral regularities among offenders. The first one (Petersilia, Greenwood, and Lavin, 1977) involved 49 "armed robbers" in a California prison—offenders who had been singled out as robbers because their current prison commitments were for that crime. Most were in their late thirties and had been criminally involved for some time. Asked to report the number of times they had committed any of nine specific crimes since becoming involved in lawbreaking, they confessed to over 10,000 offenses, or an average of 214 per person! More important, they admitted collectively to 3629 drug sales, 2331 burglaries, 1492 auto thefts, 995 forgeries, 993 grand thefts, and 855 robberies. Clearly, these were not specialists in armed robbery; instead, they were "jack-of-all-trades" offenders.

The second study (Peterson, Braker, and Polich, 1980) involved over 600 prison inmates who were asked to indicate the number and kinds of crimes they had committed during the three years prior to their present incarceration. For each type of crime, most of those who reported doing it said they did so infrequently, but a minority confessed to engaging in the crime repeatedly. The researchers concluded that there are two major types of offenders: occasional criminals and broadly active ones. Few prisoners claimed to have committed a single kind of crime at a high rate; thus *there appeared to be few career specialists in prison.*

The third study (Chaiken and Chaiken, 1982) involved 2200 jail and prison inmates in Texas, Michigan, and California who were given a lengthy questionnaire that included self-report crime items. They were asked to report the number of times they had committed robberies, assaults, burglaries, forgeries, frauds and thefts, and drug deals. About 13 percent of the prisoners said they had committed none of the offenses during the previous two years, while the remainder, who reported involvement in one or more of the offenses, most commonly indicated that they had done them at relatively low rates. In other words, most of them had dabbled in crime and were not career criminals, but a sizable minority admitted having committed one or more crimes extremely frequently prior to incarceration. Many of the prisoners reported offense versatility (crime switching); hence criminal specialization was not common among them.

Although specialization in specific crimes is not characteristic of most offenders, the other side of the coin should be mentioned. Some criminologists (Gottfredson and Hirschi, 1990) have suggested that the evidence on lawbreaking patterns indicates that, having committed one offense, lawbreakers are equally likely to commit any of the myriad acts that are defined as criminal in the statutes. In other words, persons who have committed a burglary, for example, may commit rape, embezzlement, arson, drug sales, misrepresentation in advertising, or virtually any other crime as a second offense. Indeed, the thrust of the Gottfredson and Hirschi thesis is that many of these offenders may also engage in other forms of deviance or become involved in accidents. In short, some have contended that involvement in particular kinds of lawbreaking or deviance is random and unpredictable. But, most of the evidence noted above points in a different direction. Although offenders engage in a varied repertoire of illegal acts, most of them do *not* range across the entire body of criminal statutes. For example, the Chaiken and Chaiken (1982) data suggest that persons who commit robberies often engage in assaults, other predatory offenses, and drug sales as well, but those data do not indicate that drug-selling robbers commonly engage in homicide, white-collar crimes, sexual assaults, or various other crimes.

### Offender Typologies: An Assessment

What can be said, in conclusion, about offender classifications? Skepticism is in order regarding simple systems that assign offenders to a relatively small number of types. A number of these schemes are fuzzy and ambiguous, so they are difficult if not impossible to verify through research. By contrast, the role-career perspective is relatively clear and explicit. But, as we have seen, the degree of patterning of offense behavior and other definitional characteristics in it (and in others noted in this discussion) is greater than what exists in the world of criminality. Some lawbreakers closely resemble the "naïve check forgers," "semiprofessional property criminals," or "aggressive rapists" who appear in typologies, but they are mixed in with a much larger number of offenders who defy classification.

## CONCLUDING COMMENTS

After having guided the reader through the complexities of crime classification and offender typologies, I would like to now be able to pull a conceptual rabbit out of my hat by revealing that I have well-developed and sophisticated typologies of crime and of criminal offenders to offer to criminology. Alas, I have no such rabbit! However, I have outlined a classification of crime forms which does have some promise as a scheme for structuring criminological analysis. The review of efforts to identify offender types ended on a relatively pessimistic note, but at the same time, it seems premature to conclude that meaningful schemes for sorting offenders into reasonably clear groupings cannot be constructed. Shannon's (1991) efforts and Kempf's (1987) attempt to find offense trajectories in the case of "garden variety" offenders suggest that the criminality is not entirely unpatterned. On this same point, recent work by Knight, Carter, and Prentky (1989), sorting child molesters into relatively homogeneous types, is promising, as is true of the attempt by Knight and Prentky (1990) to sort forcible rapists into a set of subtypes. The message is that criminologists ought to be aware of taxonomic efforts by others and ought to build upon those efforts.

## NOTES

[1]Not all contemporary criminologists agree that crime is heterogeneous and that separate theories are required in order to account for the myriad forms of lawbreaking. The most detailed statement of an opposite position has been made by Gottfredson and Hirschi (1990: 16), who contended that "the vast majority of criminal acts are trivial and mundane affairs that result in little loss and less gain." Additionally, they argued that criminality has much in common with accidents and with other forms of deviant behavior. According to these theorists, criminals, deviants, and persons who are prone to accidents all exhibit low self-control, which is the major cause of their behavior.

[2]Although it is not precisely a classification of crime forms, Cressey's (1972) typology of six hierarchical forms of criminal organization bears mention. He distinguished among six categories of organized illegality, arranged in a pattern resembling a Guttman scale; that is, each was identified by a special role found in the types which preceded it but not present in those that followed. Cressey's typology is instructive regarding categories for criminological attention. While criminal organizations are involved in violations of the criminal law, these are sociological rather than legalistic categories. The statutes do not speak of "criminal organizations."

[3]Still another complication is that many feminist writers argue that offenses such as forcible rape which are identified in the legal codes as "sexual" offenses are, in fact, crimes of violence. This argument holds that even in criminal episodes where offenders have engaged in forced intercourse and/or other acts which the statutes treat as sexual crimes, the real motives behind these acts have to do with violence and intimidation of women, rather than eroticism. There is no denying that "sexual" crimes are also violent ones. The issue of the motivation behind criminal acts is a thornier one. Identification of the motives underlying these offenses is an empirical problem. The existing evidence suggests that motivations that are involved in specific instances of sexual misconduct probably vary from one offender to another.

[4]The savings and loans collapse and the demise of brokerage firms such as Drexel Burnham Lambert in the 1980s are examples of another point, to wit, public perceptions of "legitimate" organizations may change independent of the activities of the organizations themselves. The misconduct by Don Dixon, Charles Keating, Ivan Boesky, Dennis Levine, and Michael Milken preceded their "fall from grace" in the public eye.

[5]Another version of this scheme has been put forth by Glaser (1992), in which he discussed five patterns of criminality: adolescence-transition criminality, vice-propelled criminality, professional criminality, legitimate-occupation criminality, and passion-driven criminality. These categories have the ring of plausibility but are not explicitly defined.

[6]The typology of delinquents involved nine alleged types of juvenile offenders, defined in the same way as were the adult types, that is, in terms of offense behavior and social-psychological characteristics that were alleged to characterize juvenile lawbreakers. But, the research evidence on delinquents which has accumulated since 1965 casts a great deal of doubt upon the argument that juvenile offenders fall into a number of fairly distinct types (Gibbons and Krohn, 1991: 61–64). Rather, what the data indicate is that (a) juveniles vary on delinquent involvement along a kind of scale, with youths who report few or no offenses at one end, and "high rate" offenders on the other. Also, (b) offense *versatility* rather than specialization characterizes most delinquents. Low-rate and high-rate offenders alike frequently show a pattern of offense variability (Shannon, 1991).

[7]I don't want to be charged with reinventing history here. It would be misleading to suggest that my typologies are supported by a complex theoretical substructure and that they were developed as a result of a lengthy process of explication. The fact is that these schemes developed out of groping attempts by Donald L. Garrity and myself to find some kind of structure around which to organize our criminology lectures when we were graduate students at the University of Washington. These notions about behavioral and social-psychological dimensions of social roles were fairly naïve ones. Further, the two typologies of juvenile and adult offender patterns that appeared in *Changing the Lawbreaker* were drawn more from a combination of existing research findings, along with our own hunches and conjectures, than they were from this sketchy conceptual background. For more discussion of the conceptual framework, see Gibbons, 1992a: 204–9.

[8]The role-career scheme also included comments about the background characteristics of offender types, organized within four broad categories: social-class origins, family background variables, peer-group associations, and contacts with defining agencies. Defining agencies are official and semiofficial agencies responsible for detecting, apprehending, punishing, and rehabilitating offenders. In some cases, persons may be driven further into criminality as a result of employment difficulties and other problems they encounter because of social stigma. In other cases, contacts with defining agencies may have positive effects, leading deviants out of deviant conduct. See Gibbons and Jones, 1975.

# CHAPTER 5

# Causal Explanations and Theories in Criminology

## INTRODUCTION*

Chapter 1 spoke briefly about criminological inquiry, pointing out that theorizing and research are two sides of the same coin. Theories tell us what to look for in the way of factors that may explain or account for some phenomenon about which we are perplexed, while research methodology and procedures operate in the service of theory. Theory-guided research is intended to produce data which either will lend confirmation to the theory or, when the findings are not as predicted, will lead to revisions of the theory and to further research. Parenthetically, the commentary in Chapter 1 also indicated that inquiry sometimes unfolds in a different order, with exploratory research leading to theorizing. But in either event, our aim is to discover explanatory formulations which will survive the test of evidence.

Chapter 1 also provided a brief characterization of the nature of theories, identified as symbolic accounts, either verbal or written in form, which in the case of criminology, purport to capture the nature of lawbreaking and its causes. Theories are symbolic portrayals of "how things work."

Finally, Chapter 1 noted that criminologists who have tried to uncover causal relationships have frequently followed a division of labor in which

* A large part of this chapter first appeared in Don C. Gibbons, "Talking About Crime and Criminals: Some Comments on the Structure of Criminological Theories," paper presented at the Pacific Sociological Association meetings, 1991.

some of them have probed specific instances of the *social structure and criminality* question, while others have centered their efforts on the *origins of criminal acts and careers* query. These matters were also identified by the shorthand "the rates question" and the "Why do they do it?" query.

However, the remarks in Chapter 1 were too brief. Criminological inquiry is a complex and multifaceted topic which requires extended discussion. As we have seen in Chapters 2 and 3, while criminological investigation has been most frequently carried on by criminologists, representatives of a variety of disciplines have worked on the criminological enterprise. Sociological criminologists have generally restricted their theorizing and research work to sociological factors and processes of one kind or another, psychologists have mainly concentrated on probing the psyches of offenders, and biological scientists have been on the lookout for biological and sociobiological variables. As a result, textbooks such as *Society, Crime, and Criminal Behavior* (Gibbons, 1992a) have often sorted the work of these persons into three categories: *biogenic, psychogenic,* and *sociogenic* approaches.

Although the biogenic-psychogenic-sociogenic scheme is roughly accurate, it does not capture all of the complexity of the criminological enterprise. For one thing, there are a variety of specific forms of biological, psychological, or sociological theorizing and/or research. Then, too, some instances of theory development or of research are difficult to assign to these groupings. For example, in recent years a number of economists have been articulating a rational choice perspective on lawbreaking, but it does not fit precisely in any of the three categories above. Additionally, some criminological investigators have constructed causal formulations that draw upon more than one of these orientations; thus there are sociobiological-psychological variants of theory with which we must contend (e.g, Eysenck and Eysenck, 1970; Wilson and Herrnstein, 1985). Parenthetically, the fact that a criminological worker is a sociologist, for example, does not guarantee that that person will be engaged in the exploration of sociological variables!

Another facet of complexity in criminology is that there are myriad causal "models" that are employed by theorists and researchers, particularly when "Why do they do it?" queries are concerned. By "models," I mean different ideas that are held by particular criminologists about how causal processes unfold, rather than the more formal or quantitative representations of causal patterns that are associated with such statistical tools as path analysis.

One final point regarding the complexity of causal approaches is that criminological formulations vary markedly in the degree to which their concepts are clear or murky, their central propositions are hidden in a mass of verbiage or are explicitly stated, and they are either discursive and rambling in form or rigorous and formalized in statement.

This chapter is structured around these problems and issues in criminological theorizing.

## THINKING ABOUT CRIME AND CRIMINALS[1]

### Social Structure and Crime Rates

Let us look more closely at the social structure and crime rates matter. Chapter 1 took note of a recent case of this kind of theorizing and research, namely Baron and Straus's (1990) investigation of state-by-state variations in forcible rape. Those investigators drew upon existing theory and research on forcible rape and identified four explanatory ideas that have been advanced in the literature: gender inequality, pornography readership, "cultural spillover," and social disorganization. The gender inequality thesis suggests that rape rates may be higher in states where gender or sexual inequality is relatively pronounced and lower in states where the sexes have attained greater equality. The pornography hypothesis is that the wide availability of pornographic forms of media is conducive to the spread of male attitudes that devalue women, and in turn, to forcible rape. The contention about "cultural spillover" is that in states where legalized forms of violence exist, such as the spanking of unruly children in the schools, this approval of violence will encourage aggression against women. Finally, social disorganization is that state of affairs in which social ties among citizens are relatively attenuated. Baron and Straus argued that these factors may contribute to rape and that they may have an interactive effect; thus rape should be particularly frequent in states where two or more of these influences occur together.

After laying out this formulation, Baron and Straus proceeded to operationalize it by gathering aggregate data for various indicators of inequality, sanctioned violence, pornography, and social disorganization. For example, gender inequality was gauged by indicators having to do with the proportion of women in professional jobs, readership of pornographic publications was measured through figures on newsstand and subscription sales of "soft core" magazines such as *Playboy*, cultural spillover was measured by corporal punishment in schools, and the like, and social disorganization by indicators that included divorce rates and church membership for the individual states. Because they recognized that other variables that were not part of their explanatory model might also affect rape rates, Baron and Straus gathered data on a number of control variables, including the proportion of state populations residing in metropolitan areas, the percentage of blacks in the state, and the like. Finally, these data were subjected to multivariate statistical analyses, which indicated that states which were high on gender equality tended to have lower rape rates, while pornography readership and social disorganization were directly related to rape rates. Legitimate violence was not associated with variations in the incidence of reported rape.[2]

My reason for devoting space to the Baron and Straus theory and research is not because of a strong interest in the topic of sexual assault, although I do regard this study as an important substantive contribution to the literature on rape. (And I should add that as a plain citizen, I regard aggressiveness of any kind directed at women with a great deal of concern.) Rather, the study is highlighted here because it nicely illustrates the interplay of theory and research in the process of criminological inquiry. In addition, it is a clear example of the kind of research that is common when queries regarding crime rates of one kind or another are posed. These kinds of questions are often addressed through official crime statistics, through various kinds of secondary data that serve as indicators of concepts that appear in an explanatory formulation being examined, and through sophisticated statistical procedures.

Other examples of "rates question" studies are easy to locate.[3] In the case of predatory crime rate variations, particularly across states or metropolitan communities in the United States, some investigators have examined the hypothesis that variations in unemployment are linked to predatory offenses (e.g., Chiricos, 1987; Kohfeld and Sprague, 1988), while others have probed the argument that predatory crime rates reflect variations in levels of income inequality (e.g., Danziger, 1976; Braithwaite, 1979). Another approach to accounting for predatory crime rates is "routine activities theory," in which it is argued that levels of predatory crime are significantly influenced by the supply of motivated offenders in particular communities, but most particularly by the supply of goods to be stolen and the presence or absence of "capable guardians" in particular communities or neighborhoods. Capable guardianship refers to the extent to which neighborhood residents engage in watching over the houses and property of their neighbors and in related activities. Studies in this genre include those by Cohen, Felson, and Land (1980) and by Cohen and Felson (1979). Finally, some studies (e.g., Carroll and Jackson, 1983) have explored the possibility that income inequality and routine activity factors may be jointly implicated in predatory offending.

There is also a relatively large collection of research on homicide and assault rates and social and economic factors that might account for variations in these rates. One line of inquiry has centered on the routine activities thesis (Messner and Tardiff, 1985), while other researchers (e.g., Blau and Blau, 1982; Messner, 1980) have sought to determine whether income inequality is related to violence, including homicide. A different line of investigation has probed the "subculture of violence" thesis (Erlanger, 1974; Loftin and Hill, 1974), which holds that regional variations in attitudes favorable to the use of violence in dealing with interpersonal conflicts have an impact on levels of violence, beyond the influence exerted by variations in poverty and the like.

To a considerable extent, the research of criminologists is "driven" by the available data. Extensive information on "garden-variety" predatory crime and violence is routinely collected by local police agencies and collated into national statistics by the FBI. Even though there are serious deficiencies in these data, criminologists have often utilized them in the kinds of studies described here.

Adequate data for assessing theoretical formulations about other forms of crime, such as organizational–white-collar crime or organized crime, are harder to locate. As a result, while some theoretical formulations about these kinds of lawbreaking have been put forth, such as Coleman's (1987) "integrated theory" of white-collar crime, to be taken up later in this chapter, little or no research specifically directed at them has been conducted.

## The Origins and Development of Criminal Acts and Careers

Why do individuals engage in lawbreaking or refrain from misconduct? What are the major forces that impel some persons into lawbreaking and that restrain others from it? Questions of this kind are encountered everywhere, for as Glaser (1983: 307) has indicated: "Causal explanation is one of those primarily verbal activities by which humans represent the world to themselves." Note that Glaser spoke inclusively of humans, rather than linking causal analysis only to sociologists and criminologists. Causal thinking is a ubiquitous feature of everyday life.

Although laypersons and scientists both engage in causal thinking, this is not to say that their views coincide. When they endeavor to make sense of criminality, laypersons frequently opt for a crude free will argument which contends that lawbreakers make willful and deliberate choices to be "bad," or, less commonly, they embrace a rigid deterministic view of human conduct, in which humans are seen as having little or no control over their destinies.

Deterministic claims are not entirely absent in criminology; instead, examples of these views can be identified in some sociobiological formulations, as well as elsewhere. However, most social scientists, including criminologists, favor explanations of human behavior which emphasize what David Matza (1964) has termed *soft determinism*. This term draws attention to the possibility that while humans are to a considerable degree constrained or influenced by social or environmental forces that surround them, they are at the same time *reactive* individuals who are able to exercise some degree of freedom of choice over their behavior. As Matza (1964: 9) put it, "human actions are not deprived of freedom because they are causally determined." Rather than being human billiard balls, buffeted about by forces over which they have no control whatever, individuals often exert countervailing influence over their life circumstances.

The implications of soft determinism as a basic assumption undergirding causal theories are vast. If human actors are able to exercise some independent influence over social-structural pressures that play upon them, some degree of indeterminancy will probably always characterize causal explanations offered by social scientists. Allowance will have to be made in those arguments for the operation of choice and freedom in human actions; thus complete predictability of human behavior may never be achieved in scientific theories.

When laypersons go about interpreting the current behavior of others, whether deviant or otherwise, they usually attribute it to the earlier life experiences of the individual. Thus, for example, the delinquent acts of a teenager are linked to parental abuse that occurred a number of years earlier. This same "model" or broad view of causation can be detected in one form or another in many of the formulations of criminologists and other theorists who have endeavored to address the "Why do they do it?" question. Although the arguments of psychologists and psychiatrists are considerably more complex than those of laypersons, both are launched from the underlying premise that present behavior reflects past experiences. In much the same way, sociological theories as diverse as differential association (Sutherland, Cressey, and Luckenbill, 1992) and low social control (Gottfredson and Hirschi, 1990) involve a core assumption that the past has largely determined the present.

The possibility of alternative ways of looking at causal processes was briefly entertained but ultimately rejected by Sutherland and Cressey (1978: 79–80) many years ago. On the one hand, they acknowledged that it is possible to think about etiological matters in two different ways. They noted that "scientific explanations of criminal behavior may be stated in terms of the processes which are operating at the moment of the occurrence of crime or in terms of processes operating in the earlier history of the criminal. In the first case, the explanation may be called 'mechanical,' 'situational,' or 'dynamic,' in the second, 'historical' or 'developmental.' "

What Sutherland and Cressey had in mind by a situational explanation could be illustrated by a homeowner failing to fortify his or her dwelling against an assault by a potential burglar, thereby providing an opportunity for a motivated person to burglarize the dwelling. However, Sutherland and Cressey minimized the significance of situational factors and argued that, absent motivation to engage in burglary or some other kind of lawbreaking, situational inducements to lawbreaking are of relatively slight importance. Put another way, after acknowledging the possibility of situational-mechanistic kinds of explanations, they proceeded to reject this "model" on the grounds that criminal acts do not occur in the absence of motivational pressures.

Consider a relevant example: Some years ago my car was stolen while I was on a weekend trip to Seattle. It was parked in an unattended lot on the waterfront and the personal belongings were visible through the window. Presumably, if Sutherland and Cressey were still alive and available to be queried, they would say that had I been more careful where I parked my car, it would not have been stolen. But they would apparently also argue that my car would not have been stolen in either location if a motivated potential car thief had not driven by and identified it as a likely target. In short, developmental arguments posit that "the real causes" of crime have to do with criminal motivations, rather than with situational inducements and opportunities.

Although this developmental perspective is dominant in criminology, it may not always be the most appropriate one to employ. In a book dealing with causal imagery in the study of deviance, written some years ago, Cohen (1966: 41–45) noted that there are at least three "models" that may merit our consideration: (a) "kinds of people" theories, (b) "kinds of situations" arguments, and (c) combined theories.

The nature of kinds-of-people arguments becomes graphically clear when dramatic and highly publicized cases such as that of Jeffrey Dahmer come to light. Dahmer was convicted in 1992 of sexually assaulting and murdering 15 young men and boys in Milwaukee. Some of the evidence introduced at his trial indicated that he had engaged in cannibalism as well. Dahmer pleaded not guilty by reason of insanity to the charges against him but was found guilty by the jury. Most persons, whether ordinary citizens or social scientists, would probably agree that Dahmer must have undergone some kind of markedly unusual earlier life experiences which made him into a "monster."

Cohen did not deny the possibility that there may be some markedly aberrant persons within the population of deviants and that their behavior may be the result of some kind of failure of socialization. However, he also noted that some kinds of misconduct may arise principally out of situational inducements or pressures, to which most persons who are subjected to them would respond in similar ways. This is the thrust of kinds-of-situations arguments. Finally, Cohen suggested that in a number of real-life instances, deviance may be the outcome of individual characteristics *and* of situational factors operating together.

If Cohen's observations about competing models of the ways in which persons become involved in deviance are on the mark, it follows that the denial of the importance of situational factors in lawbreaking should be challenged. On this point, I explored the question of situational factors in criminality (Gibbons, 1971) and concluded that these are more important than acknowledged by Sutherland and Cressey. In particular, I argued that many real-life instances of lawbreaking involve both motivational elements that separate potential lawbreakers from other persons, and situational factors which operate, in a value-added process, as the final element in a causal pattern in which all sequential events must occur in order for criminal acts to result.[4] The similarity of this view to Cressey's (1953) account of the successive stages through which trust violators proceed should be apparent.

Others have added their voices to this discussion of alternative models of causal processes in criminal behavior. In particular, Cullen (1984) authored a book-length exploration of causal pathways in deviance and criminality. His thesis was that lawbreaking may often unfold in ways that resemble the statistician's notion of stochastic processes, in which a number of alternative behavioral sequences may develop from some initial state or starting point, each of them being the result of varied contingent events that occur following those experiences that precipitated the initial behavior in question. This idea is captured in examples such as that of a collection of youths who, for whatever reasons, become involved in flirtations with delinquency. Some of those youngsters may get caught by the police and taken to juvenile court while others manage to avoid detection. In turn, appearance in court may draw those youths further into misbehavior, while the "hidden" offenders may extricate themselves from continued deviance.

A recent investigation by McCarthy and Hagan (1991), directed at the situational causation argument, is instructive. In a study of homeless youths in Toronto, they found that the incidence of criminal acts on the part of homeless youngsters was generally higher among those youths after they had left home than before they had become homeless. McCarthy and Hagan concluded that homelessness is a criminogenic situation which induces lawbreaking on the part of youths who would probably have refrained from misbehavior had they not been homeless.

There is another modification of traditional ways of conceptualizing causal processes that also is required. Developmental-historical perspectives about which Sutherland and Cressey wrote contain an implicit assumption that etiological events are *one-directional*. In this way of thinking, poor family ties, exposure to delinquent companions, and poor school performance are causal factors in delinquency insofar as they precede misconduct. However, causal relationships may sometimes be *reciprocal* or *two-directional* ones. On this point, Thornberry and Christenson (1984) have provided evidence which points to such a pattern in the case of unemployment and criminality, for their data indicated that being unemployed often operates as a factor in initial acts of lawbreaking *and also* that problems of unemployment following involvement in criminality may increase the likelihood of further misconduct on the part of the unemployed person.

Criminological theorists and researchers have often identified these two models, the one-directional pattern and the reciprocal one, as *recursive* and *nonrecursive* processes. Nonrecursive patterns are those in which a particular variable may play a causal part in behavior at one point and may be an effect of the same behavior at a different point. Also, criminologists have begun to articulate theoretical arguments of a nonrecursive form. Thornberry's (1978) interactional theory of delinquency is a case in point.

**Causal Analysis and Research Designs**

How can we go about the development of causal arguments in criminology or engage in research scrutiny of those formulations? To begin with, clues about etiological factors arise from myriad sources, including, on occasion, accounts provided by offenders themselves. For example, a felon-turned-novelist, Malcolm Braly (1976), authored an autobiography, *False Starts*, which is a rich source of insights about factors which may pull and tug offenders both toward and away from continued lawbreaking. Jackson's (1969) *A Thief's Primer* and King's (1972) *Box Man* are other valuable works in this genre.

The most frequent approach used by criminologists to investigate theoretical formulations about causal factors is that of questionnaires and cross-sectional research designs. Hirschi's (1969) study illustrates this approach. He administered a lengthy questionnaire to a large sample of youngsters in Richmond, California. The subjects were asked to indicate whether they had committed one or another act of delinquency, and in addition, they were quizzed about a host of other matters: attitudes toward their parents and teachers, their views about their peers, participation in outside-of-school activities, and so on. The questionnaire was administered at a single point in time, although it did ask youths about experiences that had occurred to them at various points in the past. The research design was cross-sectional in that it involved a sample of youngsters who were quizzed in one single administration of the questionnaire.

Although survey methodology using questionnaires is the dominant research tactic in sociology, survey instruments and cross-sectional designs are not without problems. The limitations of questionnaires have been identified repeatedly in methodology textbooks. Many of the problems of survey instruments center on the "words and deeds" concern, which is that the responses that individuals make to questionnaire items may be inaccurate because they are shaped by the questions that are posed; that is, respondents are often forced to choose from a set of responses, none of which are sophisticated enough to capture their actual feelings or perceptions. In addition, there is the possibility of respondents occasionally offering socially desirable responses rather than revealing their real feelings, or the even more extreme possibility of outright lying on their part, as well as the concern that they may simply not be able to provide accurate information in response to questionnaire items. This last possibility is frequently a real one when juveniles are asked to provide information about such matters as their parents' incomes, parental attitudes, and kindred topics.

Cross-sectional research designs have also come under fire, particularly by criminologists who have argued that these designs often do not allow the researcher to untangle causal processes that may have taken place over a considerable stretch of time. Those who make this argument are on solid ground—cross-sectional approaches do have this limitation. For example, suppose that we observe that within a sample of juveniles, some have engaged in extensive delinquency while others have committed few if any law violations. Further, suppose that we discover that the most delinquent youngsters are on poorer terms with their parents than are the other juveniles. Although it would be tempting to argue that poor parent-child relationships are causally related to delinquency, such a claim might be incorrect, for it is conceivable that involvement in delinquency *leads to* deteriorated parent-child ties. It is often difficult to divine the direction of relationships from cross-sectional observations of this sort.

Critics of cross-sectional designs have often argued for cohort studies and longitudinal research designs of the kind represented by the Wolfgang, Figlio, and Sellin (1972) study in Philadelphia and Shannon's (1991) investigation of delinquency and its outcome in Racine, Wisconsin.

Although the strengths of longitudinal studies, which involve a number of observations of cohort members at different points in time, cannot be gainsaid, some cautionary remarks are in order about this approach as well. Suppose that we obtain a cohort of youngsters in a particular city (for example, all youngsters born in 1970), track down all of them who are still residing in the city in 1980, and beginning in that year, administer a set of questionnaires to them every two years. If the size of the research cohort is very large, the costs of carrying out such a study might become prohibitive. Moreover, as Gottfredson and Hirschi (1990: 220–40) and others have noted, there is no guarantee in this design that we will end up with data that allow us to pinpoint the nature or direction of some of the causal relationships that may be operating among youths who have moved either in a delinquent or in a nondelinquent direction. For example, we may find that between 1982 and 1984, many youngsters became on poorer terms with their parents and also that their grades in school plummeted, but we may still not be able to determine which of these changes preceded the other or whether both were the consequence of other events that we have not captured in our theory and/or research design.

This is not a book on research methods; thus I do not propose to engage in an extended discussion of research in criminology. But one point should be clear, namely that research inquiry on causal questions poses some difficult problems for the criminologist.

To this point, both in this chapter and in the book as a whole, I have offered a number of observations about the development of and current state of theory in criminology, but largely without specifying precisely what I mean by theory. To this point, I have followed an *Alice in Wonderland* practice common among sociologists—"A theory is whatever I say it is!" It is now time to take a closer look at the varieties of symbolic constructions which pass for theoretical formulations in criminology. I argue in the remainder of this chapter that some of these verbal constructions ought not to be identified as theories at all and that others of them need a good bit of explication if they are to serve as the bases for advances in criminological knowledge.

## CRIMINOLOGICAL PERSPECTIVES AND THEORIES

### Discursive Theories and Formalization

The remainder of this chapter asks: "How far have we come since the efforts of Shaw and McKay, Sutherland, and other pioneers in criminology, in the way of explicit, researchable theory?[5] My comments will be relatively critical ones, drawing to a considerable extent upon Gibbs's (1972, 1985a) observations.[6] He has argued that much of the time, sociologists and criminologists literally do not know what they are talking about, due to the fuzzy and murky nature of the *discursive* theorizing that characterizes sociology and criminology. He has written at length about the discursive mode of theorizing and has contrasted it to what he termed the *formal mode* of theory construction.

What is discursive theory? According to Gibbs (1985a: 23), "the discursive mode is merely the conventions of a natural language (such as German or English)." *Webster's New World Dictionary* offers a helpful definition, indicating that discursiveness means "wandering from one topic to another; rambling; digressive." Finally, Cohen (1989: 182) has provided a succinct description of discursive theorizing in sociology: "The typical situation embeds a theoretical assertion in an ordinary prose paragraph, where a claim is made, its meaning is discussed, and its importance is justified, all in one stream of writing." Gibbs and Cohen agree that discursive theorizing usually involves vaguely defined concepts, tautological statements disguised as empirical propositions, and theoretical arguments which lack a clear, underlying logical structure. A great many of the claims that we have reviewed in the preceding pages stand as examples of discursive theorizing in criminology. Finally, Gibbs and Cohen argued that the development of knowledge in the social sciences has been greatly impeded by discursive theorizing.

Is there an alternative to discursive theorizing? Gibbs, Cohen, and some other sociologists have asserted that we ought to move in the direction of a formal mode of theorizing. Gibbs (1985a: 23) has indicated that the sine qua non of formalization is explicit rules or logical principles that are employed in theory construction so as to produce explanatory formulations that can be subjected to empirical tests which either confirm or fail to support those arguments.

### Theorizing in the Formal Mode

There is no single recipe or set of specific directions which can be identified as *the* formal mode of theory construction; rather, as Gibbs (1985a: 23) indicated, formal theorizing involves the use of one or another set of rules designed for stating theories. In other words, there are alternative ways of formalizing arguments. Some efforts to sharpen explanatory formulations have employed symbolic logic while others have proceeded on the basis of a different logical calculus. But in either case, theorizing in the formal mode refers to efforts to explicate explanatory arguments that are more rigorous and testable than those that are produced by discursive procedures.

Although this book is intended as a critique of contemporary criminological theories rather than as a detailed exposition regarding techniques of theory construction, some additional comments are in order regarding the characteristics of formal theories. We need to identify a benchmark against which to evaluate the theoretical utterances of criminologists. Accordingly, let us explore the formal theory mode in more detail.

Let us begin with Hempel's (1952: 36) succinct characterization of theory. Although written many years ago, it still stands as an "ideal type" description of scientific theory:

> A scientific theory might therefore be likened to a complex spatial network: Its terms are represented by the knots, while the threads connecting the latter correspond, in part to the definitions and, in part, to the fundamental and derivative hypotheses included in the theory. The whole system floats, as it were, above the plane of observation and is anchored to it by rules of interpretation. These might be viewed as the strings which are not part of the network but which link certain points of the latter with specific places in the plane of observation. By virtue of these interpretive connections, the network can function as a scientific theory: From certain observational data, we may ascend, via an interpretive string, to some point in the theoretical network, thence proceed, via definitions and hypotheses, to other points, from which another interpretive string permits a descent to the plane of observation.

This portrayal by Hempel conjures up an image of precision and clarity as the hallmark of scientific theory. In sociology, Gibbs (1985a) has made the most ambitious attempt to articulate a model of theorizing that approaches the picture sketched by Hempel.

*Gibbs's Formal Mode.* There is little consensus in criminology or sociology regarding what should or should not be called a theory or upon definitions of such terms as theorems, postulates, axioms, or other theoretical components. Further, we have no agreed-upon rules for deriving propositions or for testing theoretical contentions. However, Gibbs has made a major effort to distinguish between the elements of theory and to specify the linkages between theories and empirical observations. A brief summary of his detailed and complex explication is presented below, but I urge readers to go beyond my comments and to study Gibbs's writings in greater detail.

Gibbs began by identifying the types of terms that make up theories, that is, the words that define "the stuff" to be explained and the phenomena that are to be used in these explanations. *Constructs* were identified as terms, the definitions of which are incomplete, that are used in stating theories. In other words, a construct fails to enumerate all of the features of the phenomenon in question. "Social class" and "deviance" might be offered as examples of constructs.

Some terms employed by theorists are completely specified or defined, at least in the opinion of the theorist; thus all of the varieties of the phenomena designated by those terms are identified, in which case, they are *concepts*. For example, "the 1993 official Oregon crime rate" might be nominated as a concept. When theorists have identified a computational formula for a specific measure of a concept, that element would be termed a *referential* by Gibbs. The crude birth rate for a specific state, arrived at by dividing all of the "live births" in that state during a calendar year by the total population of the state (and multiplied by 1000) would be illustrative.

Two other kinds of terms were identified by Gibbs: *unit terms*, which identify the units of analysis (e.g., cities, persons over 18 years of age, FBI Index crimes, etc.), and *relational terms* such as "varies with," "is positively correlated with," and so on. Relational terms are employed in order to construct statements specifying how two or more phenomena are connected.

Throughout his discussion of theoretical terms, Gibbs (1985a: 24–25) emphasized that in order to subject a theory to empirical scrutiny, the theorist must stipulate "(1) a computational formula, (2) the requisite data, and (3) a procedure for gathering or obtaining these data." In short, Gibbs provided a vigorous argument against those activities in which one scholar formulates a relatively fuzzy argument, leaving the task of deciphering that formulation or the research testing of it to others.

Returning to Gibbs's comments on relational statements, he observed that some of these are *axioms*, in which two or more constructs are linked. Because constructs cannot be directly measured, axioms are not testable statements. *Postulates* consist of relational statements involving at least one concept and one construct, such as the assertion that across individual states, variations in social disorganization (construct) are associated with levels of the official crime rate (concept). *Transformational statements* link concepts and referentials; that is, they specify particular measures of a concept. Finally, *theorems* are statements in which all of the terms are referentials. Theorems are essentially what many investigators mean when they speak of hypotheses.

This account of Gibbs's formal mode of theorizing may well strike some readers as arcane or strange, while others may regard Gibbs as a too demanding taskmaster. Also, my brief sketch of his views may create the misimpression that he is an advocate of an overly mechanical approach to theorizing. If so, consider his concluding remarks (Gibbs, 1985a: 33): "One great misunderstanding is the belief that a formal mode can be used to 'manufacture' theories. No mode can be substituted for a theorist's imagination and judgment; and until a theorist arrives at substantive ideas or arguments, a formal mode has no utility. Since a mode is a set of rules as to a theory's *form*, it does not even suggest the *content* of premises, definitions, or procedures" [emphasis in the original].

Gibbs's "extremist" views about sociological and criminological theorizing have not been enthusiastically received. It may be, as some have suggested, that these fields are not yet well developed enough to be amenable to the forms of theorizing he advocated. For my part, I would be willing, at least for the present, to settle for *semiformal* criminological theories that begin to approach the rigor demanded by Gibbs, even if they do not entirely satisfy his conditions.

*Cohen's Views.* Bernard Cohen's (1989) explication of the elements of theory comes close to what I have in mind. At one point (1989: 178), he offered the following definition: "A theory is a set of interrelated, universal statements, some of which are relationships assumed to be true, together with a syntax, a set of rules for manipulating the statements to arrive at new statements." At another point (p. 177), he noted: "The chief components of theories, then, include: *assumptions, scope conditions, derived propositions, primitive terms*, and *defined terms*" [emphasis in the original].

Cohen (1989: 196) also enumerated six criteria to be used in evaluating a theory:

1. The theory should be explicit and relatively precise.
2. The theory should contain explicit definitions based on primitive terms for which usage is widely shared.
3. The theory should provide a clear exhibition of the structure of the argument. In other words, the syntax of the theory should allow an examination of the logical skeleton of the theory apart from its content.
4. The theory should provide clear guidelines as to its domain of applicability; that is, the theory should contain explicit scope statements.
5. The theory should be testable empirically; when joined to a set of initial conditions, the theory should allow the derivation of observational statements, both to predict and explain.
6. The theory should formulate an abstract problem.[7]

These six criteria are fairly straightforward, although the last one is open to differing interpretations. What is an "abstract problem"? This is a matter to which I will return later, for criminologists do not exhibit unanimity on this question.

## THE QUALITY OF CRIMINOLOGICAL THEORIZING

In this book, Cohen (1989: 177) remarked: "Although many books in the last decade have dealt with sociological theory and theory construction, there is still no agreed-upon view of what theory is. The word theory is used in many different ways in sociology, and if we take the sum of sociological conceptions of *theory*, virtually the only things that would be excluded are what have been called observational statements."

Does this discouraging report apply to criminology? Do criminologists use words such as theory in the same loose way, applying them to a variety of forms of argumentation or exposition? Judging by the contents of books on criminological theory, the answer is "Yes." *The Criminological Enterprise* (Gibbons, 1979) devoted a few pages to the need for more rigor in theorizing, but it had relatively little to say about how greater precision might be achieved, and it identified, as theories, a variety of arguments that differ markedly in conceptual clarity and logical structure.

Meier's (1985) *Theoretical Methods in Criminology* might be expected to contain a good bit of commentary on theory. But, save for Gibbs's chapter, most of it dealt with broad explanatory frameworks and assumptions behind various kinds of "theorizing." In his introductory essay, Meier (1985: 15) asserted: "The term, 'theoretical methods' denotes approaches, assumptions, and techniques of theory construction." However, the techniques part of theoretical methods received relatively little attention in the book.

Williams and McShane's (1988) book also involved a broad conception of criminological theory. They offered no explicit definition of the term but dealt with the classical school of thought, biological positivism, the "Chicago School," differential association theory, anomie theory, subcultural arguments, labeling views, conflict arguments, social control theory, and social learning formulations. Although these are familiar perspectives, some of them should not be called theories. For example, labeling "theory" is a collection of "sensitizing" notions or a broad perspective about deviance and criminality rather than an explicit set of concepts and propositions. Similarly, there is no relatively formal theory regarding social conflict and crime in existence. Also, Williams and McShane remarked that a good theory should be testable and should fit the evidence, but they provided little indication of the elements that make up a testable theory.[8]

Another book on criminological theory, by Lilly, Cullen, and Ball (1989) contains many informative comments on the social contexts in which various criminological arguments have developed, along with a number of observations about the social policy consequences of these varied formulations. The authors reviewed the classical writings of Beccaria and others, the search for biological bases of lawbreaking by Lombroso and others, and other efforts to find biological or psychological differences that mark off lawbreakers from the rest of us. They also had much to say about the work of Shaw and McKay and Sutherland, along with the arguments of Merton, Cohen, and Cloward and Ohlin that we encountered in Chapters 2 and 3. Then, too, they reviewed control arguments, labeling views, conflict and radical-Marxist perspectives, and concluded with a chapter on the reemergence of conservative views, such as those of Wilson and Herrnstein (1985). However, nowhere in the book is there an explicit definition to be found; rather, the implicit sense of the term *theory* is that it refers to verbal statements of varying degrees of precision, having to do with "how things work."

Shoemaker's *Theories of Delinquency* took a truly catholic view, for he indicated (1984: 8) that theory is anything that is "an attempt to make sense of observations . . . irrespective of the sophistication of its concepts and propositions." His book covered biological explanations, psychological theories, social disorganization and culture conflict arguments, and other familiar perspectives, as well as some formulations that more closely approximate theories, such as the differential association argument. Shoemaker also discussed labeling, as well as female delinquency and middle-class juvenile misconduct, all of which are particularly difficult to defend as varieties of theory.

### Sorting Out Criminological Arguments

Let me bring some order into criminological theorizing by outlining some different forms of criminological exposition. One major dimension along which arguments can be arranged was discussed at the beginning of this chapter, namely, whether they focus on *rates* of crime or delinquency, the processes through which *individuals* come to engage in or refrain from lawbreaking, or *jointly* with both of these concerns.

There are other ways in which criminological arguments might be classified. Some theoretical statements are general ones purporting to account for a variety of kinds of lawbreaking or lawbreakers, while others are specific to a single form of crime or collection of offenders. As we have already seen, explanatory perspectives also differ in terms of the number of variables which they take into account, whether they are recursive or nonrecursive in structure, and the specific kinds of variables to which they attend (biological, psychological, or sociological ones).

While it might be possible to take these and additional distinctions deemed important in categorizing criminological arguments and to construct an elaborate multifaceted taxonomic scheme, then to struggle to place most or all of the major causal arguments into one cell or another of such a matrix, I have not attempted to do so. Such a project would consume more time and effort than is warranted; thus it would be counterproductive. While various viewpoints could be "shoehorned" into the cells of such a matrix, it is unlikely that most criminologists would agree with all or even the majority of the assignments.

What I have done is considerably less ambitious than the creation of a "master taxonomy." Table 5–1 offers a simple classificatory scheme based on two dimensions, the explanatory problem being addressed in particular formulations and the degree of discursiveness-formalism found in them. Table 5–1 contains illustrative entries, rather than an inventory of all current criminological theories. In other words, I have singled out a few examples that fit in one or another of these cells. In some cases, I have identified a body of work, such as radical-Marxist theorizing, but without listing the names of persons associated with it, while in other instances, I have noted specific arguments and the person(s) most closely associated with them. Some formulations are "in the public domain," while others, such as Katz's (1988) ruminations about "the sensual attractions of doing evil" are distinctly his own.

The vertical axis of Table 5–1 involves four forms of exposition: general perspectives, discursive theories, semiformal theories, and formal theories. General perspectives suggest some "sensitizing" concepts and ideas but lack any of the other elements of a theory. General perspectives hint at conceptual notions thought to have relevance to criminality, but many of the concepts are vague. Also, general perspectives are seriously deficient in explicit propositions. Table 5–1 identifies radical-Marxist-critical criminological arguments as one general perspective. Labeling viewpoints would also be placed in this cell.

I have already indicated the general characteristics of discursive and formal modes of theorizing, borrowing from Gibbs and Cohen. As I also noted, Cohen would apparently accept, as a theory, a set of explicit and interrelated propositions that meet certain other criteria, not the least of which is empirical testability. Gibbs's standards are more stringent and he would require a higher level of rigor for an argument to be labeled as a formal theory. I have included a category of semiformal theory in Table 5–1 in order to provide a place for arguments that approach the standards enunciated by Cohen but which fall short of those of Gibbs.

Note the scale on the left-hand side of the table, as well as the dashed lines that separate varieties of explanatory problems and forms of theoretical exposition. These are reminders that the dividing lines in the table are fluid, or put another way, that the discursiveness or formality of arguments is a matter of degree. Also, some of the entries in the table are accompanied by arrows and question marks, as for example, Katz's (1988) book. These notations emphasize the difficulty of placing arguments cleanly within one pigeonhole or another.

Table 5–1 identifies radical-Marxist notions as a general perspective, and it also categorizes "criminogenic culture" views and Sutherland's differential social organization framework (Sutherland, Cressey, and Luckenbill, 1992: 104–18) as falling in this category. Sutherland and Cressey argued that crime and delinquency in American society are related to differential social organization, along with normative conflict, high rates of mobility, and cul-

**Table 5–1** Forms of Causal Argument in Criminology

|  | Explanatory Problem | | |
|---|---|---|---|
| Forms of Theoretical Exposition | Social Structure and Criminality | Origins and Development of Criminal Acts and Careers | Combination Theories |
| General Perspectives | Radical-Marxist-Critical Views<br>Criminogenic Culture Views<br>Differential Social Organization | Psychogenic Approach<br>Biogenic Approach<br>Samenow's "Criminal Mind" View (1984) | Textbook discussions such as Personal-Social Disorganization View (e.g., R. E. L. Faris) |
| Discursive Theories | Anomie<br>Currie's *Confronting Crime* | Katz's *Seductions of Crime* (1988) ↑ ? | Gottfredson and Hirschi's General Theory<br>Coleman's Integrated Theory of White-Collar Crime |
| Semiformal Theories | Routine Activities Theory<br>Structural Criminology (Hagan et al.)<br>Income Inequality<br>Forcible Rape (Baron and Straus, 1990) | Wilson and Herrnstein<br>Differential Association/Social Learning (Akers)<br>Ellis's "Synthesized Theory of Rape" | Johnson's Integrated Theory of Delinquency<br>Braithwaite's Theory of Shame and Reintegration |
| Formal Theories |  |  |  |

ture conflict said to characterize this nation. Earlier in their book, they asserted (p. 83): "Differential social organization should explain the crime rate while differential association should explain the criminal behavior of a person."

Although the idea of differential social organization is implied in the propositions that make up differential association theory (Sutherland, Cressey, and Luckenbill, 1992: 88–90), the latter is much more explicit or formal than is the former. It is difficult to know what to say about the former, other than that intuitively, it sounds reasonable. By contrast, the differential association argument has been subjected to research, albeit with mixed or ambiguous results, due in considerable part to the fuzziness of certain of its basic concepts such as "intensity" of associations and "definitions favorable to violation of law" (see Chapter 7).

General perspectives having to do with the "Why do they do it?" question are harder to identify, but broad arguments about the importance of biological or other general groupings of alleged causal influences might be placed in this category. Also, Samenow's (1984) sweeping claims about "the criminal mind" seem to fit here.

Table 5–1 also takes note of general perspectives which deal jointly with social-structural influences in criminality and the involvement of individuals in lawbreaking. These have often turned up in textbooks, with one example being Faris's (1955) account of how various forms of "personal disorganization," including criminality, are allegedly generated by "social disorganization."

Currie's (1985) detailed commentary on the contemporary crime problem in American society is an example of discursive theorizing focused mainly on social-structural forces that lead to criminality. Differentiating it from more general forms of exposition was, first, his concentrated attention upon work and unemployment, structured inequality, and family relationships as crucial in producing criminality, and second, the fact that his analysis was informed by a substantial body of empirical evidence.

Katz's (1988) *Seductions of Crime* is a highly discursive treatment of "the moral and sensual attractions of doing evil." The dust jacket quoted certain well-known persons in the field who asserted that the book is "thrillingly original," that it offers us "new insights," and that it is "an alluring and disturbing study." While it did present a stimulating and provocative thesis, Katz was not the first person to observe that offenders sometimes reap personal, psychic rewards as well as monetary ones from criminality. But, more to the point, the book was replete with allusions to "the sensual pleasures of crime," "transcendence," "metaphors," and other undefined terms, and the central propositions of the argument were difficult to identify (for a more detailed critique, see Turk, 1991).

Let me acknowledge that sweeping and not-entirely-clear analyses have a place in criminological inquiry. Also, I do not argue that professional criminologists are the only persons who have something significant to say about criminality. As I have indicated, much can be learned from books such as Braly's *False Starts*. However, we also need to recognize the limitations, *as theoretical expositions*, of books such as the Katz volume.

A number of works fall into the discursive-combination theory category. Coleman's (1987) integrated theory of white-collar crime falls in this category. He began with the claim that organizational or white-collar crimes in the United States are encouraged by social-structural or macro factors, a major one being the "culture of competition" that drives organizations toward law violations. Additional to this competitive ethos are normative restraints upon criminality that operate in varying degrees upon different financial, business, or industrial segments in the nation. For example, the federal Food and Drug Administration responds to misbehavior in the pharmaceutical industry as well as in other organizations. At the same time, the FDA is hampered in its efforts to ensure product safety because it lacks its own testing facilities and is forced to rely on the truthfulness of its client organizations regarding product testing. Finally, Coleman argued that organizational actors are most likely to engage in law violations after they have acquired "justificatory beliefs" that allow them to reconcile their decision to engage in deviance with their conceptions of themselves as honest, lawabiding persons. Although this argument contains a good many insights and hypotheses about white-collar crime, it is a discursive formulation which might be difficult to probe through research.

Gottfredson and Hirschi's *A General Theory of Crime* (1990) is another relatively discursive combined theory. Its central proposition is straightforward, namely that criminal offenders and other deviants are characterized by low self-control. Social-structural influences in lawbreaking were also discussed but were generally discounted as unimportant. Their relatively small book is complex, thoughtful, provocative, and controversial. My own copy has marginal notations on nearly every page, some expressing agreement with the authors and others raising questions about the accuracy of the claims they offered. They argued that "ordinary crime" consists mainly of criminal acts that are trivial and mundane, and they also described "the typical or standard robbery," "the typical or standard burglary," and the typical forms of a number of other crimes. Also, they claimed that embezzlement of large amounts of money by older employees in positions of trust is a "rarity." However, the reader is left to ponder such questions as "how typical? how trivial? or how rare?" More important, their basic claims must be teased out of a discursive narrative in which they are embedded, so it is reasonable to describe this as discursive theorizing (for further comments on this argument, see Chapter 10).

Table 5–1 contains several illustrative cases of semiformal theory devoted to social-structural processes in crime. One of these is the research of Hagan and his associates (1989), informed by what they termed power-control theory. This argument, stressing the interaction of class and family influences both in the causation of delinquency and in the processing of offenders in the justice system, was spelled out in detail, particularly in the specific studies that have been conducted by Hagan and his co-workers.

Routine activities theory also appears in Table 5–1 as a semiformal theory, as does the income inequality line of investigation. The study of state-by-state variations in forcible rape rates by Baron and Straus (1990) is another conceptually guided piece of work that I have categorized as a semiformal theory.

There are probably a number of places in Table 5–1 where criminologists would disagree with these entries. The assignments of the routine activities argument, the income inequality and unemployment formulations, and the gender inequality argument as semiformal theories are particularly debatable.

Quite probably, a number of persons would prefer not to call these theories, on the grounds that they are too narrow; that is, they focus on only a small slice of lawbreaking, such as predatory crime. Additionally, some might contend that these formulations fail to specify all of the relevant variables that have an impact on the dependent variable(s). Finally, some might deny that these are adequate theories because they are silent on the issue of how social-structural influences "get inside the heads of offenders," so to speak. Stated another way, some might argue that unemployment, income inequality, and rape arguments are incomplete because they do not identify the causal analogs of these variables that operate at the individual level.

However, it is difficult to establish, *a priori*, that the focus of an explanatory argument is "too narrow" (or "too broad"). Instead, this judgment is more appropriately made *after* the research evidence is in, telling us whether a particular approach has succeeded or failed to uncover information which improves upon our ability to explain and predict the phenomena under scrutiny. Regarding the incompleteness of arguments, it would be desirable to have a large number of clearly articulated theories that deal jointly with structural and individual processes, but that some formulations are restricted to the former is not a compelling reason for rejecting them out of hand. A number of these inquiries have added incrementally to our understanding of criminality.

Table 5–1 lists three examples of semiformal theorizing about how individuals become involved in criminality or refrain from it, one of which is Wilson and Herrnstein's (1985) *Crime and Human Nature*, which, contrary to what is implied by its title, in actuality was restricted to garden-variety predatory crime, rather than dealing with lawbreaking in all of its forms. In the chapter which presented a theory of criminal behavior, they argued (Wilson and Herrnstein, 1985: 61):

The larger the ratio of rewards (material and nonmaterial) of noncrime to the rewards (material and nonmaterial) of crime, the weaker the tendency to commit crimes. The bite of conscience, the approval of peers, and any sense of inequity will increase or decrease the total value of crime; the opinions of family, friends, and employers are important benefits of noncrime, as is the desire to avoid the penalties that can be imposed by the criminal justice system. The strength of any reward declines with time, but people differ in the rate at which they discount the future. The strength of a given reward is also affected by the total supply of reinforcers.

At first glance, this looks like an explicit argument in propositional form. Wilson and Herrnstein (1985: 531–35) also included what they referred to as a mathematical version of this theory in the appendix of their book. This "mathematical" statement included a number of "equations" designed to identify the propositions of the theory.

However, *Webster's New World Dictionary* defines mathematics as "the group of sciences . . . dealing with quantities, magnitudes, and forms, and their relationships, attributes, etc. by the use of numbers and symbols." Although there are a variety of symbols in this mathematical statement, there are no *values* in it; thus it appears to be a modern version of the "mathematical sociology" of Stuart Carter Dodd (1940), who contrived a large number of equation-like statements in order to "quantify" sociological knowledge, but who was not able to supply a dictionary by which competent observers were able to assign values to these equations. The sterility of this effort is reflected in the fact that Dodd's name has disappeared from the roster of important figures in post–World War II sociology.

The remainder of Wilson and Herrnstein's book was discursive and endeavored to show that constitutional and biological factors play the most important role in producing persons who have difficulty in deferring gratification, planning for the future, and refraining from criminality. Reviewers have offered negative evaluations of their book, arguing that they distorted or misrepresented much of the research evidence on which they drew for support (see, for example, Gibbons, 1987). But of most relevance here is Gibbs's (1985b) review, which took them to task for the conceptual flabbiness of their argument.

Although Sutherland's differential association formulation (Sutherland, Cressey, and Luckenbill, 1992: 88–90) is now "long in the tooth," having appeared in its final form in 1947, it still serves as a relatively explicit account of the processes through which persons come to engage in criminality or refrain from it. It is appropriately designated as a semiformal theory, even though there are a number of conceptual ambiguities that plague it (Gibbons, 1979: 56–61; also see Chapter 7). Cressey's (1960: 57) summary judgment is on the mark: "It seems safe to conclude that differential association is not a precise statement of the process by which one becomes a criminal."

Akers (1985) has rewritten the theory of differential association in terms of social learning principles rather than the cruder associational learning perspective on which Sutherland built. In the process, the argument was made somewhat more precise, but at the same time, conceptual problems continue to limit its explanatory usefulness. Krohn and I (1991: 150–54) have concluded: "It has yet to be demonstrated that differential reinforcement is more amenable to operationalization than is differential association or the ratio of definitions. The minimal amount of research generated by the theory may be reflective of the difficulty in measuring these concepts in the social arena."

Several semiformal theories which attend both to social-structural influences and the processes through which individuals become involved in misbehavior can be identified, including Johnson's (1979) "integrated theoretical" statement.[9] After reviewing the delinquency literature, he created a causal model in the form of a path diagram, in which social class, family relationships, school influences, perceptions of future opportunities, delinquent associates, delinquent values, and perceptions of risk from involvement in delinquency were knit together into an explicit and fairly complex causal argument. However, while his argument incorporated social-structural variables, it was pitched mainly at the individual level, so it is not an entirely satisfactory example of a combination theory.[10]

Table 5–1 also identifies Braithwaite's (1989b) general theory, centered on the notion of reintegrative shaming, as a semiformal, combination theory. His formulation drew upon control theory, labeling viewpoints, subcultural and learning arguments, and opportunity theory, to which he added the concept of reintegrative shaming, by which he meant (p. 55) "expressions of community disapproval, which may range from mild rebuke to degradation ceremonies, which are followed by gestures of reacceptance into the community of law-abiding citizens."

A large part of Braithwaite's analysis had to do with the conditions that lead to initial acts of lawbreaking on the part of persons, and the personal characteristics and societal conditions that encourage or discourage reintegrative shaming. He contended that persons who are cut off from intensive social ties with others are most likely to flirt with lawbreaking and also are least likely to be influenced by shaming. Also, societies such as the United States, which are low on "communitarianism" are ones in which large numbers of persons are likely to be lacking in interdependency, that is, a network of social ties that keeps them from flirtations with misbehavior. Japan, on the other hand, was identified as a society in which communitarianism is much more pronounced. Societies lacking in communitarianism are also more likely to stigmatize deviants and criminals, thus driving them into subcultural association with other lawbreakers, while societies that are more communitarian in form tend to practice reintegrative shaming.

It should be apparent that Braithwaite's theory is quite complex. Also, his book included both a relatively formal summary of the theory and a relatively discursive elaboration of it.

It bears repeating that the distinctions in Figure 5–1 are not razor sharp ones. Criminological theories are more or less discursive and more or less formal. In the case of Braithwaite's formulation, one reviewer (Scheff, 1990) has likened him to a "new Durkheim" and has concluded that Braithwaite's theory "will, I believe, generate new ideas and research into the forseeable future." On the other hand, I have drawn attention to some places where the formulation is less than clear (Gibbons, 1991; also see Chapter 10).

One entry in Table 5–1 that has not been discussed so far is Ellis's (1989: 79) "synthesized theory" of rape. His argument involved these claims:

1. Rape is sexually motivated, and, as all sexual behavior tends to be, is motivated by (a) a drive for erotic sexual experiences (the sex drive), and (b) a drive for bonded sexual relationships (the drive to possess and control one or more sex partners).
2. While the motivation for sex is almost entirely the result of unlearned neurological processes, the actual techniques involved in committing rape are largely learned through operant conditioning (and only secondarily through imitation and attitudinal factors).
3. Natural selection has favored stronger sex drives and stronger tendencies to orient drives to possess and control multiple sex partners in males than in females, while females have been strongly favored for resisting forceful copulatory tactics because it effectively prevents them from discriminating in favor of males who will help care for offspring after they have been conceived.
4. Exposure of the brain to androgens helps to produce strong sex drives and strong tendencies to attempt to possess and control multiple sex partners, while it also helps to reduce sensitivity to any aversive consequences of one's actions.

Although it consists of four relatively explicit claims or propositions, there is also a good deal of haziness, equivocation, and the like in this argument.[11] As a result, I have placed it in the semiformal category. The difficulty in classifying theories is well illustrated by Ellis's argument.

## CONCLUDING COMMENTS

On rare occasions, a piece of criminological theorizing appears on the scene and has a major impact upon criminological work. Cohen's *Delinquent Boys* (1955) was such a product, for although few research investigations of gang delinquency in the 1960s focused directly on propositions from it, it nonetheless had the effect of stimulating a resurgence of criminological interest in gangs and played a seminal role in encouraging the outpouring of gang research that occurred in the 1960s. In much the same way, Hirschi's *Causes of Delinquency* (1969) was followed by a large body of research which centered partly or wholly on his social bond argument. However, many theoretical statements by criminologists have had a very short shelf life. After receiving considerable initial fanfare, they have soon disappeared without having made any lasting impact on criminological work. There are probably a number of reasons why criminological expositions have failed to stimulate research, but one of them has to do with the discursive and fuzzy character of much of what we write.

What shall we do about this state of affairs? Some years ago, Zetterberg (1965) suggested that the rigor of theoretical arguments could be improved through axiomatization, in which a large set of researchable propositions would be generated from a small set of axioms or postulates. However, critics such as Gibbs (1972) were quick to point out that little improvement in theoretical formulations could be expected if the concepts that are employed in the postulates are fuzzy or ill-defined. The propositions that result are no more amenable to research than are statements from discursive theories.

Schrag (1967: 244) offered a different kind of advice:

> Undeveloped disciplines like sociology lack the abstract and powerful vocabularies, the precise rules of grammar, and the technical dictionaries that are necessary for translating the philosophy of science into viable procedures for handling their distinctive problems . . . . Perhaps the greatest need in sociology today is for more of the modest "inference chains," "explanation sketches," and embryo theories that aim primarily at organizing selected research findings and suggesting further avenues of inquiry.

What is an "explanation sketch" or an "inference chain?" Schrag singled out the relatively discursive theory about delinquent gangs, proposed by Cohen (1955) and the subsequent theoretical exposition by Cloward and Ohlin (1960), which had a number of links to Cohen's theory. Speaking of these two "explanation sketches," Schrag asserted (1967: 249):

> The sketches of Cohen and of Cloward and Ohlin are essentially idiographic studies, rich in descriptive detail but subject to widely varied interpretations. Before they can be tested adequately . . . their concepts need to be related more specifically to empirical phenomena and decisions need to be made as to the logical form of their claimed relationships. The discursive statements must be translated into nomothetic statements.

Schrag provided a good bit of guidance on how discursive formulations might be made more precise and formal, in other words, how explanation sketches can be converted into semiformal or formal theories. Those who are persuaded of the need for greater precision as we talk about crime and criminals can find more than a little guidance in Schrag's essay (also see Cohen, 1989: 177–238).

As I indicated earlier, I contend that more work of the kind represented by the forcible rape investigation of Baron and Straus (1990) is in order. Their explication of different lines of argument regarding the causes of rape, their subsequent weaving of these themes into a synthesized theory, their portrayal of this synthesized argument in the form of a path diagram, and finally, their research investigation which probed the key claims in the argument and provided empirical confirmation of much of the theory is instructive.

The message of this chapter is that each of us must individually concern ourselves with the task of learning how to think straight.

## NOTES

[1]Causal thinking in criminology is also discussed in Gibbons, 1992: 28–46 and in Gibbons and Krohn, 1991: 78–83. Strictly speaking, Gibbs (1985a: 27) was correct in pointing out that "causation cannot be observed . . . . a causal argument is testable only when translated into an assertion of a space-time association between variables." Nonetheless, terms such as causation and etiology figure prominently in criminological discourse.

[2]Curiously, Baron and Straus suggested that the relationship between rape and pornography was spurious; that is, pornography readership by itself was not a contributor to rape. However, they did not argue that the relationships of gender inequality and social disorganization were spurious, even though the same logic would appear to apply in all three cases.

[3]A large share of these studies is discussed in Gibbons, 1992: 228–390.

[4]I have sometimes attempted to make the case for situational processes in delinquency and criminality in my undergraduate classes by relating an experience I had when I was newly out of graduate school in the 1950s. During my first full-time teaching job, I was employed during the summer in British Columbia as a probation officer. On one occasion, I was called upon to investigate a group of teenagers who had been drinking near a cemetery on a weekend, and who had dug up a newly interred body and had dragged it about the cemetery behind an automobile. As best I was able to determine, none of the youths who were involved in this incident were markedly abnormal youths; instead, their decision to engage in this seemingly bizarre activity was a spontaneous, spur-of-the-moment one. However, I have never been successful in persuading most undergraduates that "normal" persons might be capable of such "abnormal" behavior!

[5]This book concentrates on causal theory in criminology. There is a sizable body of theorizing about other matters, such as social organizational patterns in prison, the social functions of the police, and so on. John Irwin's (1985) *The Jail* is an important recent venture of this kind, but it falls outside the scope of this book. However, it should be noted that the problems of discursive theorizing about which this chapter speaks are frequently encountered in these other works of theorizing. For example, Irwin's book is relatively discursive and contains a number of unclear sections. For a critique of Irwin's argument, along with research evidence that casts doubt upon the accuracy of his claims, see Backstrand, Gibbons, and Jones, 1992.

[6]Some readers may find my remarks of little or no interest because they disagree with the basic assumption of this book, namely that criminology should be patterned after the so-called natural science model. Some who reject the natural science or neopositivist view of criminology and other fields of social science inquiry do so because they assume that, for one reason or another, these fields *cannot* be structured in this manner. More specifically, some would argue that the complexity and unpredictability of human behavior precludes us from developing formal theories that resemble those described by philosophers of science and neopositivists such as

Gibbs. Others reject the neopositivist case for formal theories in criminology and sociology, arguing that we *should not* move in that direction, even if it were possible to do so. Persons of that persuasion argue that we should be endeavoring to develop discursive forms of theory and that these have such valuable properties as being "insightful," "elegant," "nuanced," or "provocative."

In my view, such criteria as being "nuanced" are more literary than they are scientific. Donald R. Cressey on more than one occasion referred to those criminologists who favor such theories and criteria as "poets" rather than social scientists. On the whole, I agree with Cressey that we need less poetry and more rigor in criminological theory. I do not think it wise for criminologists to go into competition with "folk criminologists" such as Truman Capote or Jack Abbott!

[7]In the long run, the ultimate criterion for judging a theory is the one of empirical accuracy; that is, the claims made in a theory ought to be supported by evidence. However, "truth" is not a criterion for judging theories, in that theoretical arguments are created for the purpose of gaining knowledge about the world. In other words, when a theory is initially stated, its empirical status is in question. The theory suggests a research agenda for uncovering evidence that will either support or disconfirm the argument.

[8]Williams and McShane also commented that the trend toward more complex forms of quantitative analysis in criminology has had an adverse effect upon theory development. That discussion included the erroneous claim (Williams and McShane, 1988: 132) that Gibbs would only admit "easily measured concepts" into criminological theories, a misreading of Gibbs's arguments.

[9]An earlier instance of combined theory, but one which was more discursive than Johnson's formulation, was Cloward and Ohlin's (1960), dealing with delinquency and opportunity. A more recent illustration of combined theory is the argument of Colvin and Pauly (1983), having to do with the ways in which class relations in capitalist societies lead to child-rearing practices which, in turn, allegedly contribute to involvement in delinquency or nondelinquency. However, this formulation was also discursive in form; hence it was not placed in the semiformal category.

[10]By being pitched at the individual level, I mean that Johnson restricted his attention regarding such factors as family relationships or school influences principally to the responses of *individuals* to immediate family members, individual perceptions of schools and teachers, etc. Little or no attention was given to parent-child relationships across social classes, different patterns of school organization, or other more structural factors.

[11]Ellis's argument has received vigorous criticism from Barth (1991) and from Fish (1990).

# CHAPTER 6

# Social-Structural Theories of Crime

## INTRODUCTION

Chapter 1 indicated that two basic causal questions can be asked about criminality and criminal behavior. One of these, social structure and criminality, or what was also termed "the rates question," is directed at various aspects of crime in the aggregate. By crime in the aggregate, I mean such things as cross-cultural variations in crime rates, regional differences in forms of criminality, variations in crime rates across different socioeconomic groups, crime rate differences across urban communities, and kindred matters.

Chapter 2 observed that the brand of American criminology that grew up in the early 1900s was largely atheoretical, eclectic, and often biologically oriented; hence it paid little attention to social-structural forces in lawbreaking. However, in the 1930s, Shaw and McKay, Sutherland, Sellin, and some other sociological criminologists sketched the outlines of what might be termed the "criminogenic culture" perspective on crime. The criminogenic culture thesis is that American society is characterized by various rents and tears or structural flaws which encourage criminality. Additionally, Merton's (1938) essay on anomie and deviant behavior appeared on the scene during this period.

Chapter 3 continued the commentary on the development of modern criminology. One observation in that chapter was that a large share of the criminological theorizing by sociologists in the 1960s and 1970s was centered on the "Why do they do it?" question; thus much attention was given to control theories which focused on individuals and their family backgrounds or to labeling viewpoints, many of which similarly centered on the problems of individuals in the correctional machinery, rather than on more global concerns.

However, conflict and radical-Marxist perspectives also came to prominence in the 1970s. These theoretical viewpoints were structural in form, although as we have already seen, they came under critical attack for not being sufficiently structural. Put another way, much of the theorizing of radical-Marxist criminologists was "one-dimensional" or "vulgar Marxism," long on hyperbole but short on substance.

Chapter 4 was concerned with the long-standing interest of criminologists in crime patterns and types of offenders. Numerous theorists have claimed that the heterogeneity of criminality precludes the development of a single explanation for it, however complex that theory might be. Instead, a number of persons have asserted that a theoretically meaningful set of crime types must be identified and in turn, separate causal accounts must be developed for each of these types. Although little progress has been made in the direction of a sophisticated and widely agreed upon set of basic crime categories, criminologists have thrown some conceptual nets around a number of crudely defined crime groupings: predatory street crime, organizational or white-collar crime, folk crime, political criminality, and organized crime, among others.

The preceding chapter devoted attention to the literary quality of criminological theories. I noted that many of our most well known theoretical expositions can be described as "insightful," "provocative," "elegant," and the like, but less often as "rigorous," "tightly reasoned," or "conceptually clear." A number of current examples of criminological theorizing were briefly noted in the course of fleshing out these observations. The commentary touched upon research and theorizing about unemployment and its relationship to predatory crime and also on income inequality and routine activities explanations which have been applied principally to predatory lawbreaking. Also, recent theorizing about forcible rape, linking it to gender inequality and certain other social-structural factors, was discussed in Chapter 5 and in earlier chapters as well. Note was also taken of inequality arguments and the subculture of violence formulations that have been put forth to account for regional and other variations in rates of homicide and assault. Finally, Chapter 5 identified Coleman's (1987) formulation about the causes of white-collar criminality as another important statement about social-structural influences in lawbreaking. In short, the preceding chapters have had a fair amount to say about social-structural theorizing. Chapter 6 builds upon this material.

## IS A "GRAND THEORY" OF CRIME
## AND SOCIAL STRUCTURE POSSIBLE?

In a widely read essay on sociological theory, Robert Merton (1949) identified three forms of theorizing that were current in the discipline in the 1940s: grand theory, theories of the middle range, and limited research hypotheses. Merton's view was that sociologists should strive to develop theories of the middle range, rather than spinning grand theories or putting most of their efforts into narrow hypothesis-testing.

Merton's attack on grand theory was directed mainly at one of his mentors, Talcott Parsons, who was the leading advocate of grand theorizing in sociology in the 1940s and 1950s. Parsons was a prolific scholar who authored a number of books and a large number of essays on one or another theoretical problem, but his most influential work was *The Social System* (1951), in which he presented an extraordinarily dense exposition which was made even more difficult to understand because of the tortured prose style which he employed. The book consisted largely of an exceedingly rich conceptual structure, with Parsons creating and discussing a wealth of terminological distinctions which he believed to be crucial for understanding the workings of "social systems" of various kinds, including societal structures. Although he played a major role in the development of a conceptual language for the discipline, his systems theorizing was judged by a number of critics to be deficient because it contained relatively few propositional statements. Although concepts are important, propositions which link two or more concepts together into accounts of "how things work" are the sine qua non of theories.

Although Parson's efforts stopped short of a grand theory which indicated, in great detail, how all of the parts of American social structure fit together, some modest attempts to construct such portrayals of social processes and social organization in the United States were made in the post–World War II years. One of these was Robin Williams's *American Society*, (1950) which attempted to identify major American value patterns and to analyze the operations of major social institutions in this country.

Efforts to capture the major dimensions of American social structure have largely been abandoned in the past few decades, although from time to time, works such as *Habits of the Heart* (Bellah, Madsen, Sullivan, Swidler, and Tipton, 1985) have appeared. This book was an audacious but methodologically weak attempt to describe the key elements of "American character" and to account for major shifts in the moral and ethical commitments of Americans that have occurred since the birth of this country.

What about a grand theory dealing with American social structure and crime? Should we endeavor to construct such a theory, in which all of the major elements of societal organization are identified, in which all of the linkages and interrelationships among them are spelled out, and in which all of these are tied to various forms of criminality? More concretely, how likely is it that we can identify all of the elements of the economic structure of the nation that might be implicated in one form of lawbreaking or another? And, how likely is it that we can also specify all of the facets of political organization that may be related to criminality or responses to it? Similarly, is it reasonable to assume that we can enumerate all of the forms of family structure and all of the family interactions that enter into crime? Finally, is it reasonable to suppose that we can put all of these pieces of a gigantic social jigsaw puzzle together and assemble a single, extraordinarily complex picture of "how things work"?

In my view, it would be highly premature to engage in a venture of this sort. We simply do not know enough at present, either about the theoretically significant elements of social structure that should be included in a grand theory or about the dimensions of various forms of criminality that would be the focus of such a theoretical venture.

At least for the present, criminologists ought to continue the theoretical work that is already underway. More effort is needed in the form of "fine-tuning" such arguments as those of Baron and Straus (1990) regarding social-structural factors in forcible rape or theorizing and research which examines the possibility of causal interactions or joint effects of such factors as income inequality and variations in crime opportunities (goods to be stolen and lack of guardianship). In the case of the Baron and Straus formulation, their results suggest that the pornography-rape hypothesis needs more attention, and in other ways, their work might be built upon by another wave of theorizing and research. In the same way, while research has indicated that unemployment is importantly implicated in predatory criminality and that income inequality and variations in crime opportunities are other important factors to be considered, little or no attention has been given to interrelations among these sets of influences as they impact upon lawbreaking (but see Carroll and Jackson, 1983).

Pursuing this argument further, consider Coleman's (1987) integrated theory of white-collar crime. Chapter 6 indicated that it is relatively discursive and also that it blurs what some have argued are important distinctions between organizational crime and such activities as embezzlement. Even so, he did identify some broad influences operating at the societal level, the organizational level, and at the level of individual organizational actors, which probably are involved in white-collar offending.

One thing is clear about organizational or white-collar crime: It comes in many forms (Gibbons, 1992a: 284–317). Shapiro (1983), among others, has argued that our knowledge about white-collar crime is limited to a few studies dealing with statistical records of corporate lawbreaking, coupled with a few in-depth case history examinations of specific instances of organizational crime, such as the electrical conspiracy case of 1961 or the price-fixing case against major plumbing manufacturers in the 1970s.

Although Shapiro's observations were accurate, considerably more data on varieties of organizational lawbreaking came to light in the 1980s. This evidence can be found both in sociological studies such as Calavita and Pontell's (1990) analysis of the savings and loans scandal and also in reports by investigative journalists such as Stewart (1991), who provided a wealth of information on the securities frauds of Ivan Boesky, Dennis Levine, Martin Siegel, and Michael Milken.

Calavita and Pontell (1990) have gone well beyond simply a report on the shenanigans of Charles Keating, Don Dixon, and other savings and loans plunderers. Their analysis identified some of the major factors that gave rise to the collapse of savings and loans firms across the nation and to the subsequent government "bailout" of these firms. Along the same line, the study by Weisburd, Wheeler, Waring, and Bode (1991) of white-collar offenders who had been processed in federal courts has added empirical meat to the skeletal structure assembled by Coleman.

While the creation of a grand theory of crime and social structure would surely be a more dazzling event than would the slower, incremental gains in knowledge through a host of theoretically informed pieces of research, each directed at some part of the phenomena of crime, the latter may be the only viable course for criminology. What are some of the major social-structural factors that would be important in this endeavor? This question is the focus of the comments below.

## MAJOR DIMENSIONS OF SOCIAL-STRUCTURAL ANALYSIS

I have already spoken of economic variables as central ingredients of a number of criminological theories. These include unemployment patterns, income inequality, and the differential distribution of crime opportunities (routine activities theory). However, there are other variables that are even more central to social-structural theorizing, namely, age, sex, and racial patterns.

At first glance, it might appear that age, sex, and race are biological, not social, variables. If so, while they might be related in important ways to lawbreaking, those relationships would not be social-structural ones. And, to some extent, age, sex, ethnicity, and race are matters of biology. But is it not also true that "age" is in many ways a phenomenon made up of various social judgments? For example, the decision to measure the age of persons from the time of birth onward is essentially arbitrary, for we could just as sensibly begin to measure persons' ages from a point nine months prior to birth, that is, from conception. In much the same way, "childhood" is not a biologically determined period in the lives of persons. "Childhood" is an invention of modern times, as contrasted with the eighteenth century or earlier, in which young individuals were regarded as "adults in small bodies."

Then, too, "adolescence" is a modern social invention, for there was a time in the past when persons ceased to be "children" and became "adults" in one relatively brief period. Finally, being "old" or "not old" is a social judgment that persons make regarding themselves or that others impose upon them.

I need not belabor this point much further. It is clear that being "male" or "female" involves much more than simply human genitalia—there are numerous cases of persons whose genitalia do not match their gender self-images. Additionally, the sex roles that are assigned to persons with male or female physical characteristics have relatively little to do with biological differences between the sexes. Finally, the sexual discrimination against females that is all too common in the United States and elsewhere is certainly not a matter of biology.

Similar comments could be made regarding ethnicity. For example, black males in the United States are much more frequently involved in homicides, both as offenders and as victims, than are white males, but there is no evidence that these differences have anything to do with race per se.

### Age and Crime

In a recent book on criminological theory, Braithwaite (1989b: 44) argued that there are a number of well-established facts which any valid theory must address, one of which is: *"Crime is committed disproportionately by 15–25 year old males"* [emphasis in the original].

This claim about criminality being most often the work of older juveniles and young adults has been made in detail by Gottfredson and Hirschi (Gottfredson and Hirschi, 1986, 1990; Hirschi and Gottfredson, 1983). They contended that this age-crime pattern is universal, appearing in all countries for which we have adequate data, and also that it is a relatively consistent pattern over all varieties of criminality. In other words, they argued that crude predatory crime, embezzlement, assaultive behavior, and various other kinds of lawbreaking are behaviors for which the highest rates of involvement are for older juveniles and young adults.

Braithwaite's observation that crime is disproportionately common among 15- to 25-year-old males is not in dispute, nor is the broad contention of Gottfredson and Hirschi that the rates of many kinds of crime peak at a relatively early point on the age scale. Furthermore, many criminologists share a somewhat sketchy theory regarding this relationship, suggesting that the onset of crime parallels the physical and social maturation that occurs in males during late adolescence. At the same time, many of these juveniles and young adults are only loosely integrated into adult social systems and social roles: They are unmarried, out-of-school, frequently unemployed or underemployed, and in other ways somewhat detached from social arrangements that often exert social control over older individuals. As a result, they are freer to engage in deviance during this age period than at any earlier or later part of their lives. This same argument is often invoked to account for the fact that many lawbreakers experiment with misconduct but desist from it relatively quickly. One's interest in flirting with danger, "hell raising," and the like wane when a job has been secured or stable affectional ties have been established with another person, male or female. Also, these adult commitments work against continued involvement in deviance, even if the individual in question has not entirely abandoned such interests.

However, not all of the questions about age-crime relationships have been settled. Instead, some criminologists (e.g., Steffensmeier et al., 1989; Greenberg, 1985) have argued that the invariant, age-crime pattern posited by Gottfredson and Hirschi is not, in fact, invariant. For example, some have argued that embezzlers are older, on the average, than are street criminals.

Gottfredson and Hirschi have also been involved in a lively debate with another group of criminologists (Blumstein, Cohen, and Farrington, 1988; Blumstein, Farrington, and Moitra, 1985; Farrington, 1986) regarding (a) the need for or the value of longitudinal research designs and (b) the usefulness of such notions as those of "career criminals" or "careers in crime." Regarding the latter, Gottfredson and Hirschi contended that variations among lawbreakers in the number of offenses they commit or the period over which they commit them can all be explained by an underlying construct, "criminal propensity." Blumstein, Farrington, and Moitra have argued differently, claiming that it is important to differentiate between those who do little crime and those who do a considerable amount of it. Also, these scholars suggested that the factors that account for initial decisions by persons to either participate or not participate in lawbreaking may not be the same ones that account for variations in the length of "careers" in misbehavior or for termination of those pathways (desistance).

The last word on this quarrel has probably not been heard. However, one batch of evidence supportive of the position of Blumstein and his associates came from a study by Sampson and Laub (1990), who reanalyzed data originally collected by Sheldon and Eleanor Glueck (1950). The Gluecks carried out a massive comparison of 500 juvenile offenders who had been involved in relatively serious offenses and 500 nondelinquents from the same community areas as the offenders, and they also compiled outcome data on these 1000 persons, followed to the age of 32.

Sampson and Laub's perspective combined social control theory with a life course approach. They reported (Sampson and Laub, 1990: 616) that "childhood delinquent behavior has a significant relationship with a wide range of adult criminal and deviant behaviors" and also that involvement in juvenile misconduct was predictive of adult difficulties in such arenas as family, education, and employment. This observation has turned up in a large number of other studies as well (e.g., Robins, 1966). But what is of greater importance are these findings (Sampson and Laub, 1990: 618): "It appears that job stability in adulthood significantly modifies trajectories of crime and deviance regardless of strong differences in childhood delinquent and antisocial conduct" and that "social bonds to adult institutions of work, education, and the family exert a powerful influence on adult crime and deviance." In short, many of the juvenile offenders in this study, and some of the youthful nonoffenders as well, changed their propensity for lawbreaking as they encountered stabilizing or destabilizing events over the portion of the life course that was examined in the research.

### Sex and Crime

The marked disparity of crime rates for males versus females in the United States has often been commented upon in criminology textbooks, followed often by virtual silence regarding the low rates of lawbreaking on the part of women. Put another way, female offenders have been relatively invisible in criminological theorizing, with their low rates of participation being taken as justification for inattention to lawbreaking on their part and to efforts to account for it.

The official data on female offending in the United States are clear (Gibbons, 1992a: 368–71). In 1989, males comprised 81.9 percent of the arrests for all crimes, and they were involved in 98.8 percent of all forcible rape arrests, 91.4 percent of robbery arrests, 88.1 percent of nonnegligent manslaughter arrests, 69.6 percent of the arrests for larceny-theft, 89.8 percent of those for motor vehicle theft, and 86.4 percent of the arson arrests. The two kinds of arrests in which women were more numerous than men were prostitution and commercial vice (69.0 percent) and runaway (56.0 percent). In both of these cases, these figures are heavily influenced by differential enforcement against women, rather than being true indicators of male-female differences in participation. In other words, although males can be arrested for prostitution when they are customers of female prostitutes, and although males are not infrequently involved in criminal acts as male prostitutes, they are rarely arrested and charged with those offenses. In much the same way, juvenile males who are apprehended for running away from home are much less likely to be arrested or referred to juvenile court than are female runaways.

Although arrest rates are much higher for males than females, the numbers of females arrested in 1989 as compared to 1980 increased more dramatically for most offenses than did the arrests of males. In other words, while participation in criminality, as reflected in arrest figures, is less common for women than for men, in relative terms, crime rates for women increased much more during this 1980–1989 period than did those for men (Gibbons, 1992a: 369). For example, women showed relatively larger rate increases for seven of the "index offenses" tabulated by the FBI (murder and nonnegligent manslaughter, forcible rape, aggravated assault, robbery, burglary, larceny-theft, motor vehicle theft, and arson). Murder and nonnegligent manslaughter was the only category in which the percentage change in arrests between 1980 and 1989 was higher for men than for women.

As the statistical evidence on the increasing participation of women in crime began to accumulate in the 1970s, theorizing about the underlying factors in this trend also began to appear. One of the most controversial theses was advanced by Adler (1975), who claimed that a "new woman criminal" had appeared on the scene. This new woman criminal was said to be engaged in "masculine," aggressive crimes. Further, according to Adler, this alleged trend toward "masculine" forms of lawbreaking is related to the women's liberation movement that has been blurring traditional sex-role distinctions.

Adler's argument was challenged by a number of other criminologists, including Simon (1975) and Steffensmeier (1978). Most of these critics noted that (a) the most pronounced increases in female criminality involved property crimes, not crimes of violence, and (b) the increases began to occur well before the women's movement became a force in American society. The most common argument that has surfaced regarding increases in female crime attributes most of these changes to increased labor force participation on the part of women, which has had the effect of increasing the number of crime opportunities available to them.

These interpretations of trends in female crime which center on changes in sex roles and female rates of participation in the labor market have been criticized by feminist scholars as too narrow or limited, in that they ignore the structural sources of sex-role inequality and the inferior status of women in historical or cultural terms. Stated differently, advocates of a radical-feminist view of female criminality and reactions to it charge that liberal theories do not go far enough toward uncovering the social-structural sources of oppression of women in capitalist societies (Simpson, 1989; Daly and Chesney-Lind, 1988; Messerschmidt, 1986). Chapter 9 takes up radical and socialist feminist arguments in more detail, but I would comment at this point that no full-blown feminist theory that deals with female crime and reactions to it has yet emerged.

### Race and Crime

This brief chapter regarding social-structural analyses of crime would be incomplete without some mention of race and crime, and in particular, criminality on the part of American blacks. The facts revealed in official statistics are clear (Gibbons, 1992a: 89–90): Blacks accounted for 30.8 percent of total arrests in the United States in 1989. Moreover, blacks were involved in 56.4 percent of the arrests for murder and nonnegligent manslaughter, 46.6 percent of the forcible rape arrests, 65.0 percent of those for armed robbery, 40.9 percent of the aggravated assault arrests, 32.3 percent of those for burglary, 33.3 percent of the larceny arrests, and 42.5 percent of those for motor vehicle theft.

Criminologists are also of a single mind regarding the general explanation for these high rates of involvement in lawbreaking, particularly in "street crimes" (Gibbons, 1992a: 117–19). Black crime is *not* a manifestation of a biologically based propensity to criminality characteristic of black citizens; instead, it is related to a number of *criminogenic* features of American society. Some criminologists have argued that these high crime rates significantly overstate the involvement of blacks in lawbreaking because they are, in part, a reflection of *differential law enforcement*. In other words, black citizens are subjected to overly zealous police surveillance, discriminatory decision-making by the police, and racially biased actions at most other stages in the criminal justice machinery.

Most criminologists argue that although differential enforcement is a partial explanation for high crime rates among blacks, the "root causes" of black lawbreaking are found in racial discrimination, particularly in the form of economic exploitation, that has been visited upon blacks from the time of slavery to the present. As Wilson (1987) has put it, blacks make up a very large part of "the truly disadvantaged," that is, inner-city ghetto residents who are mired in the secondary labor market and toiling at "dead end" jobs, or even worse, who are chronically underemployed or without jobs or job prospects.

There is no question that blacks are structurally disadvantaged compared to whites. Although some improvement in income levels of blacks has occurred in the past several decades, mean income figures for blacks continue to lag behind those for whites. The scholarly quarrels in this area center on quibbling about precisely the size of the income gap, the extent to which a black middle-class has arisen, and matters of that sort, rather than on the existence of income inequality between blacks and whites.

One other point at issue among those who have examined the economic situation of blacks has to do with a "culture of poverty" thesis which places much of the blame for lack of progress on blacks themselves. Banfield (1974) is a well-known spokesperson for the culture of poverty view, arguing that various alleged traits of lower-class citizens are major impediments to social and economic progress, while Wilson (1987) is one of many scholars who find the lower-class values argument to be unconvincing.

In my opinion, the "criminogenic culture" theorists have much the better of the evidence. The "root causes" of inordinately high crime rates among blacks are to be found principally in the various and pervasive forms of social and economic discrimination that are directed at black citizens in American society. Criminological theorists who endeavor to account for high black crime rates can find considerable guidance in such sources as Blauner's (1969) "colonialization" account of the social and economic position of blacks in the United States and in more recent analyses such as

Wilson's (1987) extended essay on "the truly disadvantaged." Finally, it is fair to say that considerably more criminological theorizing and research is in order regarding race-crime relationships.

## STRUCTURAL CRIMINOLOGY

The pages of this book to this point have been filled with a variety of criminological topics. At the same time, a subliminal message has appeared and reappeared throughout the commentary presented so far, namely, the central role of economic factors in crime and of economic position as a major determinant of law-abiding or lawbreaking conduct on the part of individuals. This message was contained in the observations in Chapter 2 regarding the theorizing and research of persons such as Shaw and McKay and Sutherland in the 1930s. Chapter 3 took note of the rise of radical-Marxist views in the 1970s, which emphasized economic oppression of the underclass and working-class citizens by the "ruling class" as the factor accounting for the lawbreaking activities of the former. Chapter 4 included a number of asides about the economic precariousness of "garden-variety" predators and of the ability of upper-class offenders to violate laws with impunity because of their greater social power. Chapter 5 took note of some more specific arguments which center on economic and class relations: unemployment and crime, the role of income inequality in lawbreaking, and Braithwaite's (1989b) general theory which emphasizes unemployment as a major determinant of initial flirtations with lawbreaking by young males. Finally, the present chapter involved additional comments about "criminogenic culture" arguments which emphasize economic precariousness as a major influence in lawbreaking. The class and economic pressures theme also appeared in the discussion of Sampson and Laub's (1990) observations regarding the adult pathways trod by the delinquents and nondelinquents who had been studied by the Gluecks years earlier. Finally, the just-concluded remarks on race and crime centered on economic discrimination and kindred problems experienced by blacks in American society.

Significant efforts to further illuminate the role of class and economic relations in criminality and delinquency have been made by Hagan and his associates (1989), in the form of what they have termed "structural criminology." Briefly described, structural criminology involves a neo-Marxist conception of stratification which emphasizes the importance of *economic* position rather than economically related *status* relationships in various social realms, including lawbreaking. In particular, Hagan et al. suggested that persons who are underemployed or unemployed are likely to also lack social power and to be vulnerable to control exercised over them by others, while those who are employed, and particularly those individuals whose monetary rewards from employment are large, are also freer to engage in deviance while escaping the punitive consequences that are often visited upon power-less groups.

Consider one instance of this line of theorizing and research based on it. Hagan, Simpson, and Gillis (1985) focused on how workplace experiences in American society affect family life and help to account for rates of male and female delinquency among different social classes. They contended that females in our society are more likely to be the objects of social control, while males are more frequently the ones who do the controlling. But recent developments in the workplace have modified these patterns among workers and their families. Where both spouses have jobs involving authority, an egalitarian household, in which husbands and wives share authority, would be predicted, while in situations where the husband occupies an authority position but his wife does not, a more traditional, patriarchal household would be expected.

In patriarchal households, females are the objects of social control, and daughters are more likely to be closely controlled and supervised than are sons. In egalitarian households, the disparity between control of daughters versus sons should be less apparent. The degree of control affects the extent to which children are willing to take risks, and risk taking is predicted to be related to delinquent conduct. As a consequence, girls from more egalitarian families are less likely to be controlled, more inclined to risk taking, and more likely to engage in delinquency than are females from patriarchal families. Additionally, this argument leads to the expectation of more nearly equal rates of participation in delinquency for boys and girls from egalitarian families than from patriarchal ones. Hagan, Simpson, and Gillis reported that the hypotheses derived from this theory were supported for less serious forms of delinquent conduct.

Hagan and his co-workers (1989) have assembled a number of pieces of research stimulated by their power-control perspective into a book on structural criminology. It contains chapters on a wide range of topics, some having mainly to do with causal analysis and others with criminal justice system processing of offenders. Both Hagan and at least one reviewer of the book (Jensen, 1990) have indicated that a full-blown statement of structural criminology, involving an interrelated set of propositions, has not yet emerged.

Hagan (1992) has continued to expand upon the central themes in *Structural Criminology*. He has argued that (1992: 1) "the simple omission of class from the study of crime would impoverish criminology." The reader would be well advised to peruse his 1992 paper, in which he endeavored to explicate the ways in which the "deprivation, destitution, and disrepute" experienced by the underclass or the truly disadvantaged lead to delinquency and criminality. That essay suggested that more inquiry of the sort represented by the Sampson and Laub (1990) study, noted earlier, is in order. Hagan claimed that the available evidence points both to the negative effects of early delinquency on later employment and to the positive impact of adult employment, marriage, and stable living upon life course trajectories and specifically, desistance from lawbreaking. He also had much to say about the ways in which access to, as well as denial of, class-structured sources of power are causally related to delinquency and crime. Put differently, he endeavored to identify some of the ways in which the greater access to resources enjoyed by employer-class persons works to free them to engage in lawbreaking and to avoid the punitive consequences of their acts.

## CONCLUDING COMMENTS

This chapter has been concerned with social-structural theories that endeavor to account for crime patterns and crime rates. The chapter drew together a number of theories that were mentioned in the preceding chapters. It also examined the question of whether it is time for efforts to outline a "grand theory" which includes all of the social-structural factors that have an influence upon levels of lawbreaking, and in which all of the linkages of these factors to various crime patterns are identified. Such an effort would probably be premature—we simply do not know enough at present to make such an effort pay off. Instead, the most productive course is likely to be the continuation of the incremental development of theories and conduct of research specific to particular forms of criminality. The final part of the chapter dealt with a number of key variables in lawbreaking: age, sex, and race, and it also examined the efforts of Hagan and his co-workers to articulate what they refer to as structural criminology.

It is now time to turn to an examination of the "Why do they do it?" question. A considerable share of the answers that have been offered to this question is examined in Chapters 7 and 8.

┌─ **CHAPTER 7** ─────────────────────┐

# Accounting for Criminals and Criminal Behavior

## SOCIOLOGICAL AND ECONOMIC MODELS

└──────────────────────────────────────┘

## INTRODUCTION

This chapter and the one that follows it make up a unit that has been somewhat arbitrarily divided into two parts. Both have to do with the "Why do they do it?" question; that is, both discuss theories, along with research studies guided by those theories, that endeavor to account for initial acts of misbehavior on the part of individuals and for lawbreaking "careers" on the part of some of them. The notion of careers refers to persistence in misconduct over a fairly lengthy time period. The "flip side" of the "Why do they do it?" question is examined in these chapters as well, in that causal theories have something to say about persons who refrain from lawbreaking as well as those who engage in it.

Chapter 6 briefly introduced the subject of causal analysis and indicated that criminologists often sort lines of etiological analysis into three broad groupings: biogenic, psychogenic, and sociogenic perspectives. Biogenic viewpoints investigate the possibility that sociobiological forces play a part in lawbreaking, while psychological theories and research deal with personality patterns and the part they play in criminality. Finally, sociogenic (sociological) perspectives center on social patterns and processes in illegal conduct.

However, the actual situation of criminological inquiry is more complex than suggested by this trichotomous classification. For one thing, a number of instances of theorizing and research can be identified in which the investigators have put forth an explanatory formulation which combines biological, psychological, and sociological factors into a larger whole. Ellis's (1989) theory regarding forcible rape is one case in point, while Wilson and Herrnstein's (1985) argument, involving mesomorphy, low intelligence, psychological liabilities, and certain social factors is another.

There is another, even more important observation to be made about explanatory approaches. Although the distinction between "psychological" and "sociological" theories often appears in one form or another in the criminological literature, this distinction is often misleading because much of the theorizing of both psychologists and sociologists is essentially "psychological" in form.

Consider for a moment the definitions of psychology and sociology that are contained in *Webster's New International Dictionary*. Psychology is identified as "the science of mind or of mental phenomena and activities" while sociology is defined as "the science of society, social institutions, and social relationships. . . ."

These definitions, which are similar to those that are encountered in sociology and psychology textbooks, imply that phenomena are psychological if they are located "inside the heads" of actors, so to speak, while they are classified as social or sociological phenomena if they are external to persons.

Now, it is true that sociologists frequently utter statements about "societal values," "social structure," and the like in ways that imply that they have directly observed such phenomena as norms, statuses, roles, institutions, relationships, and in some cases, even society or societies. On some occasions, such verbalizations are reasonably accurate, as for example, when we point to "legal norms" by drawing attention to written codes such as the Oregon Revised Statutes.

However, it is difficult to point to "societal values" or many other social facts that exist separately from individual actors. As Lemert (1972) noted many years ago in a critical essay dealing in part with Merton's (1938) claims about anomie and societal values, the expression, "societal values," is verbal shorthand standing for the aggregate of particular sentiments held by individuals. Along the same line, when we speak of social relationships, such as the nuclear family pattern of husband, wife, and a small number of children, is it not patently the case that much of this "relationship" resides in the *perceptions* of the individuals involved in it? And, were we interested in assessing the strength of that relational pattern, how would we do it without inquiring into the perceptions of the persons who make up the relationship?

Let me be clear on this point—the argument is *not* that all social relationships and social phenomena can be reduced to individual perceptions and thus sociology has no reason for existing. For example, income inequality, pornography, unemployment, and myriad other phenomena encountered in the preceding pages are social facts that are not simply or mainly reducible to mental phenomena or matters of perception. Additionally, it is reasonable to argue that perceptions and the like that are shared by a sizable number of persons represent a different sort of phenomena than do those that are relatively unique to a single person or a small group of individuals.

Having entered these disclaimers, I would reiterate the assertion that much of the theorizing of both psychologists and sociologists is essentially psychological in form, in that individual mental phenomena are central to their arguments.[1]

Nearly everyone would probably concede that, quite apart from the question of whether they are accurate or not, arguments which attribute criminality to mental disorders are psychological ones. Paranoia, for example, is a mental state, even though it can also be viewed as a relational one (Lemert, 1962). Similarly, claims about criminality being due to psychopathy or sociopathy on the part of lawbreakers are clearly psychological, for sociopaths are defined as persons with underdeveloped consciences.

The argument that persons of relatively low intelligence are particularly prone to lawbreaking is also psychological, even though there is considerable debate about the extent to which intelligence levels are determined principally by biological inheritance as opposed to being the result of social transmission.

What about rational choice viewpoints which have come to prominence in the past decade or so? Rational choice notions are pretty much described by this label: Offenders are rational actors who weigh the gains and losses (as they perceive them) from a criminal course of action before deciding to either embark upon or refrain from lawbreaking. Even though many of the exponents of rational choice arguments are sociologists and economists by training, the balancing of possible gains or pains from criminality surely qualifies as a mental process which takes place "inside the heads" of actors.

Much the same observation can be made about Sutherland's differential association argument (Sutherland, Cressey, and Luckenbill, 1992: 88–90). The key claims in that theory center on "definitions of the legal codes as favorable or unfavorable" and the thesis that persons engage in lawbreaking when they have more definitions favorable to law violation than definitions unfavorable to misconduct. If there are such things as definitions of the legal codes, where and how might we find them? Here again, we would attempt to "get inside the heads" of persons through interviews, questionnaires, or some similar technique. If so, this could be said to be a psychological theory, even though it is sensitive to social interactions, societal structure, and other factors that implicitly lie behind it.

In recent years, a number of criminologists have suggested that criminals and delinquents may not always be "driven" to lawbreaking; instead, for some of them, deviant conduct may have positive attractions. Katz's (1988) book-length discussion of "the moral and sensual attractions of doing evil" is a particularly stimulating discussion of this argument. Although Katz is a sociologist, his exposition is essentially psychological, locating the positive attractions to crime in the heads of those who engage in it.

Still another prominent statement on crime, authored by sociological criminologists, is that of Gottfredson and Hirschi (1990). These theorists put forth a general theory which is intended to account for crime in all of its various forms and which maintains that lawbreaking and a variety of other kinds of deviant conduct are most often engaged in by persons who are low on self-control. Gottfredson and Hirschi may or may not be correct in this claim, but either way, this is, at heart, a psychological argument.

Finally, let us examine a recent effort by Agnew (1992) to revise strain theory and to convert it into a general theory of lawbreaking. As he noted, earlier arguments, such as Cloward and Ohlin's (1960) theory of gang delinquency, conceptualized strain largely in material terms; thus persons whose aspirations for monetary success exceeded their expectations were said to experience strain. In Agnew's revision (1992: 49) strain was transformed into *"negative affective states—most notably anger and related emotions—that often result from negative relationships"* [emphasis in the original]. Also, Agnew listed a number of negative relationships that might lead to psychological distress (strain). Here again, while Agnew is a sociologist, his argument was heavily psychological in character.

If we turn attention to how the psychological-sociological distinction is made in actual practice, we find that it often tends, at least implicitly, to revolve around the extent to which mental states of one kind or another (motives, definitions, attitudes, and the like) are viewed as idiosyncratic to specific persons or a small group of individuals. If they are idiosyncratic, they are psychological, but if motives, definitions, or attitudes are more widely shared, they are often regarded as being sociological facts. Then, too, the psychological label is frequently used to identify "personality patterns" such as "extroversion," "dependency," and the like that are thought to be somehow different from "subcultural" or "antisocial norms" that are regarded as less central to the core personalities of individuals.

In criminological practice, the label "psychological" or "psychogenic" is often restricted to arguments which contend that lawbreakers, as well as various other kinds of deviants, suffer from various kinds of personality pathology or abnormal psychological characteristics and that their deviant conduct is attributable to these quirks and defects. By contrast, perspectives that assert that offenders are psychologically normal persons who are engaged in "normative deviance" or who are responding to "deviant norms" are more likely to be described as sociological (Gibbons, 1992: 138–92). But both of these are psychological viewpoints.

Even though a good case could be made for identifying all of the theoretical viewpoints noted above as psychological ones, Chapters 7 and 8 follow the convention of differentiating those arguments which emphasize *individual differences* from those that identify *shared problems* or *shared psychological characteristics*. Accordingly, Chapter 7 is concerned principally with differential association theory and social learning arguments, rational choice perspectives, and strain theories, while Chapter 8 deals with sociobiological explanations of lawbreaking and with psychological formulations which emphasize either personality pathology or relatively idiosyncratic personality patterns.

## DIFFERENTIAL ASSOCIATION AND SOCIAL LEARNING THEORIES

### Differential Association Theory

Sutherland's theory of differential association was mentioned briefly in Chapter 2 and the nine propositions making up that argument were noted there. Chapter 5 also contained some brief remarks which indicated that the theory is deficient as a formal argument. We begin this chapter with a more detailed discussion of differential association theory, both because of the crucial role it has played in the development of sociological criminology and because we can learn a good deal about the problems of theorizing more generally from a critique of Sutherland's argument.[2]

The reader should keep in mind that the theory of differential association was not created by Sutherland in one fell swoop; rather, it emerged in a relatively slow, incremental process. Sutherland's criminology textbook was first published in 1924, but the ideas that would ultimately be brought together in the theory did not appear until later editions of the book were published. And, it was not until 1947 that the mature version of the theory appeared. The 1947 statement continued to appear in unmodified form in the later editions of the book, most of which were coauthored by Sutherland's student, Donald R. Cressey.[3]

Sutherland's argument was constructed on a foundation of cultural conflict ideas, or what he also called differential social organization. In his words (Cohen, Lindesmith, and Schuessler, 1956: 20): "Cultural conflict in this sense is the basic principle in the explanation of crime." The social and economic changes involved in the industrialization of the Western world were believed to have generated pervasive individualism and other conditions conducive to criminality. The social influences people encounter in their daily lives are inharmonious and inconsistent; many persons have contact with carriers of criminalistic norms and become criminals as a result. This, in a nutshell, is the process of differential association.

The elements of differential association theory are these (Sutherland, Cressey, and Luckenbill, 1992: 88–90):

1. *Criminal behavior is learned.* Negatively, this means that criminal behavior is not inherited, as such. Also, the person who has not been trained in crime does not invent criminal behavior, just as the person who has had no training in mechanics does not make mechanical inventions.

2. *Criminal behavior is learned in interaction with other persons in a process of communication.* This communication is verbal in many respects, but includes also "the communication of gestures."

3. *The principal part of the learning of criminal behavior occurs within intimate personal groups.* Negatively, this means that the impersonal agencies of communication, such as movies and newspapers, play a relatively unimportant part in the genesis of criminal behavior.

4. *When criminal behavior is learned, the learning includes (a) techniques of committing the crime, which are sometimes very complicated, sometimes very simple, (b) the specific direction of motives, drives, rationalizations, and attitudes.*

5. *The specific direction of motives and drives is learned from definitions of the legal codes as favorable or unfavorable.* In some societies the individual is surrounded by persons who invariably define the legal codes as rules to be observed, while in others the individual is surrounded by persons whose definitions are favorable to the violation of the legal codes. In American society these definitions are almost always mixed, with the consequence that there is culture conflict in relation to the legal codes.

6. *A person becomes delinquent because of an excess of definitions favorable to violation of law over definitions unfavorable to violation of law.* This is the principle of differential association. It refers to both criminal and anticriminal associations and has to do with counteracting forces. When persons become criminal, they do so because of contacts with criminal patterns and also because of isolation from anticriminal patterns. Any person inevitably assimilates the surrounding culture unless other patterns are in conflict; thus a southerner does not pronounce "r" because other Southerners do not pronounce "r." Negatively, this proposition of differential association means that associations which are neutral so far as crime is concerned have little or no effect on the genesis of criminal behavior. Much of the experience of a person is neutral in this sense, such as learning to brush one's teeth. This behavior has no negative or positive effect on criminal behavior except as it may be related to associations which are concerned with the legal codes. Such neutral behavior is important especially in occupying the time of a child so that he or she is not in contact with criminal behavior while engaged in the neutral behavior.

7. *Differential associations may vary in frequency, duration, priority, and intensity.* This means that associations with criminal behavior and associations with anticriminal behavior vary in those respects. Frequency and duration as modalities of associations are obvious and need no explanation. Priority is assumed to be important in the sense that lawful behavior developed in early childhood may persist throughout life and also that delinquent behavior developed in early childhood may persist throughout life. This tendency, however, has not been adequately demonstrated, and priority seems to be important principally through its selective influence. Intensity is not precisely defined but it has to do with such things as the prestige of the source of a criminal or anticriminal pattern and with emotional reactions related to the association. In a precise description of the criminal behavior of a person, these modalities would be rated in quantitative form and a mathematical ratio be reached. A formula in

this sense has not been developed, and the development of such a formula would be extremely difficult.

8. *The process of learning criminal behavior by association with criminal and anticriminal patterns involves all of the mechanisms that are involved in any other learning.* Negatively, this means that the learning of criminal behavior is not restricted to the process of imitation. A person who is seduced, for instance, learns criminal behavior by association, but this process would not ordinarily be described as imitation.

9. *While criminal behavior is an expression of general needs and values, it is not explained by those general needs and values since noncriminal behavior is an expression of the same needs and values.* Thieves generally steal in order to secure money, but likewise honest laborers work in order to secure money. The attempts by many scholars to explain criminal behavior by general drives and values, such as the happiness principle, striving for social status, the money motive or frustration, have been, and continue to be, futile, since they explain lawful behavior as completely as they explain criminal behavior. Such drives and values are similar to respiration, which is necessary for any behavior but does not differentiate criminal from noncriminal behavior.

The first three of these statements asserts that criminal behavior is learned in an interactional or associational process within intimate personal groups, while the fourth claims that the content of the learning includes both techniques of committing crimes and criminal motives and drives. But note that the next one shifts attention from motives and attitudes to "definitions of the legal codes as favorable or unfavorable."

Propositions 6 and 7 are the most central ones. Sutherland's argument was that crime is carried out by persons who have acquired enough sentiments or definitions in favor of law violation to outweigh their prosocial or anticriminal conduct definitions. In turn, individuals get their prosocial and procriminal definitions through associations with others in their environment.

This argument has sometimes been criticized as a simple associational learning one, holding that individuals become like the persons with whom they associate. However, Sutherland developed the theory at a time when most socialization or learning perspectives were relatively simple in form. Further, proposition 7 contends that associations vary in frequency, duration, priority, and intensity. In general, associations with the greatest impact are frequent, lengthy, early in origin, and relatively intense or meaningful to the individual. These dimensions along which differential associations were said to vary represented Sutherland's attempt to go beyond simplistic claims about learning processes.

In his discussion of the theory (Sutherland and Cressey, 1978: 82), Sutherland indicated: "It is not necessary, at this level of explanation, to explain why a person has the associations he has; this certainly involves a complex of many things." However, he maintained that cultural conflict (differential social organization) characteristic of modern societies generates a wide range of both deviant and conformist associations.

Sutherland's formulation was a major effort by a sociologist to develop a general theory which could explain the occurrence or nonoccurrence of criminal conduct of various kinds. Also, it was stated in terms of a small group of core social concepts and arguments. The sociological perspective emphasizes social experiences which provide persons with standards of conduct and belief that guide their activities. Sociologists portray persons as driven by "motors" that the social process has placed inside them. No wonder that Sutherland's formulation quickly gained wide acceptance in criminology.

However, the theory is not without faults (Sutherland, Cressey, and Luckenbill, 1992: 91–99). Like much sociological exposition, it lacks clarity and precision. The problem is not that its claims are false but rather that they are ambiguous or unclear. For example, while the idea of "definitions favorable to violation of law" has the ring of plausibility to it, there is no specific explication of this key term to be found in the theory. It is not at all unlikely that were criminologists to go about doing research on these definitions, considerable disagreement would arise as to whether particular verbalizations of persons qualify as indicators of the definitions.

Additionally, consider the contention that persons become engaged in lawbreaking because of an excess of conduct definitions favoring law violation. Should we interpret this claim literally, so that the sheer *number* of conduct definitions is the major determinant of behavior, and criminality should result whenever the ratio of an individual's criminalistic definitions to law-abiding ones becomes 101/100, or some other ratio? Perhaps, but it is conceivable that under some circumstances, a few, critical conduct definitions might be more compelling than others; a few criminalistic attitudes might overpower a large number of prosocial sentiments. This possibility is captured in the notion of lawbreaking that is due to overwhelmingly stressful circumstances which drive an otherwise law-abiding person to a desperate act of criminality. If we cannot agree on which interpretation is the correct one, and if we cannot spell out the nature of the relationship suggested by the theory, we cannot carry out research that would provide an unequivocal test of the argument.

Another unclear assertion is the fourth one, which speaks of motives, drives, rationalizations, and attitudes. These also appear in the fifth statement but then disappear from the rest of the theory, suggesting that motives and drives are a kind of sociological phlogiston. Phlogiston was a hypothetical element formerly believed to cause combustion, but physicists eventually found that it was unneccessary to posit its existence because fire could be accounted for without reference to it; hence it was one concept too many! In the same way, if persons become involved in lawbreaking due to an excess of definitions favorable to violation of the law, there appears to be no explanatory role played by motives, rationalizations, drives, and attitudes.

Another question is whether "associations" refer to identifiable, physical group contacts. The relevant passages in the theory indicate that an individual's group associations exert the most important influence upon his or her behavior. Some criminologists (e.g., Glaser, 1956) have interpreted these statements to mean that associations are collectivities to which persons orient their conduct—their reference groups—so that some individuals are in association with social groups other than those with which they are in direct contact.

Regardless of the choice we make concerning the meaning of associations, there are other questions to be asked about this part of the theory. Sutherland contended that associations vary in frequency, duration, priority, and intensity. Although the first three dimensions are relatively clear, the last one is not. What kinds of associations are "intense" ones? Note that Sutherland conceded that intensity was not precisely defined and that he spoke of the prestige of different sources of definitions. All of this sounds reasonable enough—the commonsense notion of intensity suggests that some groups to which we belong are more important to us than are others. For example, I am more sensitive to criticisms of my behavior offered by my wife and children than I am to negative evaluations of my behavior coming from colleagues in the sociology department. But, even though examples of what Sutherland might have meant by intensity can easily be produced, it would be quite another thing to measure intensity empirically absent a clear definition of it.

These critical observations regarding differential association theory all have to do with unclear concepts, internal inconsistencies in the argument, and other *structural* problems. However, as Cressey (1960) indicated, over its lifetime, the theory was attacked both for alleged defects of language or structure and also for being empirically false. According to Cressey, most of the criticisms about structural deficiencies were based on an incorrect reading of the argument on the part of the critics.

Cressey noted that some persons misinterpreted the theory as declaring that persons who associate with criminals become offenders in turn. But Sutherland claimed that criminality is due to an *excess* of criminal associations over noncriminal ones. Another misinterpretation is that the theory says that criminality results from involvement with criminal *persons*, for it actually speaks of criminal *patterns*, many of which are communicated by persons who are not themselves involved in lawbreaking.

Regarding substantive criticisms, Cressey noted that some criminologists asserted that the theory could not explain certain kinds of criminality, but those negative cases were frequently left unidentified.

Differential association theory was also criticized for its silence regarding "personality traits" or "psychological variables." However, Cressey indicated that Sutherland gave considerable thought to this issue and concluded that even if personality traits are associated with certain forms of criminality, differential association still determines which persons with those traits will become involved in lawbreaking and which will not.

Sutherland's argument was also sometimes challenged on the grounds that it was not sensitive to the complexities of life experiences over time as they unfold in different ways due to previously encountered life events. To put the matter another way, different early life experiences may affect the *meaning* or significance of later ones that are common to a group of individuals. For example, children from families in which parental and parent-child conflicts have been common may be more susceptible to the influence of adult peers with antisocial definitions than might persons whose childhood experiences were more harmonious. As we saw in Chapter 5, these ideas or themes have become familiar in recent years, in the form of arguments about nonrecursive processes and the like in etiology.

Cressey also drew attention to the problems surrounding the contention that persons become involved in criminality through an excess of definitions favorable to violation of law. He noted a number of examples in which researchers were unable to accurately measure definitions favorable, or unfavorable, to violation of law.

Sutherland, Cressey, and Luckenbill's (1992: 102) summary judgment of the theory is on the mark:

> At the same time, it seems safe to conclude that differential association is not a precise statement of the process by which a person becomes a criminal. The idea that criminality is a consequence of an excess of intimate associations with criminal behavior patterns is valuable. For example, it negates assertions that deviation from norms is simply a product of being emotionally insecure or living in a broken home, and it indicates in a general way why only some emotionally insecure persons and only some persons from broken homes commit crimes. . . . Yet the statement of differential association is not precise enough to stimulate rigorous empirical testing, and it therefore has not been proved or disproved.

### Revisions of Differential Association Theory

Some attempts have been made to revise and improve upon differential association theory. In one of these, DeFleur and Quinney (1966) restated Sutherland's argument in the logically more rigorous language of set theory and in the process, turned up several points of ambiguity in the original theory. Set theory involves a notational system for designating concepts in a discursively stated theory, along with formal rules for combining the concepts into explicit propositions. DeFleur and Quinney's most important conclusion from this exercise was that a testable version of differential association theory would require a classification of criminal types or role patterns because there probably are a number of forms of differential association, each of which is related to specific varieties of lawbreaking. In short, DeFleur and Quinney argued that differential association is a broad perspective that involves an assortment of more specific experiences that are involved in law-breaking.

Commenting on the efforts of DeFleur and Quinney, Weinberg (1966) argued that personality factors must be incorporated into the theory. However, neither his recommendation nor that of DeFleur and Quinney made any noticeable impression on other criminologists. The major reason for the set theory revision having no impact is that it merely substituted symbolic notation for a set of concepts that were not clearly defined in Sutherland's original argument. What the revision did *not* do was to sharpen the original concepts, with the result that the revised version of the theory was also plagued with ambiguity.

### Differential Association and Learning Theory

Several criminological formulations have appeared in recent years, in which modern operant conditioning or social learning principles have been employed (Pearson and Weiner, 1985; Wilson and Herrnstein, 1985). However, the most significant of these was that of Akers (1985), using the language of modern social learning theory. Akers endeavored to restate the principles of differential association in social learning terms. He has provided the following summary of the revision (Akers, Krohn, Lanza-Kaduce, and Radosevich, 1979: 637–38):

> The primary learning mechanism in social behavior is operant (instrumental) conditioning in which behavior is shaped by the stimuli which follow, or are consequences of the behavior. Social behavior is acquired both through direct conditioning and through *imitation* or modelling of others' behavior. Behavior is strengthened through reward (positive reinforcement) and avoidance of punishment (negative reinforcement) or weakened by aversive stimuli (positive punishment) and loss of reward (negative punishment). Whether deviant or conforming behavior is acquired and persists depends on past and present rewards or punishments for the behavior and the rewards and punishments attached to alternative behavior—*differential reinforcement*. In addition, people learn in interaction with significant groups in their lives evaluative *definitions* (norms, attitudes, orientations) of the behavior as good or bad. These definitions are themselves verbal and cognitive behavior which can be directly reinforced and also act as cue (discriminative) stimuli for other behavior. The more individuals define the behavior as good (positive definition) or at least justified (negative definition), the more likely they are to engage in it. [emphasis in the original]

Akers observed that while reinforcers can sometimes be nonsocial, such as the direct effects of drugs or alcohol, the major reinforcers are group associations, because it is in primary groups such as the family and peer groups that effective reinforcement or punishment of behavior is most likely to occur.

Although the language of social learning theory is less familiar to both laypersons and sociologists, Akers's claims parallel those originally put forth by Sutherland. The formulation has been used, for the most part, as an ex post facto explanation of a wide variety of deviant behavior. However, it was also subjected to research scrutiny in an investigation by Akers and his associates (Akers, Krohn, Lanza-Kaduce, and Radosevich, 1979) of adolescent drinking and drug use. That study involved a self-report questionnaire administered to over 3000 male and female junior and senior high school students in seven communities in three midwestern states. Some of the questionnaire items had to do with drug and alcohol use; others were designed to tap imitation, differential association, conduct definitions, and differential reinforcement—key concepts in the theory. The data indicated that each of these ingredients of social learning was to some extent involved in drug or alcohol use or nonuse, but the single most important factor was differential association with peers who either engaged in alcohol and/or drug use or who abstained from it.

## CONTROL THEORY, LABELING, SITUATIONAL FACTORS, AND RISK-TAKING REVISITED

Not all of the contemporary viewpoints on causes of lawbreaking are discussed in detail in this chapter; rather, the emphasis is upon relatively well developed theoretical expositions which are, at the same time, dominant or influential arguments. However, we need to pause for a few comments on control theory, labeling arguments, situational factors, and risk taking, the first three of which have already appeared in preceding sections of this book.

Control theories, and particularly Hirschi's (1969) social bond argument, were discussed in Chapter 3. That commentary took note of Hirschi's general argument, including his four elements of the social bond: attachment, commitment, involvement, and belief. That discussion mentioned some of the problems that have been encountered with the theory and also pointed out that the argument has been applied principally to juvenile offenders.

However, Gottfredson and Hirschi (1990) have advanced a general theory of crime in which lack of self-control was identified as the major causal factor in a variety of forms of deviance, including criminality. Chapter 5 included some brief observations about this general theory, having principally to do with the validity of the claim that most forms of deviance and lawbreaking are variants of a single broad form of simple, mundane, and unplanned behavior. The Gottfredson and Hirschi formulation is one of a number of efforts that have been made in recent years to develop integrated and/or general theories of crime. Further discussion of their theory is postponed until Chapter 10, which is devoted to these recent ventures.

Chapter 3 examined labeling theory and concluded that it is more properly described as a broad perspective or set of sensitizing notions than as a developed theory. Additionally, a number of criminologists have concluded that the advocates of this perspective oversold it; that is, claims about the deleterious effects of labeling experiences have turned out to be, at the very least, exaggerations of a much more complex reality. Finally, Chapter 3 took note of Braithwaite's (1989b) incorporation of labeling notions into his general theory. It is likely that labeling insights will continue to pop up from time to time as elements of some larger, more complex formulation.

Chapter 5 observed that many specific theories regarding the origins and development of criminal behavior are historical-developmental in form, in which current behavior is attributed to experiences that have occurred some time ago. Years ago, I suggested (Gibbons, 1971) that situational inducements to lawbreaking have been given short shrift in criminological theorizing. More recently, Cullen (1984) has developed a fuller version of this argument.

Two things can be said about the contention that situational factors need to be incorporated into causal analyses. First, these influences certainly have not been woven into most analyses of different forms of crime, even though they do play a part in embezzlement and employee theft, sexual offenses and other forms of violence, and myriad other varieties of lawbreaking. The potential of a situational perspective has yet to be fully realized.[4] But second, elements of a situational view of things are contained in many of the analyses of rational choice theorists that have appeared in recent years and which are examined later in this chapter.

One other set of ideas about causal processes ought to be mentioned, namely, Lemert's (1972: 71–73) conjectures about "risk-taking" processes in the emergence of lawbreaking activities. In an insightful but relatively brief discussion of this idea, he suggested that individuals often get involved in deviant behavior as a result of conduct having several potential outcomes, one of which is deviant. This nonconforming behavior cannot be linked to clear-cut deviant motives, for at the outset, the individual did not specifically intend to become involved in deviance. Lemert pointed to the example of "suicidal" actions on the part of residents of the south Pacific island of Tikopia as illustrative of risk taking. These persons often go out to the open sea in small boats, not with the intent to perish in the process, but nonetheless with some awareness that if things go badly, drowning may be the result. Further, Lemert claimed that his research on naïve check forgers indicated that a number of them had become caught up in a line of action such as gambling, in which they had written bad checks to cover wagers, risking the possibility that they might well not be able to cover those checks before they arrive at the bank.

The risk-taking conjecture is well worth pursuing further. I have suggested (Gibbons, 1992a: 244–45) that driving while intoxicated may often be a form of risk taking, in which drunken persons set off in cars, hoping to arrive home without being stopped by a police officer, but recognizing that they are running a significant risk of being apprehended and charged with a serious crime. At the same time, there is no well-developed theory of crime causation in which risk-taking ideas have been explicated in detail.

## RATIONAL CHOICE THEORIZING IN CRIMINOLOGY

### Background

Rational choice formulations assume that human actions are based on rational decisions, in which persons consciously weigh the gains from a possible course of action against the costs and ultimately embark upon, or refrain from, that behavior, depending upon the calculus of gains and costs they perceive. Put another way, persons take informed actions, either de-viant or lawful ones, which maximize payoffs and minimize costs to themselves.

In his examination of rational choice views in criminology, Akers (1990: 653) argued: " 'Rational choice' theory, which is derived mainly from the expected utility model in economics, has become a 'hot' topic in criminology, sociology, political science, and the law."[5] Akers (1990: 654) also rendered the summary judgment that "thus far, no new general theoretical concepts or propositions have been added to criminological theory by rational choice studies."

### Rational Choice Perspectives in Criminology

The following paragraphs provide a brief sketch of rational choice perspectives. As will become evident, I share Akers's view that relatively little is new in these arguments. For one thing, many of the basic ideas in current rational choice notions have been in existence for a long time under other labels. For example, Sutherland's arguments about criminality resulting from an excess of definitions favorable to lawbreaking over definitions unfavorable to law violation are not entirely unlike rational choice contentions. Additionally, there is as yet, no well-developed rational choice theory; rather, what exists is a broad point of view or batch of sensitizing notions. A well-developed rational choice theory would identify the kinds of lawbreaking in which rational decisions are frequent, it would spell out the ingredients of criminal decision making, and in other ways, it would go beyond current formulations.

In his commentary, Akers (1990: 661) identified a pristine version of expected utility theory, in which individuals are seen as making highly informed, rational choices to engage in or refrain from criminality after carefully weighing all the costs and benefits of lawbreaking, unrestrained by any other considerations. Although some economists (e.g., Becker, 1968) have developed economic models of lawbreaking involving relatively strict rationality views of offenders, many of them have offered, instead, a "soft rationality" argument, in which the decisions of individuals are seen as constrained or modified by lack of information, structural factors, values, and other "nonrational" factors; thus, rational choice arguments often assert that decisions to engage in lawbreaking are "more or less" rational in nature.

Consider the following passage from an essay by economist Raaj Sah (1991: 1274), having to do with $p$, which refers to the perceptions of a specific individual regarding his or her likelihood of being punished for a criminal choice:

> An individual's $p$ is an endogenous outcome of the nature of the information available to him [sic]. This information is, in turn, generated within the economy. However, there is no source in the economy from which the individual can in practice get the accurate information. He may receive raw data from several sources, but each source has its own costs, inaccuracies, and randomness. For example, casual contact or hearsay yields unreliable data. The individual's own past experiences and those of his acquaintances are more reliable, but for reasons noted later, they provide limited information.[6]

Let us examine the rational choice views of Cornish and Clarke (1986), two of the leading advocates of this position. Like Sah, Cornish and Clarke did not argue for a pristine rational choice model of offender-nonoffender decisions. Instead, they (Cornish and Clarke, 1986: 1) contended that

> offenders seek to benefit themselves by their criminal behavior; that this involves the making of decisions and choices, however rudimentary on occasion these processes might be; and that these processes exhibit a measure of rationality, albeit constrained by limits of time and the availability of relevant information. . . .

In his commentary on the views of Cornish and Clarke, Akers (1990: 667–68) indicated that these theorists contrasted their approach to what they identified as "traditional criminology," said by them to emphasize "irrational" or "pathological" motivations that lie behind acts of lawbreaking. Akers described this alleged traditional viewpoint as a caricature, for few if any "traditional criminologists" can be identified who claim that criminality is usually the result of pathological or irrational motives. Instead, Akers (1990: 663) contended that the limited or conditional rationality posited by Cornish and Clarke is found in a great many other criminological theories as well. This is true, not only for sociological criminologists, but for the theorizing of a number of psychologists as well.

Akers's summary judgment (Akers, 1990: 665) regarding the degree of rationality assumed in these arguments was that "rational choice theory does not assume that all or even most criminal acts result from well-informed calculated choices. The rational choice models in the literature leave room for all levels of rationality, except the most mindless, pathological, and irrational."

In his critique, Akers (1990: 669–70) noted that many of the competing causal arguments place less emphasis upon the balancing of rewards and costs by potential offenders than do rational choice formulations. But he also argued that rewards and costs are central elements in social learning theories such as his own, which we examined earlier in this chapter. Indeed, according to Akers, social learning formulations take into account a wider range of both formal and informal rewards and punishments; hence rational choice is a more limited perspective and offers few new ideas to criminology.

Akers (1990: 670–71) also scored rational choice arguments for their inattention to values and moral judgments as elements in the decision calculi of criminal and noncriminal actors. Also, those rational choice models that do make room for various "moral costs" such as the sting of conscience, or which also include other variables such as social background, peer influences, and the like, then become difficult to distinguish from existing etiological formulations which have been judged to be unsatisfactory by advocates of rational choice views.

### Decision Making by Offenders

Strange as it may seem, analysts of deviance and criminality have often proceeded without adequate answers to the fundamental question, "What do deviants and criminals *do*?" In other words, a considerable share of the theorizing about the causes of lawbreaking and deviance has been based upon a limited amount of information regarding the nature of the behavior to be explained.[7] However, in recent years, information about the activities of deviants and offenders has begun to accumulate, partly because of the appearance of rational choice formulations. Clearly, rational choice views require ethnographic and other data on the actual decision-making activities of lawbreakers.

The accumulation of evidence on the criminal activities and decisions of lawbreakers is a welcome development, quite apart from how one views rational choice notions. Some recent studies on offender behavior, and in particular, the activities of predators, are those of Rengert and Wasilchick (1985); Cromwell, Olson, and Avary (1990); Åkerström (1988); and Tunnell (1992). These investigations, added to some earlier inquiries into offender behavior (e.g., Petersilia, Greenwood, and Lavin, 1977), provide considerable empirical support for a "limited rationality" view of decision making by lawbreakers.

### Situational Crime Prevention

If many offenders, and predatory offenders in particular, weigh at least some of the potential risks against the gains they anticipate from lawbreaking, criminal acts may often be deterred by making them riskier or harder to carry out. Indeed, lay citizens act as "folk criminologists" when they go about fortifying their dwellings by such means as barred windows, burglar alarms, and kindred techniques. In much the same way, self-service gas stations could be said to be implementing criminological principles when they install pumps which can only be activated by the station cashier *after* the customer has paid for the gasoline, thereby making it virtually impossible for motorists to drive away without paying for gasoline (Brodsky, Bernatz, and Beidelman, 1981). Additionally, these pumps are programmed to shut off when the amount of gasoline prepaid for has been delivered.

Rational choice theorist Clarke (1992) has drawn 23 research reports on situational crime prevention efforts into a book with this same title. Although there is little to quarrel with in the proposition that "target hardening" can dissuade some potential lawbreakers from attacking specific targets, such as a well-lit house which also has signs attached to it, announcing that it is protected by burglar alarms, we are less certain whether these actions merely "displace" the criminal activity to another residence.

## CONCLUDING COMMENTS

The opening comments in this chapter indicated that it is the first of a set of two that examine theoretical arguments regarding the factors and processes involved in criminal conduct on the part of individuals. Chapter 8 turns to the unsettled status of sociobiological views in criminology. That commentary is followed by a relatively detailed scrutiny of a number of psychological arguments that differ, in degree, from formulations considered in this chapter.

## NOTES

[1]There is a large body of work by psychologists that is physiological in nature, e.g., research on hearing, psychomotor responses, visual perception, and the like. The efforts of sociologists rarely if ever overlap with this kind of psychological inquiry.

[2]This discussion of differential association theory is similar to the commentary in Gibbons, 1992a: 177–82.

[3]According to one unverified account, Cressey made no revisions in differential association theory in the editions of the book which he coauthored after Sutherland's death because of stipulations in the book contract and the wishes of Sutherland's widow. Also, only a few, minor changes in wording were made by Luckenbill in the most recent edition (Sutherland, Cressey, and Luckenbill, 1992: 88–90).

[4]For one recent effort to investigate the situational causation argument, see McCarthy and Hagan, 1991. In a study of homeless youths in Toronto, these investigators found that the incidence of criminal acts on the part of homeless youths was generally higher among these youngsters after they had left home than before they had become homeless. McCarthy and Hagan concluded that homelessness is a criminogenic situation which induces lawbreaking on the part of youths who quite probably would have otherwise refrained from misbehavior.

[5]Readers would do well to examine, firsthand, Akers's essay, in that he identified a large share of the literature on rational choice, as well as providing a detailed critique of much of this work.

[6]This extended essay by Sah is, in my opinion, a good example of arid, sterile theorizing in a pseudomathematical form, regarding criminal behavior. Although the paper is full of formulas which the author described as "mathematical derivations," there were no values assigned to the notations in these "equations." Furthermore, various questionable assumptions about offenders and their motivations characterized this elaborate exercise. Then, too, a number of "propositions" were offered in the essay, but these contentions were more commonsensical and empirically uncertain than they were verified assertions that have been proven to be true by the "mathematical" exercise. For example, one of them asserted (Sah, 1281): "An individual's current propensity for crime is higher if during a past period of his [sic] life the crime participation rate was higher or fewer resources were spent on the criminal apprehension system. The propensity is also higher if the current relative payoff from crime is larger" [emphasis in the original]. The validity of this claim was established by fiat, rather than by evidence. Sah also made assertions such as the following one (p. 1292): "The present analysis . . . shows that, although the environment matters, the current crime participation rate will be lower if apprehension and punishment have been more efficacious in the past." In other words, Sah claimed that punishment deters persons from crime. This contention may be true in the sense that it followed logically from other arguments in the paper, but it may also be *empirically false*. Another example of this sort of argumentation, in which statements were put forth as though they are matters of well-established fact but are actually conjectures, can be found in Tuck and Riley (1986: 161). These writers asserted the following:

> More formally, behavior (B, any conscious action) is preceded by a behavioral intention, and this behavioral intention (BI) is itself a result of two and only two measurable variables: the attitude to the behavior ($A_{act}$) involved (not the attitude to the object with which the behavior is concerned but the attitude to the act or behavior itself) and the individual's subjective norm (SN) concerning the act. The term *subjective norm* refers to perceptions that most important others think the person should or should not engage in the act. The weighting of subjective norms and attitudes in the formation of behavioral intentions is held to vary both across individuals and across acts in ways that can be determined empirically. The theory is expressed in the regression equation:
>
> $$B \, ( - BI) = A_{act} + SN$$

I would not deny in principle that subjective norms and attitudes can be determined empirically, but it is also true that no one has done a satisfactory job of measuring them to date. Accordingly, to describe the formula above as a "regression equation" seems unwarranted.

[7]For example, until relatively recently, discussions of homosexuality by psychiatrists and by some sociologists frequently alluded to "passive" and "active" homosexual roles or to "insertees" and "insertors," thus suggesting that homosexual behavior is narrowly structured and that gay persons specialize in particular sexual acts. However, some critics noted that, in practice, it was often difficult to sort specific acts out as either "active" or "passive." Even more to the point, we have subsequently learned that many gay persons engage in a variety of sexual acts over time; thus many of these descriptions of homosexual conduct have turned out to be incorrect.

Another illustration can be found in the criminological literature of the 1950s and 1960s, in which criminologists often assumed, incorrectly, that most offenders were specialists in particular forms of crime. As I noted in Chapter 4, research studies in the past three decades have indicated that crime switching and involvement in a fairly large collection of different offenses is most common among those lawbreakers who engage in criminal "careers."

Finally, it is not just students of deviance and criminality who have engaged in theorizing without solid knowledge about the phenomena to be explained. It would not be difficult to identify a number of examples of sociological speculation regarding social activities about which the theorist has been uninformed.

# CHAPTER 8

# Accounting for Criminals and Criminal Behavior

## DO INDIVIDUAL DIFFERENCES MAKE A DIFFERENCE?

## INTRODUCTION

The preceding chapter began by indicating that there is a large and varied collection of explanatory arguments in criminology that are psychological in form. These psychological explanations center on factors that are "inside the skins" or "inside the heads" of persons, so to speak. The claim that psychopathy is a major factor in lawbreaking is clearly a psychological one, in that "psychopathy" or "sociopathy," if they exist, are mental states or personality configurations that are characteristic of certain individuals. Psychopaths are said to be characterized by severe lack of conscience and concern for the rights of others. Most persons would be quick to agree that the psychopathy thesis is a psychological one, but fewer might be inclined to identify differential association theory or rational choice notions as psychological. Even so, Chapter 7 contended that these are properly classified as psychological arguments because they posit certain mental states on the part of offenders: an excess of criminal conduct definitions over law-abiding ones in the case of differential association, and more perceived rewards from crime over perceived costs or pains, in the case of rational choice viewpoints.

This chapter presents the second half of the story regarding psychological views. In particular, it takes up the thesis that psychological differences among persons play a considerable role in determining the kinds of behavior, criminal or otherwise, in which they engage. While some versions of this viewpoint have stressed personality pathology as distinguishing offenders from nonoffenders, we will also examine the possibility that lawbreakers and nonoffenders differ in terms of less marked variations in personality patterns. For example, the former may sometimes show greater "dependency" than the latter, but in either case, these individuals cannot be described as suffering from serious personality disorders or pathology.

However, before turning to psychological explanations of lawbreaking, we need to give some attention to the unresolved issue of the role of biosocial biological or sociobiological factors in lawbreaking.

## WHAT ABOUT BIOLOGY?

One nagging problem in criminology is the inattention paid by social-science trained theorists to the possibility that biological factors are involved in criminality. One indication of this inattention turned up in an effort by Pearson and Weiner (1985) to integrate criminological concepts within a social-learning framework. They began this attempt at conceptual integration with the claim that criminology is an eclectic science, drawing its sustenance from a multiplicity of disciplines. If so, it is strange that they made no mention of biological forces in lawbreaking, for it surely cannot be said that the research literature on hypothesized biological causes of criminality is a meager one. Rather, as recent reviews (Ellis and Hoffman, 1990; Fishbein, 1990; Trasler, 1987; Wilson and Herrnstein, 1985; Knoblich and King, 1992) have made clear, there is a large and growing body of research studies that have probed specific hypotheses about biological or sociobiological influences upon lawbreaking.

One indication of the status of biological factors in criminology is in a report by Ellis and Hoffman (1990). They sent a questionnaire to a random sample of attendees at the 1986 meeting of the American Society of Criminology, asking them to indicate the factors that they considered to be etiologically important and also, which ones had the strongest research support. Less than half of those who were sent questionnaires returned them, but of those who did, the majority said that they favored such variables as poor home supervision and economic deprivation. Relatively few exhibited enthusiasm for the proposition that genetically influenced traits are related to criminality or for kindred arguments. Curiously, in light of these responses, a fair number of individuals said that the research support for biosocial hypotheses was fairly strong!

Why do criminologists reject biological theories and hypotheses? Ellis and Hoffman claimed that a major reason is that most of them are poorly trained in biology, especially in the area of brain functioning. Actually, Ellis and Hoffman were charitable in this claim, for many criminologists have no training whatever in the area of biological functioning.

Ellis and Hoffman also suggested that rejection of biological claims occurs frequently on ideological grounds, for many of us wish to eschew notions that "blame the victim," whether such ideas are correct or not. In other words, criminologists are attuned to identifying societal causes of criminality and find uncongenial, arguments that suggest that crime is the result of flaws and defects on the part of persons who engage in it.

Criminology textbook writers usually feel obliged to nod in the direction of acknowledging the research carried on by biologically oriented scholars. However, most of them then move with alacrity to poke holes in the methodology of studies such as those that have probed the XYY chromosome explanation of male violence. The most positive conclusion that appears in most textbooks is a grudging acknowledgement that "there may be something there," coupled with a second claim, "but if so, no substantial evidence has yet been produced."

It is sometimes possible to unlimber our methodological weapons and fire a withering blast at specific pieces of biologically oriented research. Take the modest study by Ellis and Burke (1990), having to do with sexual orientation and criminal and violent behavior. These researchers quizzed 197 females and 279 males, ranging in age from 20 to 47, about their sexual orientations and their involvement in criminality and violence. "Sexual orientation" was measured through questions asking respondents to indicate the frequency with which they fantasized about sexual relations with members of the same sex as opposed to persons of the opposite sex. By this measure, males who said that they imagined sexual relations with other males one percent or more of the time were classified as "bisexuals," while those who imagined sex with other males 100 percent of the time were designated as "male homosexuals."

The self-report data on violence and criminality indicated that males were more involved in these activities than were females (classified as heterosexuals or lesbians, with the latter being persons who said they imagined sex with same-sex partners at least one percent of the time). Further, the researchers reported that while "heterosexuals" were more involved in crime and violence than were "homosexuals," "bisexual males" were even more criminal and violent than were "heterosexuals." This finding led them to conclude that a conventional "sex role" explanation of male crime is inadequate, and they hinted that there may be some biological basis for these differences.

Clearly, most persons would treat these findings gingerly. The research involved no measurement of the actual sexual behavior of the respondents. Additionally, as the researchers themselves conceded, their definition of "bisexuality" was a very "liberal" one. It very well could be that considerable numbers of males who have no sexual contact with other males do nonetheless fantasize about such a relationship at least on a few occasions.

However, it will not do for criminologists to continue to utter a blanket rejection of biological research on the grounds that some of these studies are methodologically inadequate. By that same logic, critics of sociological criminology could argue that "there is nothing there."

A recent illustration of this tactic for disposing of unwelcome findings from sociobiology can be found in Gottfredson and Hirschi's (1990: 47–63) book in which they presented their general theory of crime. In a chapter devoted to attacking what they termed "biological positivism," they began by criticizing the biological research of Lombroso, Ferri, and Goring, which took place in the late 1800s and early 1900s. Their criticisms of these early works have merit, but they may have little relevance to the work of modern sociobiological investigators. The remainder of the Gottfredson and Hirschi chapter consisted of an incisive critique of studies of adopted identical and fraternal twins. It is clear that those investigations were flawed, far from convincing, and provide little support for claims that criminality is transmitted in the form of inherited biological predispositions.

However, the problem with Gottfredson and Hirschi's commentary is that, after criticizing the twin studies, they concluded (Gottfredson and Hirschi, 1990: 61–62) that "biological positivism has produced little in the way of meaningful or interpretable research." This conclusion would be in order if biological positivism consisted entirely of twin studies. But it is a non sequitur because contemporary biosocial inquiry involves a large number of lines of investigation not dealt with by Gottfredson and Hirschi.

I make no attempt to provide a detailed review of biosocial investigations in criminology or a critical analysis of these studies in this chapter. A number of comprehensive surveys of the evidence on biological factors in lawbreaking have already been produced and are readily available to the reader. Further, I agree with Ellis and Hoffman that most criminologists are poorly trained in biology and are ill-equipped to evaluate biosocial findings. Indeed, I am one of those criminologists about whom they spoke! Even so, it seems clear that criminological theorists cannot continue to ignore evidence that biological factors play a part in lawbreaking. They are going to have to become more sophisticated about the biological foundations of human behavior.[1]

Consider an illustration of the problem faced by those who are uninformed on biological matters. Ellis (1989) has authored a book on forcible rape, in which he reviewed a large body of evidence having to do with influences that may play a part in rape. One factor in the "synthesized theory of rape" that he assembled from this research is high androgen (male hormone) levels. According to Ellis, persons who become rapists have been exposed to high levels of androgens during the organization phases of brain development. His critics (Fish, 1990; Barth, 1991) have suggested that he may be wrong in this claim, but how are we to assess this contention if we are ignorant about such matters as hormonal functioning?

What do we need to do in order to address biological contributions?

The answer is that in some way or another, sociological criminologists are going to have to become more biologically informed, probably through undergraduate and graduate coursework in their academic training.

## MENTAL PATHOLOGY AND CRIME

### Mental Disorder and "Monsters"

As I indicated in my criminology text (Gibbons, 1992a: 23–24), feeble-mindedness enjoyed considerable popularity as a major explanation of crime in the early 1900s. But research results from World War I testing of military draftees produced results that showed that garden-variety criminals exhibited much the same IQ levels as did a cross section of the American population. Subsequently, attention shifted to the hypothesis that lawbreakers were characterized by mental disorders rather than impaired intelligence.

A number of inquiries in the early part of the century turned up reports that large numbers of criminals, and in particular, prison inmates, were mentally disordered. But as more careful studies were conducted, it became apparent that the early claims said more about the biases of the psychiatrists than they did about the mental health of offenders. As I concluded earlier (Gibbons, 1992a: 150): "It is now clear that few criminals are psychotics . . . criminality and mental disorder are different and independent forms of deviance."

Although mental disorder is not a general explanation for criminality, this is not to say that mental pathology never plays a part in lawbreaking. There are some "monsters" among the offender group, that is, individuals who are "socialization failures" and who, by any reasonable definition, are markedly abnormal persons. Consider a few examples of these "monsters." One recent case from Oregon involved a male in his thirties who was convicted of kidnapping and eventually killing a number of prostitutes, after first subjecting them to a variety of protracted and extremely painful physical attacks which arose out of some idiosyncratic forms of sexual motivation. Also, American newspapers frequently report on the criminal activities of others of this ilk: Ted Bundy, John Gacey, Richard Speck, Angelo Buono, the unapprehended "Green River Killer" in Washington state, and one of the most recent "monsters," Jeffrey Dahmer.

Parenthetically, many of us are familiar with the names of American "monsters" and probably assume that pathological offenders are particularly common in the United States. But "socialization failures" turn up in other nations as well. A recent case is that of Andrei Chikatilo, a Russian citizen who was sentenced to death for murdering 53 women and children in a series of cannibalistic sex crimes between 1978 and 1990. According to newspaper accounts, Chikatilo mutilated and killed 53 boys, girls, and women, dismembering some of them while they were still alive. He also gouged out his victims' hearts and stomachs, cut off their fingers and noses, and ate their genitals and tips of their tongues.

Quite probably, many persons would argue that while mentally abnormal offenders do exist, and while their crimes are particularly disturbing, these individuals comprise only a small part of the offender population; thus socialization failure and aberrant personality patterns are relatively infrequent in criminality.

I have no quarrel with such a response, as far as it goes. At the same time, I argue that criminologists ought to have something to say about the causal influences that give rise to a Jeffrey Dahmer or a Ted Bundy.

There is no shortage of "experts" who are willing to offer ex post facto pronouncements about the "causes" for the criminal acts of various "monsters" once these persons have been apprehended. For example, a number of "experts" claimed to see etiological significance in the "sexual abuse" that Dahmer had allegedly undergone from a male peer when he was relatively young, while others opined that clues to Dahmer's sexual crimes could be seen in his childhood interest in collecting animal bones. Perhaps these conjectures are correct, but it might also be that Dahmer did not engage in sex acts with another youngster, or if he did, he was not negatively affected by the experience and it was irrelevant to an understanding of his adult criminality.

Many years ago, I wrote a paper dealing with the inattention on the part of criminologists to sexual criminality (Gibbons, 1965b) which drew attention to the fact that sex crimes and sexual offenders were rarely mentioned in most criminology textbooks and then endeavored to account for this criminological silence regarding sexual misconduct. I argued that sociological theorizing more generally was "asexual" and that explanations for sexual criminality must await the development of a social-psychological account of sexual socialization.

Much the same point about the lacunae in the area of sexual learning was made by Gagnon and Simon (1973: 36) some years later. Speaking to the question of the causes of homosexuality, they asserted that "the problem of finding out how some people become homosexual requires an adequate theory of how others become heterosexual; that is, one cannot explain homosexuality in one way and leave heterosexuality as a large residual category labeled 'all other.' Indeed, the explanation of homosexuality in this sense may await the explanation of the larger and more modal category of adjustment."

There has recently been some criminological attention focused on violent and/or sexual crimes, and in particular, on so-called serial killers. These efforts are to be welcomed, even though one might voice some reservations about some of them. For example, it may eventually turn out that the notion of "serial killer" is a misleading and not entirely useful one. For one thing, it may slur over some important differences between persons who kill adults as opposed to killing children, or those who kill persons of one sex rather than the other. Then, too, some serial homicides appear to be sexually motivated, but others arise out of diffuse feelings of hostility toward others and kindred influences. Finally, the concept of "serial killer" may divert attention away from the possibility that some individuals who kill only one other person are motivationally similar to individuals who engage in multiple killings, if for no other reason than that the former may simply not have yet had time to engage in multiple killings.

On the whole, relatively little progress has been made in the development of criminological explanations of the kinds of "aberrant" activities discussed in this section. And this failure seems in considerable part to be due to the lack of movement toward an adequate explanatory scheme which identifies the crucial experiences that are involved in sexual socialization, whether "normal" or "deviant" in form.[2]

### Psychopathy and Crime

Another psychological perspective claims that many juvenile and adult offenders are driven by a form of psychological pathology called *psychopathic personality*, or more recently, *sociopathy*. Clinical definitions of these terms that have been offered by psychiatrists and psychologists stress egocentricity, asocial behavior, insensitivity to others, hostility, and lack of conscience as the hallmarks of this syndrome or pattern. Some authorities have suggested that psychopaths at first glance often appear quite normal, but when under stress, they exhibit a number of signs of being poorly socialized, indifferent, and affectless persons who feel little or no guilt for acts of deceit or betrayal directed at others.

I have reviewed a number of the definitions of psychopathy or sociopathy that have been put forth by psychiatrists (Gibbons, 1992a: 155-56) and have indicated that most of them are similar to the description above. I also noted that most of these involve a set of relatively general and unspecific symptoms or identifying characteristics said to be common to psychopaths or sociopaths.

Although there is a good deal of fuzziness in the notion of psychopathy, workers in the criminal justice system have frequently invoked it as a label to attach to some of their charges or clients. Faced with offenders who are uncooperative, who lie, or who engage in various and sundry other kinds of negative and/or deviant conduct, the diagnosis that these persons are "sociopaths" sometimes becomes a convenient and seemingly meaningful one, for at first glance, it seems to provide an explanation for their deceitful or negative behavior. In a parallel way, some of us who have had bad experiences with automobile salespersons are sometimes tempted to conclude that

that occupation is filled with individuals who suffer from serious character defects.

However, as critics of psychopathy-sociopathy notions have pointed out, there is a good deal of circularity involved in these everyday usages of labels such as "psychopath." Under close examination, it often turns out that the evidence on which a person has been identified as a "sociopath" is the same behavior that the diagnosis is intended to explain. In other words, chronic delinquency or repetitive acts of deviance are the bases for identifying a person as a psychopath, following which, that diagnosis is used to account for the undesirable behavior!

Many sociological criminologists have been chary of the psychopath argument, for the reasons noted above. Still, some scholars continue to find value in the idea of psychopathy. Some have claimed to see persuasive evidence of sociopathy in a sophisticated investigation by psychiatrist Lee Robins (1966). She traced the adult adjustments of 54 persons in St. Louis 30 years after they had been in a child guidance clinic, and of 100 normal school children grown up. Over 70 percent of the guidance clinic youngsters had been referred by the juvenile court for "antisocial conduct," such as running away, truancy, or theft. The researchers obtained interview data on 82 percent of those who had lived to age 25, either from the individuals themselves or from their relatives.

The clinic subjects who had been referred for neurotic behavior showed satisfactory adult adjustments closely similar to those of the control subjects. However, the antisocial youngsters showed a number of adult arrests for criminality and drunkenness, numerous divorces, occupational instability, psychiatric problems, and dependency on social agencies. For example, 44 percent of the male antisocial youths had been arrested for major crimes, as contrasted to only 3 percent of the controls. In short, the clinic subjects exhibited generally messed-up adult lives.

A major part of this study concerned the extent of sociopathic personality among the subjects. To be judged a sociopath, an individual had to show maladjustment in at least five of nineteen life areas. That is, the person had to exhibit some combination of poor work history, financial dependency, drug use, sexual misconduct, and so on. The judgment that a subject was a sociopath rested with psychiatrists, who made clinical judgments from the interviews. In all, 22 percent of the clinic cases and 2 percent of the controls were so designated.

Those who are skeptical about the sociopath concept would probably not be persuaded by this study. Robins asserted that some kind of "disease" or personality entity was behind the symptoms that were used to identify sociopaths, but no convincing evidence of this elusive entity appeared in her report; instead, the sociopath argument seemed tautological. Although this study clearly showed that many youngsters who end up in juvenile courts and guidance clinics live disordered lives as adults, there was little direct evidence that these individuals were pathological; indeed, some findings under-mined the sociopath concept. For example, the data suggested that antiso-cial children who avoided juvenile court or training school were less likely to become sociopaths than those who had been through these agencies. Could it be that the crude machinery of these organizations, rather than socio-pathy, contribute to botched lives? Further, about one-third of the putative psychopaths had given up much of their deviant activity by the time of the follow-up investigation. Sociopaths are supposed to be particularly intrac-table and unamenable to change; thus this finding raises questions about the diagnosis.

It is difficult to escape the conclusion that *psychopathy* or *sociopathy* is often a pejorative label hung upon lawbreakers because of their non-con-formist behavior, rather than a diagnosis of clear-cut psychological impair-ment. In other words, these terms are euphemisms for behavioral deviance. Persons have been identified as psychopaths or sociopaths because of their involvement in criminality, drug addiction, or some other troublesome behavior, and "explanations" of their behavior as a function of psychopathy have followed.

## PERSONALITY PROBLEMS AND INDIVIDUAL DIFFERENCES[3]

### Personality Problems and Criminality

Even though the evidence indicates that mentally disordered persons are uncommon in the population of offenders, and even though it does not appear that most lawbreakers are psychopaths or sociopaths, it might still be true that personality problems of one kind or another do differentiate law violators from lawabiding citizens. Moreover, the thesis that criminality is fre-quently an indicator of personality inadequacies on the part of offenders has enjoyed wide popularity among workers within the criminal justice system, as well as among many psychologists and psychiatrists.

Early support for the personality problems–criminality thesis came from Healy and Bronner's (1936) study, which compared 105 delinquents with 105 of their nondelinquent siblings in New Haven, Boston, and Detroit. Healy and Bronner (1936: 122) concluded that 90 percent of the delin-quents but only 13 percent of the controls were unhappy and discontented in their life circumstances or extremely emotionally disturbed. However, this finding was open to criticism on the grounds that the differences between the offenders and controls were probably exaggerated. The staff members who reported on the personality characteristics of the subjects were psychia-trists and social workers who were predisposed to the belief that emotional problems are a major cause of delinquency. The clinical judgments were subjective and no attempt was made to conceal the identity of the youths prior to the psychiatric examinations; thus knowledge of the delinquency status of the subjects may have contaminated the findings.

Those who favor the personality problem argument have often cited the Gluecks' (1951) investigation as support for their views. The 500 delinquents and 500 controls in that research were subjected to psychiatric interviews and Rorschach testing. Regarding the results, the Gluecks (1951: 240) reported that 48.6 percent of the delinquents and 55.7 percent of the nondelinquents showed "no conspicuous pathology." However, they also declared that the delinquents were "to a much greater degree socially assertive, defiant and ambivalent to authority; they are more resentful of others, and far more hostile, suspicious, and destructive; the goals of their drives are to a much greater extent receptive (Oral) and destructive-sadistic; they are more impulsive and vivacious, and decidedly more extroversive in their behavior."[4]

These Rorschach findings were not clearcut. Some of the characteristics that were identified as more common among offenders were not clearly signs of maladjustment, for impulsiveness, assertiveness, and vivacity could be regarded as positive signs. At the same time, the Gluecks were clear as to their interpretation of the evidence. At one point, they asserted that (1951: 240) "a statistically significant difference exists between the delinquents and nondelinquents in the incidence of mental pathology . . ." and at another (1951: 241): "Even a simple review of the traits and tendencies under consideration shows that they are of a nature to facilitate uncontrolled self-expression."[5]

There has been a host of other inquiries into psychological characteristics of offenders, with many of them producing equivocal results, at best. Several reviews of these studies have been produced, including one by Schuessler and Cressey (1950). They reviewed 113 studies conducted up to 1950 and concluded (Schuessler and Cressey, 1950: 476) that "of comparisons [of criminals and noncriminals] 42 percent showed differences in favor of the noncriminal, while the remainder were indeterminate. The doubtful validity of many of the obtained differences, as well as the lack of consistency in the combined results, makes it impossible to conclude from these data that criminality and personality elements are associated." Waldo and Dinitz (1967) updated this review and also found no psychological factors that were clearly associated with criminality, nor did Tennebaum (1977) and Arbuthnot, Gordon, and Jurkovic (1987) in more recent reviews.

### Individual Differences and Criminality

Even though the evidence overall seems negative, the last word has not been heard on psychological factors in lawbreaking.

One body of positive data came from studies using the Minnesota Multiphasic Personality Inventory (MMPI). This inventory includes eight scales; certain responses to questions in each scale are indicative of particular personality patterns. For example, persons with high scores on the *Pa* (paranoia) scale respond similarly to individuals clinically diagnosed as suffering from paranoia.

In one study (Hathaway and Monachesi, 1952), this inventory was administered to over 4,000 Minneapolis ninth-grade students in 1948. In 1950, these children were traced through the police department and juvenile court to determine which had acquired delinquency records. Of the boys, 22.2 percent had become delinquent, and of the girls, 7.6 percent had become known to the police or the court. The researchers reported that 27.7 percent of the boys with high *Pd* (psychopathic deviate) scale points were delinquent, as were 25.4 percent with high *Pa* scores. However, it should be noted that the items making up the *Pd* scale were originally derived from a group of training school inmates and they centered around feelings of being picked on and the like. Of the boys with *Invalid* responses, indicating uncooperativeness, lying, and so on, 37.5 percent were delinquent. Similar results were obtained with girls. Thus, delinquent youngsters showed somewhat disproportionate numbers in some of the scales of the MMPI.

Another study of the personality characteristics of juvenile offenders used the Jesness Inventory, which, like the MMPI, is an instrument that involves a number of scales or dimensions (Jesness, 1962). The data from investigations of delinquents and nondelinquents, using this instrument, indicated that the offenders and nonoffenders did *not* differ on some of the scales, but they did differ on authority attitude, with delinquents showing greater hostility toward authority figures. The delinquents were also more suspicious and more concerned about being normal. They exhibited more marked feelings of isolation, were less mature, lacked insight, and tended to deny that they had problems.

Conger and Miller (1966) studied tenth graders in Denver in 1956. Youngsters who had appeared in juvenile courts made up a subgroup among the students. Both delinquents and nondelinquents were studied retrospectively through school records and teachers' ratings of them. Conger and Miller found that teachers had viewed the delinquent youths as less well adjusted than the nonoffenders as early as the third grade. Also, personality tests administered to the two groups indicated that the delinquents were more immature, egocentric, impulsive, inconsiderate, and hostile than the nondelinquents.

Turning to adult lawbreakers, the work of Harrison Gough on psychological factors in criminality is particularly instructive, in that his research was informed by a theoretical argument, rather than being an atheoretical search for psychological correlates of lawbreaking. Many years ago, he (Gough, 1948) offered a theory regarding the conditions that lead to the development of psychopathy, in which he argued that psychopaths are defective in role-taking ability; thus they do not experience such emotions as embarrassment, contrition, sympathy for others, or loyalty.

Gough's 1948 essay was in the genre of psychiatric claims that sociopaths or psychopaths are an identifiable group of persons who exhibit marked personality pathology. However, his subsequent endeavors (Gough, 1960) reconceptualized psychopathology as a point on a socialization continuum, so that a representative sample of the population at large would include personality patterns ranging from well-socialized, exemplary citizens at one end of the scale to markedly asocial individuals at the other. Further, he argued that these are the products of variations in socialization and role-taking experiences. Finally, he argued that we should expect that well-socialized individuals would occupy social positions of trust and high repute, while relatively asocial persons should end up as criminals and other deviants. At the same time, he cautioned (Gough, 1960: 23) that "discrepancies are of course to be expected in individual instances between the sociological baseline and the psychological measurement, if for no other reason than that the culture will occasionally make mistakes, in putting some men in prisons and others in positions of trust and responsibility."

Now, a sociologist might argue that these notions about social allocation processes that consign well-socialized individuals to desirable social niches and impaired persons to deviant roles are altogether too sketchy. Even so, this is a coherent argument which was involved in Gough's subsequent development of his California Personality Inventory, and in particular, the *So* (Socialization) scale in that inventory.

The *So* scale consists of 54 items, of the following kind:

1. Before I do something I try to consider how my friends will react to it.
2. I often think about how I look and what impression I am making on others.
3. I would rather go without something than ask for a favor.
4. I find it easy to drop or "break with" a friend.

The 54 scale items tap role-taking deficiencies, insensitivity to the effects of one's behavior on others, resentment against family, feelings of despondency and alienation, and poor scholastic achievement and rebelliousness (Gough and Peterson, 1952). These differentiate poorly socialized persons from well-socialized ones, although it should be emphasized that persons who receive relatively low scores on this scale exhibit only mild forms of undersocialization. Put another way, individuals who say that they find it easy to end a friendship, and so on, are in many cases probably not markedly deviant individuals.

Gough tested a number of groups on the *So* Scale—"best citizens" in a high school, various occupational groups, and known delinquents and prison inmates. These groups exhibited clear differences in mean scores, that is, the average number of positive or "socialized" responses (the range of scores on the *So* Scale is 0-54). "Best citizens" in a high school had a mean score of 39.44, a group of college students had a score of 37.41, and military inductees showed a mean of 32.83. Deviants showed lower scores: County-jail inmates had a mean score of 29.27, prison inmates had a mean of 27.76, and a group of federal reformatory inmates had a score of 26.23. Indeed, the results for these conventional and deviant citizens were remarkably consistent with the argument that a social sorting process operates to allocate the most well-socialized individuals to the most desirable social niches and the least socialized persons to disvalued social positions.

### Other Considerations

Supporters of psychological views would probably be quick to cite these investigations using the MMPI, the Jesness Inventory, or the work of Gough as support for the proposition that criminality and delinquency represent responses to personality factors. Moreover, that interpretation may be correct, at least in a number of individual cases.

However, we need to acknowledge another possible interpretation of these findings. If we find that *prison inmates, training school wards,* or other *incarcerated* offenders differ from seemingly noncriminal or nondelinquent individuals, such a finding may *not* be evidence of a causal link between personality factors and misconduct. Instead, hostility, negative attitudes, and antagonism toward authority figures, in particular, may be byproducts or the *results* of correctional experiences such as incarceration. Criminologists have often argued that the experience of being incarcerated is likely to have negative effects upon the attitudes and self-perceptions of prisoners. A number of persons have conjectured that a common technique for fending off self-condemnatory feelings stemming from the experience of being segregated in a penal institution with other "bad" people is to project blame onto "the system" instead of oneself. And the incarceration experience of "doing time" may lead to deterioration of the prisoners' self-images as they come to grips with the negative views that are directed at them by persons outside of the prison. Along this same line, other experiences with the social control machinery, such as placement on probation, may also create attitudinal and self-concept changes. In short, some of the psychological differences between offenders and nonoffenders may be the *result* of involvement in law-breaking, rather than the other way around.

This "labeling" interpretation of personality-crime linkages is a plausible one, but hard evidence supporting it is not readily available. Relatively little research has been conducted on psychological changes brought about by correctional experiences. Even so, we would do well to remind ourselves that there are two different, plausible possibilities which cannot be adjudicated through cross-sectional data of the sort that has most often been collected in the research cited above.

**New Directions**

One recent effort to reinvigorate inquiry into psychological patterns and individual differences as factors in lawbreaking is in an exchange between Andrews and Wormith (1989) and myself (Gibbons, 1989). According to Andrews and Wormith, many sociological criminologists have denied the significance of individual differences in criminality because of moral, professional, and/or ideological reasons. They also contended that criminologists have engaged in "knowledge destruction," employing verbal legerdemain to make significant research findings disappear. Finally, they reviewed evidence on personality factors and lawbreaking and argued that much of it supports their claim that we ignore psychological factors at our peril.

I was identified as a "knowledge destroyer" in the Andrews and Wormith paper. However, in my response, I noted that much of the evidence that they invoked in support of psychological hypotheses had been cited in my own criminology textbook (Gibbons, 1992a)! I also drew attention to shortcomings in some of this research that weaken their claims about criminological knowledge destroyers. Further, I pointed out instances where Andrews and Wormith employed some of the "knowledge destruction" techniques about which they complained (see note 4). However, my most important point was that they were on the mark in urging greater attention to personality factors and individual differences in criminality.

I have spoken to the question of personality differences in another book (Gibbons, 1979: 212–16):

> Sociological criminology has not succeeded in resolving the issue of psychological forces and personality factors in crime and delinquency. That criminology has been deficient in this regard should come as no surprise, given the fact that the psychological question is a perennial and nagging one that has not been solved in sociology. . . .
>
> Sociological criminologists have been on solid ground in concluding that no convincing evidence of psychological forces, particularly in the form of aberrant personality patterns and the like, has yet been uncovered. At the same time, it is clearly a non sequitur to imply, as many criminologists have done, that personality factors play no part in criminality. It is entirely conceivable that there are important psychological forces that have yet to be uncovered. . . .
>
> There is little more that can be said about psychological correlates in criminality at the present time, given the paucity of attention that this question has received in criminology. But, there are hints contained in some of the personal accounts of criminal careers that have been provided by actual offenders that these "qualities," as Inkeles has termed them, do play a part in lawbreaking. . . . More such linkages between social conditions and psychological states are likely to be uncovered if and when criminologists begin the task of "bringing men [sic] back in."

This is not the place for a detailed presentation of a research agenda regarding psychological factors in lawbreaking, but some additional comments are in order.

To begin with, criminology is rich in analyses of secondary data, but criminologists have had considerably less to say about what is "inside the heads," so to speak, of rapists, predators, white-collar criminals, and other lawbreakers. For example, although many criminologists suspect that income inequality, which refers to the distribution of total income within some population group, has an analog in the form of feelings of "relative deprivation" on the part of lawbreakers, particularly those who are unemployed or who earn low incomes, there is little direct evidence to support this suspicion. In much the same way, although there have been research studies of sexual attitudes, sexual self-images, propensities to violence, and the like, of apprehended rapists and groups of putative nonrapist males, we do not have an overabundance of this kind of information.

Consider some other personality dimensions that may be involved in criminality. It is conceivable, indeed, likely that individuals differ with regard to willingness to engage in risk taking, living life on the edge, pursuing excitement, and similar characteristics. Such sources as Jackson's *A Thief's Primer* (1969) hinted that some criminals are attracted to lawbreaking because of the excitement it provides them. Then, too, some of the studies of decision making by offenders that we examined in Chapter 7 (see pp. 124–25) also suggested that some predators prefer lawbreaking pursuits over noncriminal ones for these same reasons. John Irwin, a former offender and now a prominent criminologist, has reported that a number of his former acquaintances from the world of crime asserted that they were drawn to lawbreaking in part because of the excitement and stimulation it offered them.

Speculation and evidence that not all offenders are driven into crime and that lawbreaking may satisfy certain personality needs of lawbreakers are scattered throughout the criminological literature. However, Katz (1988) developed this theme in detail in a richly textured analysis that centered on the "sensual pleasures" of crime. His book dealt principally with psychological rewards in garden-variety homicide; burglary and shoplifting by teenagers; armed robberies by "badass" street criminals; and "senseless murders," such as those by Gary Gilmore or Richard Speck.

Katz claimed that garden-variety homicides offer a way for persons to transcend feelings of deep humiliation created by those they end up killing. Although the murderer may ultimately come to feel remorse or shame for his or her act of violence, at the moment of the act it serves to relieve the offender's feelings of having been denigrated by the victim.

According to Katz, some juveniles are attracted to the "sneaky thrills" of burglary and shoplifting for the pleasure of "getting away with it," of breaking free of the restraints of adults. Those who have engaged in juvenile "pranks," such as breaking street lights with rocks and then watching the intense light of the bulb just before it goes dark, or who have engaged in myriad other kinds of "hell raising" as youths, would probably concede that this line of argument by Katz has a ring of accuracy to it.

"Badass" street elites who engage in armed robbery do so in part for monetary gains, but equally important, so said Katz, violent robbery is a way of rising above societal demands for dull, routine social conformity. Persons who engage in the "badass" style, which includes considerably more than involvement in armed robbery, are endeavoring to demonstrate that they have not been beaten down by racial discrimination, economic problems, and other exigencies of life that are experienced by the urban underclass.

Finally, Katz argued that "senseless" murders make sense to those who carry them out. These homicidal acts allow the violators to overcome deep feelings of cowardice and failure that have dogged them in their lives.

Katz's exploration of "the moral and sensual rewards of doing evil" was discursive and vague at points, and some of the evidence he invoked in support of this theme was relatively weak. Even so, his book was a welcome addition to a fairly meagre literature. It is clear that he has drawn attention to an aspect of criminality that warrants considerably more scrutiny.

How should we proceed in the business of uncovering psychological correlates of lawbreaking? New directions are called for, in the form of hypotheses that spell out the *specific* personality ingredients that are thought to accompany some specific pattern of criminality. The theorist will also have to indicate the mediating factors that operate, along with personality elements, to produce criminality or law-abiding conduct. In other words, it is likely that certain personality patterns contribute to lawbreaking, but only when they are accompanied by other contingent factors.

Consider one hypothetical case. There may be large numbers of individuals who can be described as "dependent" personalities because they lack various social skills in dealing with personal problems and because they make demands on others to extricate them from difficulties. It may be that some dependent persons get involved in writing bad checks or in other forms of lawbreaking and others do not, depending upon whether they experienced other identifiable life experiences, such as acquiring gambling debts or becoming caught up in other financial difficulties.

I have pasted the preceding example together from separate studies by Lemert (1953, 1962), which suggest that the illustration is more than simply hypothetical. In an investigation of amateur forgers who write "bad checks" against their own bank accounts, Lemert (1953: 298) argued that "naïve check forgery arises at a critical point in the process of social isolation, out of certain types of social situations, and is made possible by the closure or constriction of the behavioral alternatives subjectively held as available to the forger." He studied the case files of over 1000 naïve or amateur forgers in Los Angeles and conducted interviews with a sample of them. Most of these persons had little or no contact with persistent criminals, were nonviolent, and appeared to be likable and attractive but impulsive. Most of them were white, middle-class males.

Most of the check writers had been socially isolated prior to their offenses, with many of them experiencing unemployment, alcoholic sprees, estrangement from their spouses and families, or kindred life events. Lemert (1953: 303–4) also reported that immediately prior to their acts of forgery, most of the offenders had become embarked upon what he termed "certain dialectic forms of social behavior." They had become engaged in a course of action involving a clear beginning and end and also involving pressures to carry the activities to their conclusion. A night of gambling with one's peers serves as one illustration. Once a person becomes engaged in this activity, he or she comes under some pressure to remain in the game until, by mutual agreement, all of the participants decide to bring it to a close. That individual who has suffered large betting losses may nonetheless find it difficult to extricate himself or herself from the game without losing face with the other players.

Lemert (1953: 304–5) argued that forgers found relief from situational tensions by a social-psychological process of *closure*. They opted to write a bad check because they were unaware of more acceptable solutions to their financial difficulties, and they "closed upon" this solution by convincing themselves that they would be able to get to the bank, deposit additional funds in their accounts, and thereby avoid becoming dealt with as a check forger; or by persuading themselves that writing a check against insufficient funds was "not really crime" because "you can't kill anyone with a fountain pen."

What about "dependency" as an ingredient in check forgery? First, I have often heard probation officers offer the claim that many check forgers are dependent personalities who make excessive demands upon their time. Of course, it could well be that this conjecture by probation workers is incorrect. But some tangential evidence in support of it can be found in Lemert's (1962) inquiry into dependency as a predispositional factor in alcoholism. He studied a collection of alcoholic patients in a state mental hospital setting and found evidence favoring this contention in a sizable proportion of the cases he studied. The link between this research and Lemert's study of naïve check forgers is that a substantial number of the latter were persons whose social isolation was related to alcoholic behavior.

My argument is *not* that dependency has been shown to be causally related to check forgery; rather, this argument is simply an illustration of the kind of theorizing and research that is required if we are to learn more about the role of psychological patterns in lawbreaking.

Improvements in theory and innovations in research procedures are necessary if we are to make progress. For one thing, the search for psychological correlates of offender behavior calls for construction of research instruments specific to the hypotheses under study. In the past, researchers have often proceeded in an atheoretical fashion to administer a batch of personality tests to samples of offenders and nonoffenders in an attempt to discover significant differences between the two groups. However, a great many personality variations may have little or nothing to do with criminality/ noncriminality. For example, there is no readily apparent reason to suppose that a masculinity-femininity scale would differentiate between offenders and law-abiding citizens, or between types of lawbreakers. Masculinity-femininity is probably a personality dimension that is uncorrelated with criminality. To confirm specific psychological hypotheses, researchers must use instruments suitable to the formulation under investigation, and in a number of instances, we may need to develop those instruments because appropriate ones do not now exist.

### Process Psychology and Criminal Behavior

As I indicated earlier in this book, comprehensive analyses of criminality and crime causation in the form of textbooks and other publications have largely been the work of sociological criminologists. By contrast, the efforts of psychologists and psychiatrists have often appeared in more narrowly focused journal articles and the like, although the psychological literature includes psychiatric tomes such as Karl Menninger's (1968) *The Crime of Punishment,* along with a few psychological textbooks such as the one by Bartol and Bartol (1986).

A new contribution to the psychological literature appeared in 1992 in a book by Pallone and Hennessey, in which they presented what they termed a "process psychology analysis" of criminal behavior. Although the dust jacket declared that this book "is virtually unique in providing a comprehensive paradigm that fits across variant species of crime," its general thesis is relatively similar to the viewpoint expressed in the preceding paragraphs.

Pallone and Hennessey began by contrasting "process psychology" with two existing explanatory traditions. First, they labeled as differential psychology that perspective which assumes that variations among individuals result in differences in behavior between them. In the study of criminality, differential psychology is represented by that largely unfruitful tradition of searching for psychological traits that differentiate between those who violate the law and those who are conformists, and by the companion hypothesis that lawbreaking is commonly a response to psychopathological personality elements.

According to Pallone and Hennessey (1992: 4), there is another approach "which undergirds much of contemporary empirical sociology" and which assumes that behavioral variations are solely due to the different stimuli experienced by persons and not at all to "differences between behavers." In all likelihood, a considerable number of sociological criminologists would take issue with this characterization and would contend that they attend *both* to individual differences and to variations in social settings and social influences that also affect persons.

Having laid out these two polar positions, Pallone and Hennessey proceeded to identify the core assumptions of process psychology, namely that behavior, criminal or otherwise, is the result of *multivariate processes*, that is, a number of variables interacting with each other, rather than some single causal force or influence. Additionally, they contended that the process of "emitting" behavior, criminal or otherwise, involves *dynamic interaction* between the person and the environment, that is, personality elements such as tastes, dispositions, motives, and the like, along with the varied social influences that play upon individuals.

Pallone and Hennessey's framework differs from differential psychology in that it does not assume that psychological predispositions to behave always result in the same behavioral outcome. For example, while it might be possible to locate a collection of persons who exhibit some psychological characteristic in common, such as "risk aversion," "dependency," "taste for risk," or some other pattern, we should not expect to find that all of those who are characterized as "risk aversive," for example, act out that interest in the same way.

Pallone and Hennessey also disassociated themselves from that collection of psychologists and psychiatrists who have argued that lawbreaking is usually a symptom of personality pathology of one kind or another.

Although this social process theory was put forth in the technical language of social learning theory, the thrust of the argument can be stated simply. Pallone and Hennessey contended that four elements make up the process that precipitates criminal behavior: *inclination, opportunity, expectation of reward*, and *expectation of impunity*. In other words, crime occurs on the part of persons who are motivated in some way toward lawbreaking, who have opportunities to engage in crime, who anticipate rewards from misconduct, and who believe that they will "get away with it." Further, they asserted (Pallone and Hennessey, 1992: 24): "*For formally criminal behavior to be emitted, four process elements that interact with and potentiate each other in varying ways must be present and activated in the behavioral situation*" [emphasis in the original]. They offered a number of other assumptions about how these influences interact with each other, but it is less than certain that all of their assumptions are correct.

The first chapter of the Pallone and Hennessey book presented their "paradigm" for understanding criminal behavior. That chapter was followed by three additional ones dealing with conceptual, methodological, and operational constraints on the study of criminality. Chapters 5–8 dealt with various aspects of homicide, while Chapter 9 examined the evidence on larceny in order to determine the "fit" between their formulation and the data. The final chapter considered some refinements and applications of the process perspective.

There are a number of things to be said about this book. For one, the authors' discussion (Pallone and Hennessey, 1992: 137–204) of homicide included a review of an extensive body of evidence regarding neuropsychological factors in human violence, leading them to the conclusion that these biological and neurological influences play a major part in many instances of criminal homicide and/or assaultive conduct. Although sociological criminologists often find more congenial, those hypotheses that link violence to social influences of one kind or another, it would be difficult to dismiss this body of evidence reviewed by these authors. And, this seemingly impressive collection of biogenic findings presents a case in point of the problem identified at the beginning of this chapter, namely the challenge posed to sociological criminologists to become more knowledgeable and sophisticated about biological research findings.

Although there are other thought-provoking arguments in this book, there is less that is new or novel in it than is suggested by the dust jacket or implied by the authors. For one thing, while this process psychology framework *may* have the potential to illuminate a broad spectrum of forms of criminal behavior, the application of it was confined to homicide and larceny; thus its applicability to white-collar crime, sexual offenses, and myriad other kinds of lawbreaking remains to be demonstrated. On this same point, the marshaling of evidence on homicide and larceny serves more to illustrate the potential utility of the framework than it does to demonstrate the accuracy of it.

On this same point, while a large number of names appear in the book, the authors apparently were unaware of contributions by sociological criminologists who have already explored a number of the lines of explanation that appear within this perspective. For example, at one point (Pallone and Hennessey, 1992: 310–11), they commented on "kleptomania" and suggested that rather than being a compulsive crime arising out of psychopathology, many instances of shoplifting which have been labeled as "kleptomania" may be less senseless, purposeless, or irrational than that label would suggest. However, nowhere in this commentary was there any mention of Cressey's (1954) critique of the notion of compulsive crimes, in which he pointed out that labels such as "compulsive" or "kleptomania" are often assigned to instances of lawbreaking which are goal-directed and which make a good deal of sense to the actor but which are not understood by the observer.

An even more glaring omission from the book was any mention of Ronald Akers (1985) and his well-developed version of social learning theory. All of the key elements of this process psychology formulation can be found in his statement of social learning theory and in a form which is at least as precise as the argument of Pallone and Hennessey.

I do not mean to suggest that there is nothing of value in this process psychology exposition, and I have already suggested that the material on neuropsychological factors in agression warrants close study. A good deal of additional commentary in the book merits a close reading and serious consideration. However, I also agree with an assertion that appeared at the beginning of the book (Pallone and Hennessey, 1992: 2): "Formulation of a broad-gauged, widely applicable, and *scientifically-anchored* psychology of criminal behavior remains at a relatively-primitive stage" [emphasis in the original].

## CONCLUDING COMMENTS

Chapter 7 considered a number of approaches that have been taken by sociologists to account for the initial involvement in, or persistence in, criminal conduct by individuals. Chapter 8 continued that examination, looking first at the body of theory and evidence on biological factors in lawbreaking. The major conclusion from that discussion was that criminologists cannot continue to dispose of these inconvenient findings regarding sociobiological influences simply by poking holes in the methodology by which they were obtained. Instead, we are obliged to take the evidence seriously, which among other things means that most of us are going to have to become more literate and sophisticated regarding the sociobiological foundations of human behavior.

Another message contained in Chapter 8 is that even though most criminality is carried on by relatively normal individuals, some recognition must be given to the existence of pathological "monsters" within the offender population, that is, persons with idiosyncratic and disturbed personalities whose behavior is a reflection of abnormality. However, the largest share of this chapter centered on the large and complex issue of the extent to which individual differences in personality and psychological makeup interact with social influences and lead to lawbreaking on the part of some individuals.[6]

This chapter has tried to identify some key conceptual and theoretical issues that must be addressed if we are to arrive at more satisfactory answers to "Why do they do it?" questions.

To this point in this book, my concern has been principally with what I have termed "mainstream criminology," by which I mean the theorizing and research activities that are characteristic of the majority of persons who are engaged in the criminological enterprise. However, a number of scholars have expressed strong misgivings about mainstream criminological analysis and have advocated major shifts toward new perspectives and new ways of thinking about lawbreaking. Chapter 9 turns to these "new criminologies."

## NOTES

[1]On this point, I have been advised by a biologically oriented criminologist, Lee Ellis, that I should include a more comprehensive treatment of biosocial theories and research in my criminological writings. In a prepublication review of this book, Ellis commented that it shortchanges readers on many recent developments in biosocial approaches. One response to Ellis's criticism would be that the book is not intended as an undergraduate textbook and that a broad review and critique of biosocial theories and research would go beyond the stated purposes of the

book. But I also want to acknowledge Ellis's point that criminologists need to confront the evidence on sociobiological influences in lawbreaking.

In his communication to me, Ellis asserted that *arousal theory* is one of the most highly developed biosocial theories in the area of lawbreaking. Further, he offered this summary of arousal theory:

> Arousal theory contends that a substantial proportion of human behavior is oriented toward maintaining a preferred (or optimal) level of arousal. The theory also assumes that people's brains differ with respect to how much environmental stimulation they need to maintain an optimal arousal level.
>
> According to this theory, behavior patterns such as hyperactivity in childhood and sensation-seeking behavior later in life basically reflect attempts by people whose brains are getting insufficient stimulation to increase their stimulus input. These same brain-functioning patterns may affect the probability of criminality.
>
> Consider a model involving three hypothetical persons under normal environmental conditions. Person A feels "over-aroused," and thus would be rewarded for withdrawing to more secluded places (such as a quiet church service or the security of his or her home). Person B is representative of the majority of persons in society, who would usually feel comfortable under normal environmental conditions, and neither seek to increase or decrease his or her level of stimulation. Finally, person C should have an unusually high probability of being hyperactive. And in adolescence and adulthood, he or she should be motivated to frequently toy with new and potentially dangerous experiences, including the taking of substantial risks (e.g., gambling for high stakes), trying neurologically active drugs, and victimizing others.
>
> Arousal theory, of course, remains a theory in the sense that people's arousal levels cannot be directly observed. Nevertheless, it is consistent with evidence that childhood hyperactivity and conduct disorders are considerably more common among persons who later manifest high levels of delinquency and criminality. The theory is also consistent with evidence suggesting that criminals have slower average brain activity (beta waves) than persons in general.

My problem with this advice from Ellis regarding biosocial arguments generally and arousal theory specifically is that I am unprepared to offer an *informed judgment* about them. Moreover, I suspect that a large number of other criminologists would also be unable to make an informed judgment about the merits of various biosocial arguments and findings.

[2]Gagnon and Simon's book (1973) contained a large number of valuable insights and hypotheses regarding the major dimensions of sexual socialization.

[3]In the comments in this chapter, "individual differences" refer to personality characteristics that may be shared by a significant number of persons, but which separate them from others who do not exhibit those characteristics. In other words, "dependency" or other personality patterns may be common among a number of lawbreakers and less common among conformists. Also, this is what is usually meant by individual differences in most psychological discussions of these factors in criminality. The notion of individual differences does *not* refer to personality patterns that are unique to some specific individual.

[4]In this passage, the Gluecks were guilty of a common error of interpretation, in which findings showing differences between delinquents and nondelinquents in terms of the *numbers* of youths showing defiance, hostility, and the like were incorrectly stated in terms of *intensity*. The Rorschach results in their study only referred to the number of youths who exhibited particular patterns and not variations in the intensity with which they exhibited particular traits. Accordingly, the Gluecks were in error in asserting that their data showed that delinquents were "more assertive" or "more extroversive" than were the nonoffenders.

[5]In a recent discussion of personality factors and crime, Andrews and Wormith (1989: 297) argued that the Gluecks produced evidence that the effects of personality pathology on delinquency were relatively weak and that the personality variables that distinguish delinquents from nondelinquents were "not pathological traits but a lack of conscientiousness and a distinct taste for excitement . . . unreliability and carelessness . . . and nonsubmissive-

ness, defiance, and vivacity. . . .'' Although these were the characteristics that differentiated the two groups, the *conclusions* of the Gluecks do not seem to be accurately described by Andrews and Wormith.

[6]Blackburn's *The Psychology of Criminal Conduct* (1993) was published after this book had gone into production. Blackburn's book is intended for an audience of professional psychologists and advanced students. The book ranges over a number of topics, including the classification of offenders; social, economic, familial, and other correlates of lawbreaking; biological factors in criminality; individually oriented and integrated theories regarding criminality; personality attributes of offenders; aggressive and violent offenders; sexual deviation; and mental disorder and crime. Blackburn's book presents a wide-ranging, thorough, and incisive review and critique of the research literature on these topics. Additionally, many of his conclusions regarding personality factors in criminal conduct parallel those that are offered in this book. In short, Blackburn's book is an important recent contribution, particularly regarding biological and psychological factors in lawbreaking.

# CHAPTER 9

# The "New Criminologies"

## INTRODUCTION

Chapter 2 indicated that it is not possible to specify a precise date at which criminology was created and also that we cannot single out one person as its founder. But whatever one might designate as the beginning point of the criminological enterprise, Chapters 2 and 3 made it clear that additions to and alterations in criminological theory have been continuous from the early days of the field.

In the late 1800s and early 1900s, some American sociological criminologists advocated eclectic and atheoretical approaches to criminality, while others simply adopted the biological views of nineteenth-century European investigators. However, in the 1930s and 1940s, sociological perspectives and theories began to emerge, gradually replacing the relatively crude biological viewpoints. Chapter 3 indicated that a dramatic proliferation of theories about criminality and delinquency occurred in the period following World War II.

Nearly all of these theoretical contributions were predicated upon some shared assumptions about the real world, the pursuit of knowledge, and criminality. More specifically, most criminologists assumed that the world of experience is orderly and directly observable; that as trained observers, we can usually trust our perceptions regarding that world; and that it is possible to construct theories that accurately capture the causal dynamics behind criminality and other forms of social behavior.

There have been many twists and turns in criminological thought, particularly in recent decades. Some of the innovations in criminological theory have become incorporated into the mainstream, while other new viewpoints have faded away, but in either case, criminologists have rarely called their operating assumptions into question. Instead, they have concluded that human fallibility accounts for shifts in criminological viewpoints, in which a particular theory has arisen, enjoyed initial acceptance, and later has been declared to be defective. Put another way, most persons have concluded that advocates of rejected theories had erred in some way, either by incorrectly identifying the phenomena under scrutiny or by failing to collect and examine all of the relevant facts bearing upon the argument.

The rise and fall of social disorganization viewpoints in criminology is illustrative of such theoretical changes. Those arguments were common in the 1950s and centered on claims that American society was malintegrated and that crime and other forms of socially disapproved conduct were produced by this lack of societal coherence. However, the idea of social disorganization virtually disappeared in the decade that followed, being replaced by claims that stressed "differential social organization," that is, value pluralism and social conflict, as central to understanding of criminality in modern societies. Although one perspective was rejected in favor of a newer one, the underlying operating assumptions behind sociological inquiry were not challenged; instead, the social disorganization theorists were judged to have been mistaken in their observations.

Turning to the recent past, some new forms of criminological thought have arisen in the past decade. As we shall see as this chapter unfolds, some of these "new criminologies" are "newer" than others, in that some of them involve claims that are more at variance with mainstream criminology than do others. But even more important, these "new criminologies" are all predicated at least to some degree *on a different set of assumptions about reality, inquiry, and criminality than those that guide mainstream criminology*.

To this point, I have offered some brief remarks about the neopositivist assumptions behind mainstream criminological work. Before taking up the claims of the new, alternative criminological perspectives, a more detailed examination of these assumptions is in order so that we can contrast them with the alternative assumptions about reality and criminality upon which the newer views proceed.

## ONTOLOGY, EPISTEMOLOGY, AND MAINSTREAM CRIMINOLOGY

Most practicing criminologists go about their day-to-day work without giving much thought to the logical and philosophical assumptions that are basic to their endeavors. Philosophers of science are at home with strange-sounding words such as "ontology" and "epistemology," but most investigators of crime and criminal behavior probably feel uncomfortable with such terms and rarely think about the ontological and epistemological assumptions that undergird their work.

To what do these terms refer? *Webster's New World Dictionary* indicates that ontology is "the study or theory of the nature of being or reality," while epistemology is "the study or theory of the origin, nature, and limits of knowledge." Although these are reasonably clear definitions, they hardly capture the complexities that surround the discussions of ontology or epistemology in which philosophers of science engage. These matters can only be touched upon here, but let me try to capture some of the sense of these topics.

Philosophy has often been described, whether accurately or not, as a discipline that endeavors to address questions of the sort: "If a tree falls in the forest and no one is around, does it make a noise?"[1] Consider this query, for it provides a simple illustration both of ontological and of epistemological issues. Although most readers would probably be quick to assert that trees exist and that we know this to be true because we have all seen trees, other ontological possibilities can be entertained. Perhaps trees do not really exist; rather, it is only molecules that are real (or in the same way, perhaps "persons" do not really exist, only human cells do). Still another ontological position would be to argue that trees do not really exist at all.

Assume for a moment that we agree that trees are real, basing this agreement on the claim that we have all observed trees via sensory perceptions of sight, smell, or hearing. If so, what about the unobserved falling tree? Does it make a noise, absent an observer who can hear a noise? If our answer is "Yes," it is based on an epistemological position in which we assume, first, that our sensory observations are the bases on which we accumulate knowledge of reality, and second, that phenomena which have been consistently observed in the past can be assumed to occur again in the absence of direct witnesses.

In a brief comment in Chapter 1, I indicated that this book is "unabashedly neopositivist" in its orientation, and I also remarked that one of the identifying characteristics of neopositivism is the insistence upon clearly stated theoretical arguments. Let me add that, although I have no hard evidence on this point, my guess is that the majority of contemporary criminological investigators are exponents of neopositivism, whether they acknowledge that fact or not.

At least a few brief comments are in order regarding positivism and neopositivism. Like ontology and epistemology, positivism and other perspectives on scientific inquiry are difficult to describe in a few words or paragraphs. *Webster's New World Dictionary* offers this definition: "the system of philosophy of Auguste Comte, based solely on observable, scientific facts: it rejects speculation on ultimate origins." This is not very helpful unless one has already been introduced to the history of ideas and the philosophy of science. In particular, the definition immediately raises another thorny question: "What is an 'observable, scientific fact?' " Additionally, as Cohen (1989: 43) has indicated, "the term itself has a number of different usages ranging from an unanalyzed curse word to a name for a specifically defined philosophical position."[2]

The basic assumptions upon which positivism is based were enumerated many years ago by Lundberg (1939: 8–9; also see Lastrucci, 1963). Lundberg was one of the major spokespersons for positivism in sociology during the 1930–1950 period. According to him:

> The basic postulates regarding the nature of "reality" and "knowledge" upon which all sciences proceed may be briefly stated as follows:
>
> 1. All data or experience with which man can be concerned consists of *the responses of organisms-in-environment.* This includes the postulate of an external world and variations both in it and the responders to it.
> 2. Symbols, usually verbal, are invented to represent these responses.
> 3. These symbols are the immediate data of all communicable knowledge and therefore of all science.
> 4. All propositions or postulates regarding the more ultimate "realities" must always consist of inference, generalizations, or abstractions from these symbols and the responses which they represent.
> 5. These extrapolations are in turn represented symbolically, and we respond to them as we respond to other phenomena which evoke behavior.

Persons who adopt these postulates assume that a world exists apart from themselves. That reality includes other actors or persons. Individually and collectively, we "know" (learn about) the world through sensory observations or responses, which we communicate through shared symbols, usually in the form of written or spoken language. An additional assumption is that the world is relatively stable and unchanging; thus it is possible to obtain knowledge about it that is not simply ephemeral.

Although positivism is a notion that is laden with various meanings, most of those who have endeavored to identify its features have zeroed in on the use of objective evidence as central to it. Positivists insist that hypotheses and theories be tested through "facts," that is, carefully gathered observational evidence (Cohen, 1989: 43–46). Regarding criminological positivism, Hagan (1985: 89–90) has asserted that "the hallmark of criminological positivism is the formulation of predictive propositions, using data derived from efforts at the objective measurement of variables." In short, those who advocate a positivist approach in the social sciences, including the field of criminology, contend that we ought to adopt the objective procedures and practices that are followed in the basic or "hard" sciences.

Although the majority of American sociologists either became avowed positivists or at least engaged in activities that looked more or less positivist in nature in the decades preceding and following World War II, a significant number of "anti-positivists" also surfaced. Some of these persons rejected, in principle, the idea of social sciences based on the natural science model, arguing that social behavior cannot be studied by the methods of science. Others contended that even if these methods could be applied to the study of social behavior, they would yield only puny results. Positivists were also said to be guilty of crude operationalism, in which they claimed that concepts have no meaning apart from how they are measured. They were charged with uttering such nonsense as the claim that intelligence is whatever IQ tests measure or that income inequality is whatever the Gini coefficient measures.

Some of these critical observations about early positivism were valid ones. Some early positivists were insufficiently appreciative of the role of theory in the process of inquiry, and much of what passed for social research was relatively atheoretical. Some early positivists, including many who wanted to distance themselves from the "grand theorizing" represented particularly by the writings of Talcott Parsons, in which empirical evidence played little or no part, embraced an equally extreme position. Some of them operated as though theories are unnecessary, the business of social science is to go about "getting the facts," and facts will speak for themselves.[3]

In addition, some of the measurement-oriented early sociologists did seem insufficiently sensitive to the problems of measurement, a well-known one being the "words and deeds" issue. This term draws attention to the fact that persons who offer responses about their "attitudes" and the like on social survey instruments often behave in ways quite different from what "the data" suggest. For example, there is good reason to suspect that the extent of marital infidelity, recreational drug use, and other acts of "deviance" is far greater than what is revealed in surveys. Respondents are often either unable or unwilling to provide accurate information when responding to questionnaires or interviews. Finally, a closely related complaint about early positivists was that some of them appeared to dismiss as unimportant, those sociological variables that are difficult if not impossible to examine through "hard methodology."

I have already noted that Bernard Cohen (1989: 43) has indicated that positivism is sometimes used as an unanalyzed pejorative term. On this same point, Turner (1992: 1509) has contended: "Most frequently, at least within sociology, positivism is associated with such undesirable states as 'raw empiricism,' 'mindless quantification,' 'antihumanism,' 'legitimation of the status quo,' and 'scientific pretentiousness.' With few exceptions, sociologists are unwilling to label themselves as 'positivists.'"

Turner (1992: 1509–12) also noted that raw empiricism, mindless quantification, antihumanism, and the like were *not* ingredients of positivism as it was outlined by Comte; rather, he stressed the need for theories to guide research efforts to discover natural laws.

One does not have to search for long to find contemporary examples of mindless quantification in criminology, in which, for example, defective data are subjected to complex statistical manipulations that are not warranted with those data. Then, too, pretentiousness is not entirely absent from sociological and criminological writings. In short, positivists have sometimes deserved the criticisms that have been directed at them.

However, many modern-day positivists in criminology and sociology are better described as "neopositivists," in that many of them embrace a "soft" or modified position regarding epistemology and scientific inquiry. Neopositivists emphasize the continuous interplay of theory and research. They argue that explicit theories are required and that they must be subjected to empirical confirmation or disconfirmation. If the evidence fails to support our theoretical conjectures, we are obliged either to revise or to abandon those hypotheses, rather than jettisoning the uncomfortable facts.[4]

Modern-day neopositivists do not deny the existence of phenomena such as "attitudes," "motives," and the like that are not directly observable. Then, too, most of them concede that quantitative manipulation of statistical evidence is an appropriate methodological approach to some of the research questions we pose, but also that there are other phenomena that require the use of qualitative ("soft") methods.[5] The discussion of causal thinking and criminological analysis in Chapter 5 presented a fairly detailed characterization of neopositivist perspectives in criminology.

These remarks on ontology, epistemology, and neopositivism concern the working assumptions upon which contemporary, mainstream criminology proceeds. It is now time to move on to the "new criminologies," or what have also been lumped together under the umbrella of "critical criminology." But before doing so, let me make it clear that the remainder of this chapter ranges over a disparate collection of recent theorizing about crime and criminality. This material can be sorted into a few rough categories: left realism, feminist criminology, and peacemaking criminology. Some of these new arguments are relatively inchoate while others are more well-developed formulations (although none qualify as formal or semiformal theories). Additionally, some persons have asserted that these new variants of criminological thought, along with another that they have identified as poststructuralist criminology, make up a new paradigm that they have labeled as constitutive criminology.

Although there may be some connections between left realist notions and feminist criminology, DeKeseredy and Schwartz (1991) have argued that left realists are insufficiently attentive to feminist arguments. A final complication is that feminist criminology is not all of a single piece; rather, there are a number of versions of feminist thinking currently in criminology.

Many of the persons who are engaged in expounding one or another version of new criminology assert that their ideas are part of a larger intellectual development called postmodernism. Postmodernism itself is a term for a melange of themes, a number of which are stated in a conceptual language peculiar to postmodernists. Still, the starting point in this examination of the new criminologies should be with postmodern thought.


## POSTMODERN SOCIAL THEORY

Beginning in the 1950s, a number of sociologists and other social commentators began to argue that modern, industrialized and urbanized societies such as the United States had begun to move to another stage of development which they often termed *postindustrial society*. These persons pointed to important changes in technology and social organization, particularly computerization; the pronounced growth and influence of the mass media in modern societies; and the rise of an interrelated world system in place of relatively autonomous and independent society-states. Expansion of the welfare state and growing flaws in modern industrialization are other central features of this emerging pattern (Fiala, 1992). More recently, many of the discussions of the nature of and future of advanced industrial societies have centered on the broad idea of *postmodern society* . In turn, these analyses of postmodern society make up what has been termed *postmodern social theory* (Best and Kellner, 1991; Brannigan, 1992; Denzin, 1986).[6]

Although not of a single piece, postmodern social thought is largely the product of a collection of European sociologists and other intellectuals, including Michel Foucault, Gilles Deleuze, Felix Guattari, Jean Baudrillard, Jean-Francois Lyotard, and Frederic Jameson (Best and Kellner, 1991: 1–33). One thumbnail sketch of the major themes of these theorists has been offered by Fiala (1992: 1517), who argued that postmodern theory involves

> a view of postmodern society as a technologically sophisticated, high-speed society with access to vast amounts of information, and fascinated by consumer goods and media images. Mass consumption of goods and information is seen as facilitating a breakdown of hierarchies of taste and development of an explicit populism. Technology and speed blur lines separating reality from simulation on television, videos, movies, advertising, and computer models provide simulations of reality more real than reality. . . .

Norman Denzin (1986) has provided an explication of the major themes of postmodern social theory, in which he contrasted these arguments with the major ingredients of mainstream sociological theory work in contemporary American sociology. According to Denzin (1986: 194), mainstream theorizing has these characteristics:

> It is clear that large portions of the new theory work in American sociology share the following commitments: (1) a desire to conceptualize societies as totalities; (2) an attempt to wed the micro and macro levels of experience; (3)

an effort to form sociology into a science of society; (4) desire to speak to the conflict and crisis that appear in the post-or-late-capitalist societies. At the same time there is an undertheorizing of language, the human subject, the mass media, commodity relations in the consumer society, and the legitimation crisis surrounding science, knowledge and power in the modern world. These topics are the major problematics in postmodern social theory.

According to Denzin, postmodern social theorists eschew the search for grand-scale schemes which endeavor to conceptualize societies as totalities. They also contend that in the modern, media-dominated world, citizens often suffer from an "information overload" produced by the media, and in addition, much of that "information" is inauthentic or spurious. Those persons who occupy such positions as high-level administrators, heads of major corporations, national and state politicians, and heads of media agencies are engaged in the production of "knowledge" and representations of reality that are false. Denzin also indicated that postmodernists point to the demise of traditional "master narratives" ("metanarratives") in everyday life. Metanarratives refer to belief systems or assumptions regarding science, religion, politics, and art which have traditionally given meaning to people's lives. In particular, postmodernists reject traditional neopositivist assumptions that reality exists apart from the symbols by which it is described, that truth can be revealed through the senses, and that history is purposive and progressive. In short, postmodernists reject the neopositivist perspective which informs this book.

Faila (1992: 1517) offered much the same description of postmodern thought. He described postmodernism as an intellectual movement which views social and cultural reality, and the social sciences that endeavor to describe them, as "linguistic constructions." Put another way, postmodernism challenges the assumption that what is real can be separated from the symbols that convey it or from the activities of those who create these symbolic representations. This view rejects the idea that the symbolic characterizations of reality produced by social scientists are "privileged," that is, superior to the thoughtways of other citizens.

Much the same description of postmodernism was put forth by Best and Kellner (1991: 4–5), who asserted that

> postmodern theory provides a critique of representation and the modern belief that theory mirrors reality, taking instead "perspectivist" and "relativist" positions, that theories at best provide partial perspectives on their subjects, and that all cognitive representations of the world are historically and linguistically moderated. Some postmodern theory accordingly rejects the totalizing macroperspectives on society and history favored by modern theory in favor of microtheory and micropolitics. Postmodern theory also rejects modern assumptions of social coherence and notions of causality in favour of multiplicity, plurality, fragmentation, and indeterminacy. In addition, postmodern theory abandons the relational and unified subject postulated by

much modern theory in favour of a socially and linguistically decentered and fragmented subject.

In his essay, Denzin (1986: 203) came down on the side of postmodernists, arguing that sociologists (and criminologists) must take postmodernism and its attack on mainstream social theory seriously. He concluded:

> Theory and research must be fitted to the empirical situations of the postmodern period. Old social stratification paradigms, old theories of the family, of small groups, religion, education, science, urbanization, media, communications, demography, social organization, criminology and deviance must be rethought. These theories presumed structural causation models which could be fitted to theories of societies as totalities, which were functionally integrated at micro and macro levels.

Denzin's contention that postmodernist theories are required in criminology and deviance is clear enough. However, it is also clear that to date, no full-blown postmodern "paradigm" has emerged in criminology. Most contemporary criminological work, whether mainstream inquiry or radical-Marxist efforts, is based, at least loosely, on neopositivist foundations. But, there have been some recent developments in criminology which have been influenced, to some degree, by postmodernist thinking. "Constitutive criminology," to which I now turn, is one of these.

## POSTMODERN THEORY AND CONSTITUTIVE CRIMINOLOGY

As we have seen, neopositivists argue that knowledge of the world of reality comes from sensory observations, represented and communicated through symbolic means, usually in the form of written or spoken language. However, they do not argue that there is an inherent link between symbolic representations and the phenomena for which they stand. As the well-known popularizer of semantics, S. I. Hayakawa (1949) put it: "The word is not the thing." Further, neopositivists concede that symbolic representations of reality often turn out to be defective if not entirely false. On this point, there are probably few persons, neopositivists or otherwise, who would contend that the explanations offered by government officials, including former President Bush, for the war with Iraq should be given much credence. That conflict had more to do with threats posed by Saddam Hussein to American interests in low-cost and abundant supplies of oil than it had to do with freeing "the freedom-loving, democratic regime" in Kuwait from Saddam's "tyranny."

In the case of criminality, it is clear that there is something "out of whack" with mass media discussions and the comments of politicians regarding "the crime problem" in the United States. Much of this commentary centers on "career criminals," burglars, robbers, assaultists, and the like and ignores the existence of corporate criminality, much of which is much more serious than the "street crime" about which citizens are exercised.

There is also something "out of whack" with many contemporary criminological accounts of crime and its causes. For example, mainstream criminologists have often been oblivious to evidence indicating that women in American society are routinely subjected to myriad forms of sexual aggression directed at them, additional to forcible rape. In short, our theoretical formulations sometimes do not mirror reality. Mainstream criminologists assume that it is possible to correct these flawed representations and bring them into line with reality through the processes of scientific inquiry outlined in Chapter 5. However, this assumption has come under serious challenge in recent years from persons who have associated their views with the postmodernist intellectual movement.

### Critical Theory and Constitutive Criminology

*Critical Criminology.*  Chapter 3 drew attention to a number of attacks in the 1970s and 1980s upon mainstream criminology which were variously termed conflict, radical, Marxist, "new," and critical criminology. Although the writings of many of the critics shared a number of points in common, they also differed from each other in some important ways. Not all of these alternative perspectives were Marxist in character, and in particular, much of what was called critical criminology was only loosely tied to Marxist theory.[7] Moreover, while the advocates of Marxist criminology have fallen relatively silent in recent years, critical criminology continues to attract the attention of a number of criminologists.

What is critical criminology? Pepinsky (1983: 324) provided the following characterization:

> *Critical* is a term originally applied to members of the Frankfurt school of social thought, which arose in the 1930s. . . . Critical criminologists seek to expose and explain popular and legal myths about crime and crime control. Much of their work suggests that crime and punishment are born of self-serving myths perpetuated by officials, the wealthy, and the powerful—myths born of economic and political selfishness.

A sizable body of theorizing, in the broad sense, has accumulated in recent years and can be identified as critical criminology, but this work does not form a coherent whole, that is, a shared body of broad propositions or generalizations and supporting evidence. Instead, critical criminology is an intellectual posture around which a variety of criminological endeavors have been pursued. However, Henry and Milovanovic (1991) have endeavored to draw the fragments of critical criminology together and to synthesize them into what they referred to as *constitutive criminology*. Their proposals warrant our attention.

*Constitutive Criminology.*   Henry and Milovanovic began with the claim that critical criminology currently involves several new, competing perspectives: left realism, socialist-feminist, peacemaking, and poststructuralist criminologies. They also argued that a "paradigm crisis" in critical criminology may develop if the advocates of these competing perspectives continue to engage in internecine warfare. Accordingly, they contended that if this paradigm crisis is to be avoided, common elements of the four perspectives must be identified as the basis upon which a unified critical paradigm can be built. The label they chose for this core of common themes was constitutive criminology. In turn, they (1991: 294–95) identified the following four themes as making up this core:

> These themes are: (1) the codetermination of crime and human subjects through crime control ideology and how this ideology has the capacity to reproduce and transform; (2) discursive practices as the medium for the structuring of crime and its control institutions; (3) symbolic violence as the hidden ideological dimension of legal domination; and (4) the use, by control agencies, of sense data to construct meaning that claims space and displaces the intersubjective construction of meaning and, through this process sustains control institutions as relatively autonomous structures.

The preceding quote may strike some readers as "heavy going," that is, statements that are difficult to understand due to a number of unfamiliar words and phrases. Like much other writing in the critical genre, this essay employs terms such as "transpraxis" and the like which are peculiar to critical thought. While Henry and Milovanovic would probably argue that this unfamiliar terminology is indispensable to communication of their ideas, I have endeavored to capture the essence of their views in more familiar language in my summary of them which follows.

When they spoke of codetermination of crime and human subjects through ideology, Henry and Milovanovic meant that human agents (persons) are the basic elements of "social structure" and that they create the latter through human interaction. In the case of lawbreaking and responses to it, it is persons who have created our conceptions of "crime" (and "noncrime"); crime control institutions such as the police, the legal codes, the judicial system; and the correctional machinery that processes "criminals." In turn, once a particular set of structural arrangements becomes crystallized, it is sustained through "discursive practices" (language) which determine the images of "reality" that are entertained by newer members of society. For example, in the current social climate of the United States, most citizens have become prisoners of the imagery of "the crime problem" constructed by the authorities and the media. As a result, few common citizens are able to "see" as part of the crime problem, various harmful, crimelike forms of behavior such as employer negligence leading to industrial accidents or deaths. Similarly, crime control efforts have become dominated by "lock 'em up" sentiments, resulting in the highest prison incarceration rate in the world, and most citizens (and many criminologists) find it difficult if not impossible to visualize other approaches which might replace incarceration.

One part of these observations about the codetermination of crime and human subjects centered on what Henry and Milovanovic called "transpraxis." If it is the case that social arrangements, including beliefs and ideology about crime and its control, are produced by human interactions, it is presumably also true that new structures and beliefs—a new "reality"— can also be created by human agents. "Praxis" is the term that is often employed to refer to the use of knowledge in order to create new social arrangements, but Henry and Milovanovic (1991: 295–99) argued that it ought to be jettisoned in favor of "transpraxis," a richer term which alerts us to the complex and varied relationships between purposive human actions and their outcomes.

The thrust of this commentary was that efforts to challenge and alter current social arrangements often have the unintended effect of preserving the status quo. For example, attacks upon jails because of the squalid conditions that have often characterized them may lead to some improvements in jail conditions, but if so, these may strengthen, rather than undermine, public support for the use of jails.

The other side of this coin is that in some instances, state efforts to support and affirm the status quo may backfire, resulting in the undermining of current arrangements. For example, Henry and Milovanovic argued that the effect of governmental efforts to control economic patterns falling outside the national tax accounting system, by labeling them as the "hidden" or "underground" economy and by identifying those who are involved in these patterns as "criminals" or other nefarious creatures, may be to draw attention to rewards of these activities, thereby attracting new recruits to them. Similarly, the "Just say No" anti-drug campaign of Nancy Reagan may have induced some youngsters to just say "Yes!"

The concluding comment of Henry and Milovanovic (1991: 298) on transpraxis is worth repeating:

> Thus, the more state agencies elaborate their control talk, and the more people experience the different reality of relations subject to control, the more contempt accrues to the controllers and their control institutions. As a result, people begin to question other distinctions, such as those between theft and the legitimate acquisition of property, between honesty and dishonesty, between street crime and white-collar crime, and between hard and soft drugs. Such questioning, stemming from the attempts of control institutions to con-

trol, actually undermines that which the controls were designed to protect: the existing relations of production and the moral and social order.

Much of what has been said to this point regarding constitutive criminology has directed attention to "discursive practices," in which human actors create their views of reality, in which others challenge portions of that reality, and in which still others endeavor to create new views of what is possible in social relations. By discursive practices, Henry and Milovanovic (1991: 299–302) referred to processes through which persons make sense out of the myriad sense impressions and social experiences they encounter, by sorting them out into shared experiences and capturing them in verbal pictures. One illustrative case in point reported by Cicourel (1968) had to do with the ways in which juvenile justice system employees arrive at typifications and diagnoses of the juveniles they encounter, identifying some of them as "serious cases" and others as petty offenders. Another illustration is Van Maanen's (1978) report on how street police officers sort out citizens as "assholes," "suspicious persons," and "know nothings." The role of language and discursive practices was described by Henry and Milovanovic (1991: 299) in the following terms: "Social structures are the categories used to classify the events that they allegedly represent. As such, they are strengthened by routine construction in everyday life and by activity organized in relation to them, as though they were concrete entities." Henry and Milovanovic contended that the symbolic representations or word pictures of "reality" that become dominant within a society at any point in time largely determine how individuals will relate to the events that surround them, what they will think about them, and how they will talk about them. These discursively constructed "social structures" thus become strengthened through repeated use in everyday life.

When they spoke of symbolic violence as the hidden ideological dimension of legal domination, Henry and Milovanovic (1991: 299–302) highlighted the fact that the behavior of members of a society is channeled and controlled as much or more by the ideologies or belief systems that characterize that society to which they belong as it is by the criminal laws and the criminal justice system. Furthermore, "informal social control" of various kinds does not stand apart from "law"; rather, these are interrelated aspects of the same phenomenon. For example, when citizens refrain from "stealing" the property of others, it is in large part because they have been induced to accept the prevailing cultural or ideological views which sanctify ownership of private property. Then, too, when persons are arrested for stealing or other acts which violate formal or statutory laws, some of them may assert that they are innocent of the charges, but few of them endeavor to challenge the legitimacy of the criminal justice system which will process them because they have been socialized to accept the ideology of "the rule of law."

Finally, Henry and Milovanovic's (1991: 305–7) comments about the use, by control agents, of sense data to construct meaning dealt with the increasing influence of agencies of social control over the discursive activities which produce the "narrative constructions" (characterizations of "reality") that dominate and control the lives of citizens.

Let us examine Henry and Milovanovic's (1991: 307–8) comments:

> Constitutive criminology . . . is the framework for reconnecting crime and its control with the society from which it is conceptually and institutionally constructed by human agents. Through it criminologists are able to recognize, as a fundamental assumption, that crime is both *in* and *of* society. Our position calls for an abandoning of the futile search for the causes of crime because that simply elaborates the dimensions that maintain crime as a separate reality while failing to address how it is that crime is constituted as part of society. . . .
>
> A direct consequence of such an approach is that any "rehabilitation" from crime requires that criminologists and practitioners alike deconstruct crime as a separate entity, cease recording it, stop dramatizing it, withdraw energy from it, deny its status as an independent entity. [emphasis in the original]

What should we say about these recommendations? First, it is hard to quarrel with the contention that greater recognition be paid to the fact that crime is not some kind of aberrant activity that arises outside of the social forces and influences that create socially approved kinds of conduct. Henry and Milovanovic's claim that crime is both in and of society is valid.

The summary comments by these authors with respect to the future of criminology were not entirely clear. They appeared to call for the abandonment of criminology, but at the same time, they spoke about the shape of future criminology. What Henry and Milovanovic apparently favor is a drastically redesigned field which has been termed "peacemaking criminology" (Pepinsky and Quinney, 1991). I want to postpone the discussion of peacemaking criminology until later in this chapter, after having examined feminist and realist perspectives.

## FEMINIST THEORY IN CRIMINOLOGY

The first order of business in a discussion of feminist theory in criminology is to specify the meaning of the term *feminism*. Tuchman (1992: 695) has offered the following definition: "The term *feminist theory* is an invention of the academic branch of the mid- and late twentieth century feminist movement. It refers to generating systematic ideas that define women's place in society and culture, including the depiction of women—large questions indeed." In their discussion of feminist criminology, Gelsthorpe and Morris (1988: 94) began by noting that while there is no single agreed-upon definition of feminism, "the essence of feminist perspectives is that they reflect the view that women experience subordination on the basis of their sex."

### Pre-Feminist Theory

If feminist theory has only recently arisen, how have criminologists in the past dealt with crime on the part of women?[8] As a number of persons have indicated, women have been virtually invisible in criminological analysis until recently and much theorizing has proceeded as though criminality is restricted to men (Gelsthorpe and Morris, 1988). At the same time, it is possible to identify a number of early figures in the development of criminology or sociology, including Lombroso, W. I. Thomas, Freud, Kingsley Davis, and Otto Pollak, who put forth explanations for the low rates of lawbreaking on the part of women and hypotheses about the causes of criminality among females.

Feminist critics of this early theorizing (Klein, 1973) have pointed out that the central thesis running throughout it was that female offenders were biologically or psychologically flawed persons; thus their criminality was linked to individual defects and little or no recognition was given to social-structural factors that might account for low rates of participation in crime or for the criminal acts of those females who did engage in lawbreaking.

This sort of analysis continued well into the 1950s and 1960s. For example, virtually no mention of women and crime was made in the three editions (1948, 1955, 1962) of Cavan's criminology textbook, one of the first written by a woman. By contrast, Mabel Elliott (1952: 199–255) devoted two chapters to female offenders in her book, but her exposition was in no way a forerunner of feminist theorizing on crime. She contended that men and women live in different "worlds," that the average woman is more gullible and naïve than the average man, that women experience less frustration over failure to reach life goals than do men, and that women spend most of their lives in devoted service to their families, from which they receive emotional nurturance. This argument presumably addresses the question of why most women do *not* commit crimes, while the explanation for those who do violate the law was (Elliott, 1952: 227) that "the average woman offender is actually a rather pathetic creature, a victim of circumstances, exploitation, and her own poor judgment."

Some sociologically more sophisticated analyses of female crime began to appear in the last two or three decades, including Hoffman-Bustamente's (1973) argument that female crime is related to different sex-role expectations for men versus women and also to sex-related socialization differences, sex-related crime opportunities, access to deviant subcultures, and sex differences built into crime categories. Harris (1977) also put forth an argument regarding sex differences in lawbreaking, centered on the different sex-role expectations for men versus women in American society. Then, too, a number of sociological commentators (Simon, 1975; Adler, 1975; Steffensmeier, 1978) endeavored to make sense of the dramatic increases in crime rates for women since about 1960 in the United States. However, these contributions were not markedly oriented toward feminist theory.[9]

### Feminist Theory in Criminology

I have said nothing so far about the defining characteristics of feminist criminology. Broadly speaking, feminist perspectives probe the historical roots and contemporary forms of gender inequalities. Feminists argue that modern societies are heavily androcentric—that is, male-dominated. Male power over women leads to myriad forms of sexual discrimination, ranging from gross and blatant to more subtle forms of exploitation. Also, male domination means that only male thoughtways count; women's ideas and activities are ignored or treated as unimportant. Finally, feminist scholarship has a praxis side, for feminists are concerned about identifying the sources and forms of sexism so that these might ultimately be eradicated. Feminist criminology probes the role of gender inequality in crime. It is *not* concerned solely with female lawbreakers; rather, it asks how gender inequality is implicated in the crimes of *both* males and females and in the different responses that are directed at male or female offenders.[10]

Detailed explications of the current state of feminist theory in criminology have been provided by Gelsthorpe and Morris (1988) and also by Simpson (1989) and Daly and Chesney-Lind (1988). The discussion that follows draws heavily upon the latter two sources.

Simpson (1989: 606) offered a definition of feminism that parallels the ones I have just outlined:

> Feminism is best understood as both a world view and a social movement that encompasses assumptions and beliefs about the origins and consequences of gendered social organization as well as strategic directions and actions for social change. As such, feminism is both analytic and empirical. In its incipient form, feminist research almost exclusively focused on women—as a way of placing women at the center of inquiry and building a base of knowledge. As it has matured, feminism has become more encompassing, taking into account the gendered understanding of all aspects of human culture and relationships.

Daly and Chesney-Lind (1988: 2) put forth a similar description:

> A major element of feminist thought centers on how gender constructs— the network of behaviors and identities associated with masculinity and femininity—are socially constructed from relations of dominance and inequality between men and women. Different natures, different talents, and interests that define Western notions of manhood and womanhood rest on a string of male-centered oppositions to and negations of woman and femininity. Masculinity and men are not only defined as not-feminine, but also superior to femininity and women.

Simpson and Daly and Chesney-Lind were also quick to point out that feminism is not a single theory or perspective (also see Gelsthorpe and Morris, 1988). Simpson took note of *liberal feminism*, in which sexual inequality is viewed as amenable to eradication. By contrast, *socialist feminism* holds that gender inequality and gender oppression are central features of capitalist societies and can be overcome only by constructing a completely different society. Finally, *radical feminism* asserts that patriarchy and subordination of women are linked to male aggression and control of women's sexuality. The political agenda of radical feminists emphasizes elimination of compulsory heterosexism, in which women in male-dominated societies are compelled to restrict their sexual interests to heterosexuality and to conform in other ways to male-defined conceptions of the proper role of women in society, including narrow notions about how they should accommodate themselves to the nuclear family and child rearing.

Daly and Chesney-Lind's categories were slightly different. They included *traditional* nonfeminist views of women and their place in society. More important, they argued that *Marxist feminism*, which stresses class relations as the basis of gender inequality, should be distinguished from *radical feminism*, which emphasizes male domination, male aggression, and patriarchy. Finally, *socialist feminism* combines elements of both the Marxist and radical feminist perspectives.[11]

No complete version of feminist analysis of crime and crime control has yet been developed, but there have been some important steps taken toward a comprehensive feminist perspective in recent years. For example, Messerschmidt (1986) has produced both a critique of Marxist feminist writings and a replacement perspective, which he termed a socialist feminist one. In brief, he contended that the modern system of corporate capitalism involves two core elements. The first, the *relations of production*, is the economic system of production that gives rise to class relations and exploitation of workers by owners, while the second, the *relations of reproduction*, are the ways in which persons organize their activities so as to reproduce, socialize, and maintain the species. According to Messerschmidt, in contemporary American society, relations of production take the form of *patriarchal gender relations*—that is, social arrangements in which males appropriate the labor power of females and control their sexuality. Messerschmidt then applied this argument to various pieces of criminological evidence.

I identified a number of other recent feminist-inspired contributions to the criminological literature in another work (Gibbons, 1992a: 383–87). These building blocks are accumulating at an accelerating rate, particularly in the form of research studies such as Boritch's (1992) of gender differences in criminal court dispositions from about 1870 to 1920 in a Canadian jurisdiction.

In their review of developments in feminist criminology in Britain, Gelsthorpe and Morris (1988) asserted that the impact of feminist thinking, particularly upon male criminologists, had been relatively slight. They noted a number of recent instances of theorizing in which gender was not considered and in which the authors wrote as though crime on the part of women, the superordinate position of males, and related matters were unimportant. Even in those instances in which mention was made of female offenders or of public and justice system responses to them, much of the analysis was superficial; thus women were discussed in a "by the way" fashion or as an afterthought. Gelsthorpe and Morris's review suggested that the process of "bringing gender in" to criminology may be a protracted one. Even so, I agree with Beirne and Messerschmidt (1991: 525), who argued: "Feminist criminology, though relatively new, has made significant contributions to the field of criminology, and will continue to flourish in the future. Its criticisms of the gender bias in criminological theory are of major importance, and must be taken seriously."

## REALIST CRIMINOLOGY

Chapter 3 noted that the "vulgar" or "one-dimensional," instrumental Marxist criminology of the 1960s and 1970s eventually became toned down and gave way to a more structural version of Marxist analysis. In Great Britain, some erstwhile radical criminologists began to articulate a new view of the crime problem, labeling it as left realism or realist criminology (Matthews and Young, 1986; Kinsey, Lea, and Young, 1986; Lowman and MacLean, 1992). I indicated in another work (Gibbons, 1992a: 132):

> Exponents of realist criminology have moved away from romantic portrayals of ordinary offenders and have acknowledged that the earlier versions of radical thought overemphasized the crimes of the socially powerful. They have reasserted the seriousness of street crime and have conceded that social consensus on a core group of criminal laws does exist in Great Britain. Realist criminology also calls for greater citizen-police involvement in crime control; some of the more strident attacks on the police that characterized earlier radical thought have been toned down. Finally, these newer ideas of radical-Marxist theorists have had the effect of blurring many of the distinctions between this group and mainstream and liberal criminologists.

Beirne and Messerschmidt (1991: 498–501) have provided an account of left realist arguments (for a parallel description, see DeKeseredy and Schwartz, 1991: 156). They pointed out that some realist criminologists put forth a "straw person" to attack when they began their work with a critique of "left idealism." Some realist criminologists contended that the unnamed advocates of left idealism were of the view that economic deprivation, principally unemployment, drives people into crime and that conventional criminals are social rebels, not "real criminals." Left idealists claimed that it is members of the ruling class who are the "real criminals," so said the critics. Beirne and Messerschmidt correctly noted that while some early radical theorists did put forth romanticized descriptions of conventional criminals, converting them from "bad guys" into "noble ruffians," later ventures into radical criminology eschewed this view of street criminals as primitive rebels and as potential revolutionaries.

Beirne and Messerschmidt indicated that although left realists do not entirely ignore the crimes of the powerful, they devote most of their attention to conventional crime and assert that "we must take crime seriously." Realist criminologists reject the overly simple view that absolute economic deprivation, for example poverty, is the driving force behind conventional crime and the companion view that "garden-variety" offenders are social rebels. Instead, they suggest that these lawbreakers are motivated by feelings of relative deprivation and also by selfish, reactionary, and individualistic motives. Moreover, these offenders engage in unlawful acts that inflict serious economic and/or psychological pain upon members of their own communities.

Realist criminologists also argue that street crime is a serious problem for the working class for reasons additional to the costs to the victimized individual. Areas that are riddled with predatory street crimes and endemic violence become characterized by sundered community ties, making it difficult for the local residents to "fight back."

Because they view conventional crime as serious and threatening to community values, realist criminologists contend that crime control also must be "taken seriously." They argue that even though the machinery of the state exists in considerable part to serve ruling class interests, it can be harnessed to inaugurate effective programs of crime control. They also suggest that, among other things, these programs should emphasize *demarginalization*, that is, such measures as restitution, community service, and other sanctions that would serve to reintegrate offenders back into the community, rather than converting them into pariahs and driving them further into persistent lawbreaking. In this same vein, realist criminologists argue for minimum use of prisons, so that penal institutions would be employed only for extremely dangerous individuals.

Beirne and Messerschmidt also noted that left realists argue that realism about the police is in order. While the police must be reformed, they are essential to the maintenance of a civil society. Police organizations must be shifted away from the "crime fighter–crime control" model in which they engage in reactive law enforcement and in which they are distanced from the communities they police. A community policing model is required, in which the members of local communities would participate in establishing goals and priorities for the police and in supervision and control of police agencies.

Beirne and Messerschmidt (1991: 501) concluded that "what left realists have essentially accomplished is an attempt to theorize about conventional crime realistically while simultaneously developing a 'radical law and order' program for curbing such behavior."

I have a few remarks to add to these of Beirne and Messerschmidt. First, realist criminologists have added some innovations to criminological research, particularly in the form of local crime surveys, such as the one in Islington, an inner borough of London, which have enriched our knowledge about crime patterns in local neighborhoods. Second, the realist criminology literature has continued to grow and includes both elaborations upon the arguments sketched above and critiques of realist notions as well (Young and Matthews, 1992; Matthews and Young, 1992; Lowman and MacLean, 1992).[12] Even so, left realism can best be described as a general perspective centered on injunctions to "take crime seriously" and to "take crime control seriously" rather than as a well-developed criminological perspective. It would be incorrect to contend that realist criminology is simply "old wine in new bottles," but much of what passes for realist theorizing is paralleled in viewpoints that are fairly common among mainstream criminologists. For one thing, many of the contentions about crime and its causes that appear in the left realist literature are little different from the claims of many mainstream criminologists. On this same point, one of the architects of realist criminology, Jock Young (1992), has outlined a realist approach for local criminal justice policy which, among other things, argues for a multiagency approach to crime control and for new styles of policing. In short, this brand of "new criminology" turns out not to be particularly new or novel. Finally, it is not entirely clear as to how realist criminology qualifies as one of the "saplings of critical growth," as claimed by Henry and Milovanovic (1991: 294).

## PEACEMAKING CRIMINOLOGY

Peacemaking criminology, the last version of new criminology to be considered, was alluded to earlier in this chapter. To what does this term refer? One answer is that peacemaking criminology is a humanistic approach to crime and control of crime. *Webster's New World Dictionary* offers several definitions of humanism, one of which is "any system of thought or action concerned with the interests and ideals of people." This definition comes closest to identifying the nature of a humanistic or peacemaking criminology. In everyday usage, humanism often refers to a religious movement adhered to by persons who reject conventional notions of a Supreme Being but who at the same time argue that we should behave in accordance with the values and ideals that are embodied in the Christian tradition. In an anthology of essays on peacemaking criminology, two leading figures in this development, Harold Pepinsky and Richard Quinney (1991: ix) have declared that peacemaking criminology is "a criminology that seeks to alleviate suffering and thereby reduce crime."

In the writings of peacemaking criminologists, and particularly in the hortatory essays which endeavor to state the case for peacemaking, such as Quinney's (1991) opening chapter in the Pepinsky and Quinney anthology, much is made of human suffering, not only that which is caused by the criminal acts of lawbreakers, but also that which is experienced by those law violators. Unlike much contemporary analysis on the part of conservative commentators, in which "garden-variety" criminals in particular are denounced and calls for ever more repressive actions directed at them are voiced, peacemaking criminologists argue that although we are obliged to reject offensive behavior, we should not reject the perpetrator; instead, we should endeavor to bring the person back into the community.

In the concluding essay in the Pepinsky and Quinney book, Pepinsky (1991: 299) claimed that the essays in the anthology, and presumably the peacemaking movement in general, are anchored in three traditions: religious, feminist, and peacemaking.

I have already taken note of the humanist thrust of peacemaking criminology. When they turn attention to causal analysis, peacemaking criminologists probe the interconnections between the economy; economic and political domination of the powerless by the powerful; the criminalization of some kinds of harmful behaviors at the same time that other, more injurious acts are ignored; the involvement of persons in these activities; and the responses of the authorities to those acts that have been defined as "crimes."

Peacemaking criminology is derivative of critical analysis. The pain and suffering about which peacemakers speak includes the suffering experienced both by law violators and by those against whom they offend. It also includes economic suffering, in which a favored few citizens are able to amass immense wealth at the same time that large numbers of other citizens are homeless, unemployed or underemployed, and often deprived of basic human rights. Citizens also suffer at the hands of corporations such as automobile companies that produce cars or trucks which explode in a ball of flames in collisions, due to design defects in their fuel systems; pharmaceutical companies that charge outrageously inflated prices for drugs; and various other corporations that are engaged in unethical or immoral conduct. Women experience myriad kinds of suffering in modern, patriarchal societies in which they are under the domination of males, such that women "don't count." This litany of forms of pain and suffering could be extended much further, but the basic point is that peacemaking criminologists, like other critical commentators, view all of them as interrelated consequences of the modern capitalist, patriarchal social order.

The most distinctive feature of peacemaking criminology is its nonviolent but fundamentally radical advocacy of a dramatically altered social order, in which injustice, pain, suffering, and alienation would be replaced by a just system, alleviation of pain and suffering, and a new sense of community and interrelatedness among citizens. One of the many consequences of peacemaking would be a drastic reduction in suffering in the form of criminality and victimization.

The proposals of peacemaking criminologists have something in common with the diagnoses of the ills of American society that have been made by Bellah, et al. (1985), who have urged Americans to rediscover the community bonds that united citizens in the early 1800s in this country. Then, too, although he did not identify himself with the peacemaking movement, Braithwaite (1989b) has offered crime control recommendations that center on the need for a greater sense of communitarianism, that is, enhanced ties and linkages among citizens. Communitarianism, in turn, might lead to reintegration of offenders rather than further stigmatization of them.

Doubtless many criminologists would agree with the peacemaking thesis that American social policies toward crime control have been dominated in the past two or three decades by harshly punitive sentiments and that new and less punitive approaches are urgently needed. Then, too, many criminologists would probably concur with Elliott Currie's (1985: 276) call for new directions in crime reduction of a more global form, including the following efforts:

> Substantial, *permanent* public or public-private job creation in local communities, at wages sufficient to support a family breadwinner, especially in areas of clear and pressing social need like public safety, rehabilitation, child care, and family support.
> Universal—and generous—income support for families headed by individuals outside the paid labor force.

However, skepticism is also in order regarding proposals for massive restructuring of modern societies. On the one hand, the representative sample of essays in the Pepinsky and Quinney volume does suggest that modest steps toward a more humane society and more positive approaches to lawbreaking, in the form of reductions of sexual violence and other forms of abuse of women, alterations in the severity of incarceration, and wider use of mediation strategies in the criminal justice machinery, are possible. But massive overhaul of American society is another matter. Many persons would argue that the huge federal deficit, runaway entitlement program costs, and a host of other problems plaguing the economy and society make it almost impossible to restructure the social order. On this point, both Currie's book and the Pepinsky and Quinney volume have little to say about *how* the grand-scale changes they propose might be achieved.

## CONCLUDING COMMENTS

Only a few brief remarks are needed in order to bring this chapter to a close. The chapter began with the ontological and epistemological assumptions behind neopositivism, which is the orientation to knowledge and inquiry upon which most mainstream criminology is based. Most of the chapter was devoted to "the new criminologies." Postmodern social theory, to which constitutive criminology is related, was discussed, as was constitutive criminology. My judgment is that the latter is unlikely to revolutionize the field, although some of the insights that have been offered by critical criminologists are likely to be co-opted by mainstream theorists. We also examined feminist criminology, which is a perspective that has already had an important impact upon criminology and which seems likely to continue to be of influence. We also examined realist criminology, which turned out to be less new than advertised. Finally, peacemaking criminology was discussed briefly.

Chapter 10 moves on to consider some other recent developments in criminology, in which efforts have been made to develop theoretical statements that integrate a number of independent lines of theory or in which criminologists have endeavored to develop a general theory which can be applied to a variety of forms of lawbreaking.

## NOTES

[1] Actor-comedian Steve Martin captured lay notions about philosophy on one of his comedy records when he reported that he had taken a philosophy course as a college undergraduate, in which he (and other students) learned "just enough to screw you up for the rest of your life." Additionally, he asserted that in philosophy courses, students grapple with such questions as whether the Pope defecates in the woods!

[2] A brief but thoughtful discussion of positivist and neopositivist viewpoints in the social sciences can be found in Cohen (1989: 43–46). A detailed discussion of positivism in criminology can be found in Hagan (1985: 75–92).

[3] A relevant example in criminology is Calvin F. Schmid's (1960) research on crime rates and urban areas, in which he correlated a large number of social and economic variables in Seattle census tracts with arrest rates for various crimes in those same areas. Although the findings that came from the study were of considerable value to criminologists, this research was not informed either by an explicit ecological theory regarding urban social structure or by any explicit version of criminological theory. It is worth noting that after having obtained "the facts" regarding crime rates and census tract characteristics, Schmid added an ex post facto "theory" or interpretation of the results to his research report.

[4] Several decades ago, I devoted a good deal of effort to creation of offender typologies (Gibbons, 1965). These descriptions of alleged offender "types" were constructed from a variety of materials, including a relatively limited body of research evidence. Some years later, the emergence of a larger collection of data on offender patterns, much of which was mentioned in Chapter 4, led me to voice a number of reservations about the accuracy of many typological claims (Gibbons, 1975, 1985). Interestingly, on a number of occasions, criminologists have expressed the view that I had exhibited extraordinary candor in recanting some of my earlier views! But it has always seemed to me that we are obliged to reject questionable theories rather than uncomfortable data!

[5]In the 1960s, a new variety of sociology appeared upon the scene, called, somewhat misleadingly, ethnomethodology. Heritage (1992: 588) has indicated that "ethnomethodology is a field of sociology that studies the common-sense resources, procedures, and practices through which the members of a culture produce and recognize mutually intelligible objects, events, and courses of action." In other words, ethnomethodology examines the ways in which lay citizens "make sense" out of the world around them, by creating shared rules and interpretations of behavior so as to be able to carry on organized social life. Many of these rules are implicit and unverbalized; thus persons are often unaware of them or that others share the same viewpoints. A well-known ethnomethodological study in criminology is Cicourel's (1968) probing of the social organization of juvenile justice. He looked at the practices of police officers, probation officers, and juvenile court officials as they went about processing their juvenile charges. Cicourel reported that these officials went about their business, employing a lay theory that identifies the delinquencies of youths from underprivileged social and/or familial backgrounds as more serious than those of middle-class youngsters. This lay theory led them to engage in practices that run counter to the official ideology and policies of the juvenile justice system.

Ethnomethodologists sometimes suggested that their approach and the insights it produced represent a serious challenge to the kind of neopositivist sociology and criminology I have described here. It can be argued that ethnomethodologists made an important contribution to the discipline by reminding us that the people we study may often have a different view of the world than we assume in our theorizing. Moreover, that point has become acknowledged by most mainstream sociologists, as has the corollary that qualitative research methods may be required in order to probe many of the specific research questions posed by persons of an ethnomethodological persuasion.

[6]Postmodernism is also an intellectual movement that has influenced modern art and architecture.

[7]I refer to certain theories as Marxist because that is how they were labeled by their creators. As I noted in Chapter 3, one of the points of contention between radical-Marxist criminologists and their critics was on the extent to which these arguments were truly derivative of or based upon principles of Marxist thought as developed by Marx himself.

[8]I have reviewed both the early and the modern theoretical and research literature on female criminality in Gibbons, 1992a: 363–90.

[9]Leonard's (1982) book on women and crime is a transitional work. She produced a critique of contemporary theories concerning female crime. She contended that Simon's (1975) book contained only a superficial review of causal theories. She also argued that Adler's (1975) thesis about the new woman criminal was unsupported by firm evidence. She conceded that sex-role arguments provide insights into female crime but claimed that they are limited because they ignore the structural origins of sex-role inequality and the inferior status of women in historical or cultural terms. She also scrutinized anomie theory and found it deficient as an explanation of women's crime. She concluded that labeling notions are incomplete because they fail to attend to social-structural factors in the social position of women in contemporary society. Differential association was also criticized for its failure to deal with fundamental differences in the situation of men and women. Subcultural theory received poor marks as an explanation of crime among women, as did radical-Marxist theorizing. Leonard concluded that these theories cannot simply be modified slightly in order to deal with female criminality; instead, a truly feminist theory of crime is required. Although she argued for the development of a feminist criminology, she presented only a brief sketch of what that criminology might look like.

[10]Actually, it would be more accurate to argue, as did Gelsthorpe and Morris (1988) that feminist criminology *should* center on inquiry into the role of gender in crime and responses to it. They correctly point out that mainstream and feminist criminologists alike have rarely dealt in depth with male needs, masculinity issues, and the like when theorizing about male criminality. I share their implicit conclusion that in the long run, criminology ought to be an enterprise in which gender relationships are fully and thoroughly explored and examined.

[11]Some comments are in order regarding the methodology of feminist scholarship—that is, the procedures that are used in order to examine patriarchal relations, male oppression, and the like. Is it true, as some persons have hinted, that feminists engage in an inferior form of scholarship that produces biased, subjective, or erroneous claims? Do feminists prefer "soft" research procedures? Are these methods incompatible with those used by other scholars?

Feminism is not a single strain of thought, and there is no single feminist methodology. Some feminists have suggested that radical and subjective methods must be employed in feminist work. However, many feminists, as well as other social scientists who do not regard themselves as feminists, are committed to the pursuit of knowledge through a natural science model. They endeavor to probe the nature of the world through objective methods of observation. They acknowledge that there are special problems in the study of social behavior in that the observers are participants in the societies they endeavor to study; thus objectivity is difficult to achieve. Researchers do sometimes inject their own biases into their work and thus do not "see" social phenomena entirely accurately.

Feminists have highlighted an additional problem that is particularly acute in the social sciences. Most social scientists, including sociologists and criminologists, have traditionally been males living in an androcentric world and sharing the same biases regarding women's worlds and lives as do other men. They have unwittingly created theorizing from which women are absent. Many of these formulations which ignore women are distorted portrayals of the real world. Feminist theories endeavor to "bring women back in" and to correct the androcentric biases of mainstream social science.

In the view of feminist scholars, feminist social science is no more subjective than is male-dominated inquiry. Most of them agree that the ultimate test of feminist hypotheses should be an empirical one. Many feminists opt for an objective science stance, which implies that trained researchers, whether male or female, are capable of observing the manifestations and consequences of gender inequality. Further, feminist scholars sometimes engage in quantitative studies employing "hard data" gathered through social surveys or similar techniques. However, they do often argue that in order to probe many aspects of women's existence, qualitative procedures and direct observations are required. For example, one cannot learn much about how women perceive and deal with spouse abuse from arrest statistics. Instead, the investigator needs to talk directly to abused women, perhaps while living with some of them in a shelter for battered women. This view, that research methods should be appropriate to the problem being attacked, is widely shared among social scientists. In short, feminist methods of investigation are not unique to feminism, nor is feminist scholarship inferior to other versions of inquiry. It is certainly true that some criminological theories and research studies are superior to others. Some criminologists carry out careful, high-powered studies; others do shoddy work, misinterpret results, and write badly. There is "good" and "bad" criminology. Some bad criminology is produced by feminists, some by nonfeminists, but there is no basis for claiming that bad scholarship is more common among the former than the latter.

[12]DeKeseredy and Schwartz (1991: 156–57) have indicated that the criticisms of left realism include the charge that left realists have not addressed the power of police subcultures to undermine progressive reform. Also, left realists have been criticized for a failure to take elite deviance seriously, for defects in their views of race-crime linkages, and for putting forth overly simplified crime control proposals. Finally, left realists have been charged by their most severe critics with accommodating, rather than attacking, the draconian social control measures that were employed by the Thatcher government.

# The Prospects for General and Integrated Theories

## INTRODUCTION*

A number of persons in recent years have bemoaned the lack of theory development in criminology (e.g., Meier, 1980; Braithwaite, 1989a). But as we have seen, there is currently a good deal of interest within criminology in "theory work," that is, construction of causal generalizations and research scrutiny of them. In particular, there has been considerable attention directed at the development of general theories and/or integrated theoretical perspectives.

This chapter asks "Are general and/or integrated theories regarding criminality or delinquency possible?"[1] It is concerned with *etiological* or *causal* formulations, as contrasted with deterrence, the social functions of jails and/or prisons, the social origins of criminal laws, and various other topics that occupy the attention of some criminologists. "Theory work" having to do with explanation of criminality is *the* central task of the criminological enterprise.[2] (To reiterate, by theory work I mean *both* the formulation of theories and the research scrutiny of them.)

Why are criminologists trying to create general theories or integrated theoretical statements? In the case of general theories, a number of persons

*This chapter is an expanded version of "Talking About Crime: Observations on the Prospects for Causal Theory in Criminology," in *Criminal Justice Bulletin*, Sam Houston State University, 1992b.

appear to believe that greater criminological progress is likely if we manage to develop a "central notion" which can provide coherence to our endeavors. This view closely parallels Gibbs's (1989) advocacy of "control" as a central notion around which sociological inquiry might be structured.

Proponents of general theories sometimes point to the "natural science model" of physics and to relativity theory, which guides the work of physicists, as suggesting directions that ought to be pursued by sociology and criminology. Clearly, criminology is not now characterized by a central notion or organizing paradigm which is embraced by the majority of scholars in this field.

The arguments in favor of integrated theories are straightforward. Some have contended that the situation in criminology (including the study of delinquency) is similar to that of the blind persons touching an elephant, with each observer reporting upon different parts of the beast. Just as a more accurate description of the elephant would result from the pooled observations of all the blind individuals, a larger "bang for the buck" might come from an integrated causal theory than from various individual formulations, each of which accounts for only a portion of the variance in lawbreaking and conforming conduct. For example, this argument underpinned Johnson's (1979) integrated theory of delinquency. He argued:

> Each orientation has pinpointed certain processes that play a role in generating delinquent behavior. The either/or approach of many researchers is rejected in favor of drawing together the most useful and empirically tenable features of these major theories, incorporating them into a coherent conception of delinquency causation to be represented in a causal model, and testing the empirical tenability of the resulting model.

Are general and/or integrated theories possible? The answer depends in considerable measure on the standards by which theories are to be judged. If one is unconcerned about the *structural* and/or *empirical* adequacy of formulations, the response is obviously "Yes." However, if one takes the position that criminologists must endeavor to develop conceptually and structurally rigorous theories, the task of constructing general theories may be considerably more difficult.

Chapter 5 commented on the structural forms of criminological theorizing, drawing on Gibbs's (1972) discussions of discursive and formal theory, and arguing, as he did, that criminologists and sociologists ought to endeavor to construct rigorous theoretical statements to replace the relatively fuzzy and ambiguous ones that often pass for theory in criminology.

Chapter 5 also sorted out a number of criminological arguments into four broad categories: general perspectives, discursive theories, semiformal theories, and formal theories, although the latter category had no entries in it!

The idea of general theory is not an entirely recent one; instead, criminology has long had a surfeit of discursive, relatively broad-ranging perspectives which some persons have labeled as theories. Consider some of these "classic" arguments. Merton's (1938) anomie formulation about the origins of forms of deviant conduct was a general perspective, as were "social disorganization" views that were popular in the 1950s (e.g., Faris, 1955). Carr's (1950) argument about various causes of delinquency, Reckless's (1973) "containment theory," and Sutherland's (1947) differential association perspective are examples of somewhat more well-structured formulations.[3]

Some of the more recent ventures of criminologists toward general and/or integrated theories, such as those of Braithwaite (1989b) and Gottfredson and Hirschi (1990) are more tightly structured than were the statements of Merton, Sutherland, and others. However, as we shall see, criminologists have not yet managed to articulate a large collection of relatively formalized arguments of a general or integrated kind.

To this point, I have spoken of general and/or integrated theories as though these terms are well understood and clearly agreed upon. But in fact, considerable disagreement exists regarding these labels. Accordingly, let us examine the lay of the land regarding the various meanings of "general theory."

## SOME DEFINITIONAL OBSERVATIONS

Consider the expositions by Braithwaite (1989b) and by Gottfredson and Hirschi (1990). In the preface (p. vii) to his book, Braithwaite declared that it presents a general theory, although he also indicated that he was aware of "the need for theories of particular types of crime to complement the general theory." Along the same line, he asserted (p. 1) that "one should not be overly optimistic about a general theory which sets out to explain all types of crime." Finally, at an early point (pp. 4–5), he indicated that his intent was not to put the torch to existing theories; rather, he declared that he sees "enormous scope for integrating some of the major theoretical traditions ..." and indeed, much of the remainder of the book was given over to a conceptual blending of concepts from these traditions with his own ideas about the role of shaming and reintegration in shaping criminal pathways.

However, the major point regarding Braithwaite's book is that it did not specify the elements that identify general theories. By general theory, he apparently had in mind some kind of multivariate formulation that applies to a "significant portion" of the offender population, but not necessarily to all of it. Put another way, he apparently would argue that generality is a matter of degree. If an argument applies to a significant chunk of the lawbreaker population, it is a general theory, but if it applies only to rapists, murderers, or some other small subgroup, it is low on generality.

Turning to Gottfredson and Hirschi's *A General Theory of Crime* (1990), these authors also provided no explicit discussion of the identifying marks of a general theory. On the other hand, they asserted at various places that most (how many?) crimes require little skill and are mundane and rational and deliberate acts. They also devoted considerable space (pp. 1–44) to outlining the characteristics of "ordinary crime(s)," asserting that white-collar offenses, homicides, burglaries, and various other offenses are all relatively similar in nature; that is, they claimed that thefts, white-collar offenses, and other violations all share features in common and moreover, the persons who carry out these acts exhibit a good many shared characteristics. The Gottfredson and Hirschi general theory runs in this direction:

> Crime involves the pursuit of immediate pleasure. It follows that people lacking self-control will also tend to pursue immediate pleasures that are *not* criminal: they will tend to smoke, drink, use drugs, gamble, have children out of wedlock, and engage in illicit sex. (p. 90)

Although this thesis is by no means as simple as it might appear to be, it is a different kind of general argument than the one by Braithwaite. It is general in that it asserts that various forms of deviant conduct have much in common and that persons who lack self-control are most likely to engage in deviance. Absent from it is the appreciation of other causal factors that characterizes the Braithwaite argument.

### Tittle's Views on General Theory

One detailed discussion of issues of general theory in criminology has been provided by Tittle (1985). He began with a distinction between an "explanation" and a "theory." According to Tittle (pp. 93–95), an explanation attempts to make sense of observations regarding some specific phenomenon such as burglary, while a theory "on the other hand, is a system of interrelated ideas that answers, *for more than one phenomenon*, the question of why/how in a *general, abstract* manner" [emphasis in the original]. Regarding general theories, he argued that "although the 'generalness' of theories is really a continuous rather than a discrete characteristic, the term 'general theory' will be used here to denote a scheme of highly abstract generality designed to account for an *entire domain* of phenomena such as all individual criminal (or socially disapproved) behavior or all variations in the content of criminal laws (or patterns of social disapproval), but it will not be used to signify attempts to account for all criminological phenomena in all domains." These definitions and distinctions paralleled the implicit ones in the Braithwaite and Gottfredson and Hirschi books.

After establishing some metes and bounds around the notion of general theory, Tittle addressed the question of whether the quest for general theories is a viable endeavor. He reviewed five instances of what he termed "futilitarianism," that is, objections to the goal of general theory. One of these is that the subject matter of criminology is ambiguous, due to the relativity of laws, owing to their variability over time and from place to place. A second objection is the alleged heterogeneity of lawbreaking, which requires that separate explanations be devised for the different groupings of crimes or criminals of which this heterogeneous subject matter is composed.

A third contention regarding the futility of general theory efforts is an ethnomethodological one, to wit, that crime-related social processes are situationally problematic rather than recurrent, orderly, and concrete. As a result, we cannot generalize about them within the framework of a general theory which is based on assumptions that criminal acts, causes of lawbreaking, and responses to criminality are objective and predictable social facts.

Still another argument is that crime-related phenomena are produced by myriad and diverse factors; thus broad generalizations about causal patterns cannot be constructed. Finally, Tittle commented upon the claim that past efforts at general theory have failed; thus there is little reason to suppose that such endeavors will pay off in the future.

After presenting these views, Tittle then offered an "optimistic rebuttal" to them. His counter arguments are not easily captured in a few paragraphs, but a brief summary of his rebuttal follows.

Regarding subject-matter ambiguity, Tittle's principal contention was that the variability of legal codes over time and from place to place can be overcome if we go about developing theories dealing with human killing, for example, in which both legal and illegal homicides would be addressed. One task would identify the circumstances under which homicidal acts are likely or unlikely to be criminalized. As Tittle put it (p. 104), we should "treat crime-relevant activities as foci for testing and expanding theories about human behavior," with criminal acts being defined not as unique, but rather, as interesting variations. He also pointed out that ambiguity, orderliness, predictability, and other alleged characteristics are not inherent in social phenomena; instead, they are in the eyes of the beholder insofar as conceptualization and theorizing make sense of what would otherwise be an unstable, disorderly, ambiguous, or unpredictable world.

Tittle's reply to the heterogeneity-uniqueness attack paralleled some of the preceding comments. No two car thefts (or car thieves) are identical in all respects, nor are any two instances of any other act precisely identical. But many of these distinctions do not make a difference. It is possible to focus on common elements in car thefts, to ignore slight variations among them, and to develop accounts that provide an explanation for the acts that have been brought together under a conceptual umbrella.

Tittle conceded that ethnomethodologists have performed a service by drawing attention to the problematic nature of aspects of criminality and responses to it, but he also argued that much of their work actually highlights the *orderliness* or *predictability* of behavior. He also noted that while legal labels such as "rape" are attached to some instances of sexual conduct and withheld from other, similar ones, due to interpretive activities that intervene between the sexual activities and the labeling of them, criminologists are still free to theorize about socially disapproved forms of sexual conduct, including both the labeled and the unlabeled instances.

Tittle's rebuttal to the complexity charge was a standard one, holding that instances of some phenomenon of interest do not have to be identical in all particulars for us to theorize about their causes. Indeed, it is a central task of theorizing to identify common causal elements in different instances of criminality. Thus, while we may acknowledge that no two cases of homicide are identical, we may hypothesize that they are all attributable to some general variable such as "interpersonal insecurity," or that different instances of car theft are related to "marginality" and/or "problems of masculine identity" (Gibbons, 1966).

Tittle was not impressed by the argument that because ventures in general theory have not been successful in the past, they are not likely to succeed in the future. He argued that considerable progress has already been made in the direction of broader and more powerful theories, and additionally, he offered the theoretical integration argument that we may be able to obtain a "bigger bang for the buck" by amalgamating different lines of theory into a more general one. As one case in point, he argued that (pp. 113–14) "while neither the differential association nor the social bond system of thought is by itself a general theory . . . a general theory that accounts for criminal behavior by spelling out the interconnections among motivations, constraint, opportunities, and abilities will probably include these two formulations. . . ."

While he spoke optimistically about the prospects for theoretical gains through integrative efforts, Tittle also remarked (p. 114) that current attempts along these lines "have done little more than identify variables or processes that may be operative." I will turn to these recent integrative ventures shortly.

Tittle's essay contained additional advice and commentary about prospects and strategies for general theory. In his view, if we are to succeed in developing more general theories, we will need to emphasize abstract categorization and generalization; develop hierarchical formulations that tie various factors or variables into sophisticated accounts of causal processes; and finally, generate closer interactions between theory development and research scrutiny of the products.

Tittle also argued that the main business of criminology ought to be *collective* theory work, rather than activism, applied research, or other secondary tasks. By collective work, he meant that the field must find ways to reward persons for building upon the efforts of others, rather than implicitly encouraging them to savage the existing body of theory prior to setting out some new argument. Finally, Tittle argued that criminologists need to devote more attention to speaking and writing clearly and precisely, rather than spinning out still more dense, murky, ambiguous versions of discursive theory that will further clutter the field.

### Other Considerations

Chapter 5 indicated that the distinction made by Cressey (1960) between causal accounts focused on epidemiology and those centered on individual conduct is an important one. I borrowed this distinction (Gibbons, 1992a) and renamed the two problems as those of social structure and crime ("the rates question") and the origins and development of criminal acts and careers ("the Why do they do it" question). While some theoretical statements have paid attention jointly to social-structural factors and crime rates and to the process by which individuals get involved in lawbreaking, many criminological formulations have focused on one or the other but not both of these matters.[4] Accordingly, it makes sense to sort out theories in terms of the explanatory level at which they are pitched.

I have already noted that there has been a good deal of recent commentary having to do with general theory and/or integration of different lines of argument into a single explanatory perspective. As indicated above, Tittle's arguments also suggested that the most powerful general theories are likely to be those that are integrated ones.

Integrated-general theory can be treated as one cell in a fourfold table of theory types, or an $n$ by $n$ table if finer distinctions are made along two classificatory dimensions. This fourfold table would sort theories out as specific or general and as integrated or unintegrated. Braithwaite's (1989b) theory is a general and integrated argument, while the Gottfredson and Hirschi (1990) formulation is a general one which emphasizes lack of self-control to the exclusion of other variables; thus it is not an integrated argument. Baron and Straus's (1990) theory of forcible rape, which marries gender inequality, pornography readership, social disorganization, and "cultural spillover" arguments is a specific, integrated argument. Finally, income inequality and predatory crime formulations would be entries in the nongeneral (specific) and nonintegrated cell of this table.

One of Tittle's suggestions was that criminologists might profitably consider a strategy of developing general theories through placing some kinds of crime, such as white-collar business offenses or forcible rape, into broader theories dealing with business behavior or socially disapproved sexual conduct. However, efforts to date have all been centered on crime or delinquency rather than on more catholic groupings of phenomena. Tittle also provided a sound rebuttal to "futilitarian" views which deny the possibility of viable general theory. But while the idea of general theory cannot be rejected on logical grounds, as the saying goes, "the proof of the pudding is in the eating."[5] General and/or integrated theories may be achievable in principle but not in fact. Let us turn to what have been the results of efforts made to date in these directions.

## THEORETICAL INTEGRATION IN CRIMINOLOGY[6]

The current embarrassment of riches in the form of a large body of criminological "bits and pieces," that is, research findings that are unconnected to an overall theoretical structure or framework, has led some criminologists to conclude that it may be time to bring order to the field by drawing related lines of theory and/or research evidence together.

The idea of theoretical integration is commonsensically plausible. Such efforts might help us make sense of the existing evidence and might point to linkages between theoretical arguments that have not heretofore been apparent. Then, too, integrative efforts might generate new hypotheses and research findings. All of this is consistent with familiar notions about scientific progress occurring through the development of new "paradigms" and the interplay of theory and research. Let us look at the attempts that have been made to combine elements of different theoretical frameworks into an integrated perspective, beginning with those dealing with delinquency and followed by integrated theories regarding adult criminality.

### Integrated Theories of Delinquency

Attempts to account for juvenile delinquency have taken a number of directions. Marvin Krohn and I (1991) sorted these into biogenic and psychogenic formulations, social disorganization and social control perspectives, social status and opportunity arguments, and cultural values and social learning theories. The evidence indicates that each of them may have some contribution to make in explaining delinquency (Gibbons and Krohn, 1991; Empey, 1982; Quay, 1987); thus, some have concluded that a theory which combines elements from these specific arguments may do a better job of accounting for delinquency than will any single one of them.

One of the most ambitious integrative efforts was by Colvin and Pauly (1983: 513), who tried to construct "a comprehensive theoretical approach to understanding the social production of serious patterned delinquent behavior." They began with a critique of learning formulations, control theory, and other etiological perspectives, followed by the presentation of their own theory. Their integrative argument was a structural-Marxist one centered on the following proposition (Colvin and Pauly, 1983: 515): "This entire process of delinquency production is comprehended as a latent outcome of the reproduction of capitalist relations of production and the class structure." Krohn and I (1991: 162) have provided the following summary of their argument:

They argue that the power relations to which most lower-class workers are subject are coercive. The coercive social milieu in which the workers exist reduces their capacity as parents to deal with their children in anything other than a repressive fashion. In turn, this harsh, punitive environment hinders the bond that children form with their parents. In addition to the quality of the affective relationships between parents and the children being poorer, children also become less interested in those activities deemed important by their parents, e.g., school. Hence the general social bond is weakened and delinquent behavior becomes a likely outcome.

The Colvin and Pauly theory was painted in broad strokes and involved at least some propositions of debatable accuracy. For example, one claim centered on the deleterious effects of tracking experiences upon school children, but the evidence on the negative impact of these experiences is not entirely clear. Also, theirs was a discursive theory, rich in texture and filled with details from other lines of discursive theory on which it drew, such as compliance theory, structural Marxism, and the like. While it was "provocative" and "insightful," if judged by the criterion of theoretical rigor, the argument leaves something to be desired. Research designed to test the argument has produced mixed results (Messner and Krohn, 1990).

Johnson's (1979) integration of delinquency theories was less global. It involved the following factors: social class, family experiences, perceptions of future opportunities, delinquent associates, delinquent values, and deterrence (perceptions of risks of being apprehended for delinquent acts) which he brought together into an integrated path analytic model. This model identified a number of independent "paths" or causal sequences, involving different combinations of influences that were hypothesized to be linked to delinquent conduct. Johnson's research provided mixed support for his argument.

The integrative effort by Elliott, Ageton, and Canter (1979) linked social learning/differential association, control theory, and strain arguments into a single, relatively complex argument. Elliott and his associates also conducted a large-scale study of delinquency and drug use which employed this integrated theory as its theoretical framework (Elliott, Huizinga, and Ageton, 1985).

Although the assumption that theoretical integration will account for more of the variance in delinquency sounds reasonable, it does not have unanimous support. Hirschi (1979) has pointed out that theories can be integrated by placing them "side by side," "up and down," or by stringing them "end to end" in a hypothesized causal sequence, which is the form of the Johnson and the Elliott, Ageton, and Canter formulations. He also quarreled with Elliott over the issue of whether "the predictor variables of the last theory in the sequence absorb all of the predictive power of those theories located earlier in the sequence" (Elliott, 1985: 132). He voiced his preference for a strategy in which theories are placed in *opposition* to each other, rather than being amalgamated or integrated, claiming that we would be well advised to develop individual theories; to spell out all of the connections of the major variables in them to other, related influences; to identify ways in which they differ from competing arguments; and then to subject each of them to research test.

The thrust of Hirschi's comments was that theoretical integrations muddy the empirical waters and make it more, rather than less, difficult to disentangle causal influences and to identify the differential contribution that each of them makes to the behavioral outcome, delinquency. Finally, Hirschi (1987) reviewed the findings of Elliott, Huizinga, and Ageton (1985) and concluded that they did not provide much empirical support for the integrated theory that drove the study.

### Integrated Theories of Adult Criminality

The preceding remarks suggest that integration of delinquency theories is no small task. If so, one might wonder whether parallel formulations about adult criminality are possible at all, in that juvenile lawbreaking is considerably more homogeneous than is adult criminality. However, attempts at conceptual and theoretical integration regarding adult crime arguments have been made, including one by Pearson and Weiner (1985).

Pearson and Weiner began by surveying criminology journals and concluded that the most frequently mentioned theories were social learning, differential association, negative labeling, social control, deterrence, economic factors, routine activities, neutralization, relative deprivation, strain, normative (cultural) conflict, Marxist–critical-group conflict, and generalized strain and normative conflict.

This curious list mixed together explanatory perspectives that differ widely in the scope of what they endeavor to explain. For example, the routine activities approach speaks mainly about predatory property crimes, while differential association was proposed as an explanation for all forms of crime. Additionally, this inventory threw formulations intended to account for lawbreaking conduct of individuals into a porridge with perspectives that deal with crime rates and social-structural sources of criminality. Pearson and Weiner made no attempt to evaluate the degree of empirical support for the various theories that were to be integrated, with the result that one might wonder about the quality of the product when empirically shaky arguments are integrated with others which have considerable empirical support.

Pearson and Weiner's integration translated concepts from various theories into a common vocabulary, rather than combining different propositions into a single theory. For example, they asserted that many of the terms of differential association theory have analogs in other formulations.

Conceptual integration requires that one first settle upon a set of concepts with which others are to be "integrated." Pearson and Weiner used an operant conditioning framework, employing such terms as behavior, utilities, utility demand, and discriminative stimuli, which also included a place for rule-governed behavior that has been shaped by earlier contingency-shaped learning. Pearson and Weiner (1985: 122) summarized their integrative perspective in the following way:

> Six ideas developed above form the basis of the integrative framework: (1) utility demand, (2) behavioral skill, (3) signs of favorable opportunities (discriminative stimuli), (4) behavioral resources, (5) rules of expedience, and (6) rules of morality. These factors are antecedent, causal factors. Two kinds of antecedent factors may be distinguished: those that are internal to the person (*i.e.*, utility demand, behavioral skill, rules of expedience, and rules of morality) and those that are external (signs of favorable opportunities, behavioral resources).

There was little that was novel about this argument with which Pearson and Weiner began, but the plot thickened in their elaboration of it. They presented a graphic version labeled as a dynamic model of micro-level factors influencing the probability of criminal behavior, complete with pseudo-mathematical notation, along with narrative statements such as (Pearson and Weiner, 1985: 123) "the probability of apprehension and processing by the cjs (criminal justice system) $(K_2)$ is denoted by $Q_j$, while the probability of not being apprehended by the cjs is $1-Q_j$." They also offered a number of claims about "vectors," but they used this term much more loosely than is done in mathematics, where it has a relatively precise and quantitative interpretation.[7]

Because their social learning framework was a psychological and social-psychological one, focused on the individual level, Pearson and Weiner added constructs of "*social structural production and distribution of* (1) utilities, (2) opportunities, (3) rules of morality and expedience, and (4) beliefs about sanctioning practices" [emphasis in the original] to it in order to take account of macro-level causal theories. This resulted in a number of pedestrian observations such as (Pearson and Weiner, 1985: 125): "Crimes, particularly acquisitive property offenses, most likely will be committed where valued utilities are both located (target attractiveness) and most easily secured illegally (target vulnerability)" and also: "Behavior is partly dependent upon the legitimate role and status *opportunities* available to the individual. These opportunities are not distributed equally across all structural locations" [emphasis in the original]. At another point, they (Pearson and Weiner, 1985: 126) observed: "Suppose that a person loses a job and subsequently suffers a substantial decline in income. The resulting income deprivation should create an increased monetary utility demand."

This conceptual integration consisted, in part, of a table in which the "integrative concepts" were arranged along one axis and the various criminological theories that were to be integrated were listed along the other.

The cells were filled with check marks showing where various concepts from differential association or other theories were "mapped into" the integrative concepts. The other part involved narrative remarks which endeavored to justify the various check marks.

"Mapping" of concepts referred to a relatively arbitrary process of shoehorning concepts into spaces in a summary table. It is likely that many criminologists would take issue with a number of these mappings. For example, consider the treatment of Sutherland's theory of differential association. Pearson and Weiner (1985: 130–33) concluded that his assertions (Sutherland, Cressey, and Luckenbill, 1992: 90) that "the process of learning criminal behavior . . . involves all of the mechanisms that are involved in any other learning . . ." and that "criminal behavior is an expression of general needs and values . . ." represent an alternative way of speaking of utility demand, overlooking the fact that these were disclaimers about factors seen by Sutherland as *peripheral,* rather than core ingredients of the theory. Along the same line, they contended that "definitions favorable to the violation of the legal codes" are equivalent to rationalizations, or what they also called rules of expedience, but they missed entirely his argument that definitions *precede* criminal acts, unlike "rationalizations," which are exculpatory defenses of one's conduct invoked *after the fact.* Then, too, Sutherland's dimensions along which differential associations vary, namely, intensity, frequency, duration, and priority, were not mentioned by Pearson and Weiner. Sutherland has been dead for forty years; thus we cannot ask him whether this "integration" preserves the sense of his theory, but there is ample basis for doubt on this score.

Similar problems run throughout this entire "mapping" exercise. For example, Pearson and Weiner claimed that Hirschi's (1969) control theory dimensions of attachment, commitment, involvement, and belief could be assigned to their categories such as rules of expedience, but this does violence to control theory.

What is the message from this effort at conceptual integration? It is that there is little to be gained from exercises which merely attempt to reconcile a number of mushy and poorly defined concepts from one perspective with those of another.

Consider another integrated and general theory, presented in Wilson and Herrnstein's *Crime and Human Nature* (1985). These authors articulated what they termed a "comprehensive theory of crime" and also reviewed the evidence bearing upon it.

The book title implies that it contains a theory of lawbreaking in all of its forms, but it was actually restricted to persons who engage in "aggressive, violent, or larcenous behavior" or to individuals who "hit, rape, murder, steal, and threaten" (p. 22). Missing entirely was any mention of insider traders, violators of occupational safety regulations, plunderers of savings and loans, or other white-collar offenders; organized crime figures; political criminals; and various other kinds of criminality and criminals. Further, their contention that offenders often exhibit mesomorphic bodily structure, somewhat lower intelligence than their noncriminal peers, and impulsivity and other psychological traits that free them from restraint against lawbreaking probably has little applicability to Ivan Boesky, Don Dixon, Charles Keating, and other criminals of that ilk.

Wilson and Herrnstein's (1985: 41–66) theory of criminal behavior was an eclectic, social learning–behavioral choice formulation. The sense of it is conveyed in the following passage (Wilson and Herrnstein, 1985: 61):

> The larger the ratio of rewards (material and nonmaterial) of noncrime to the rewards (material and nonmaterial) of crime, the weaker the tendency to commit crimes. The bite of conscience, the approval of peers, and any sense of inequity will increase or decrease the total value of crime; the opinions of family, friends, and employers are important benefits of noncrime, as is the desire to avoid the penalties that can be imposed by the criminal justice system. The strength of any reward declines with time, but people differ in the rate at which they discount the future. The strength of a given reward is also affected by the supply of reinforcers.

The chapter in which they offered their theory included a number of graphs filled with pseudomathematical formulas, while the appendix (pp. 531–35) presented what they referred to as the full mathematical version of the theory. However, there were no *values* assigned to any of the symbols and equations; thus the argument has the appearance but not the substance of precision.

As Gibbs (1985b) has pointed out, most of Wilson and Herrnstein's claims about linkages between impulsivity, low intelligence, hereditary factors, family and school experiences, the effects of the mass media, and other variables were stated discursively. Given the imprecision of the argument, as well as the equivocal or incomplete nature of much of the criminological evidence, it is little wonder that reviewers have produced widely varying assessments of this book (Cohen, 1987; Sarri, 1987; Gibbons, 1987; Schrag, 1987; Kamin, 1986; Gibbs, 1985b). Some have praised it, but others have suggested that the authors either unwittingly or deliberately misinterpreted or distorted many of the findings upon which they drew, while ignoring a body of other research results which ran counter to their position.[8]

This review has indicated that integrative efforts have not been entirely successful. Colvin and Pauly's (1983) global and highly discursive argument consisted of an amalgam of claims, at least some of which lack empirical support. The integrations of Johnson and of Elliott, Ageton, and Canter were more narrowly focused, being largely developmental and social-psychological in nature. Efforts to test these arguments have led to equivocal results. One criminologist (Hirschi, 1979) argued against the strategy pursued by Elliott, Ageton, and Canter, asserting that it results in a theoretical "stew."

In Hirschi's view, we would be better advised to pursue an oppositional strategy, in which we devote our energies to the full development of specific lines of theoretical argument and to research testing of these competing theories.

The conceptual integration by Pearson and Weiner was unimpressive. Little or nothing appears to be gained from exercises of this sort, in which divergent theories and concepts are shoehorned into a smaller set of conceptual niches. Finally, Wilson and Herrnstein's social learning argument was presented in a fashion that suggested greater precision and logical rigor than it actually possesses.

## GENERAL THEORY: TWO RECENT CASES

Wilson and Herrnstein's book appeared in 1985, accompanied by considerable fanfare, including dust jacket claims that described it as "a major contribution to criminology" and as "a magisterial survey of the now very extensive literature." However, it quickly passed from the scene, in considerable part because of the flaws in it that were reported by the critics. Like a number of other "blockbuster" books in sociology and criminology, it had a relatively short shelf life.

### Braithwaite's Theory of Reintegrative Shaming

One of the more significant theoretical expositions in the last few years is Braithwaite's *Crime, Shame, and Reintegration* (1989b), which, as noted earlier, advanced both an integrated and a general theory. Dealing with the issue of whether general theories are possible in the light of the heterogeneity of criminality, he argued that (pp. 1–2) most forms of crime have one thing in common, namely, they involve "behavior that is poorly regarded in the community compared to most other acts, and behavior where this poor regard is institutionalized."[9] Further, he asserted (p. 3) that "the homogeneity presumed between disparate behavior such as rape and embezzlement in this theory is that they are choices made by the criminal actor in the knowledge that he is defying a criminal prescription which is mutually intelligible to actors in the society as criminal."

After grappling with the question of whether crime is sufficiently homogeneous that a general theory can account for it, Braithwaite reviewed the dominant, contemporary theoretical traditions: labeling, subcultural arguments, control theory, opportunity formulations, and learning theories. He concluded that there is much of value to be derived from these viewpoints, but also that they do not account for many of the facts of crime that must be explained. Braithwaite concluded that much of the current theorizing can be incorporated into a new formulation, and further, he indicated that his contribution to that integration centered on the idea of *reintegrative shaming*, which has to do with positive rather than negative reactions to law-breakers. The overall thrust of his explanation of lawbreaking was captured in the following passage:

> Let us simplify the relevance of this chapter by imagining Fagin's lair as something of a caricature of a criminal subculture. We need control theory to bring young offenders to the doorstep of the criminal subculture (primary deviance); stigmatization (labeling theory) to open the door; subcultural and learning theory to maintain the lair as a rewarding place for secondary deviants to stay in; and opportunity theory to explain how such criminal subcultures come to exist in the first place. This is the scheme supplied by the theory of reintegrative shaming for synthesizing the dominant theoretical traditions.

What are the basic facts of crime that are not adequately explained by existing theories? Braithwaite (pp. 44–50) asserted that the major ones are these:

1. *Crime is committed disproportionately by males .*
2. *Crime is committed disproportionately by 15–25 year olds.*
3. *Crime is committed disproportionately by unmarried people.*
4. *Crime is committed disproportionately by people living in large cities.*
5. *Crime is committed disproportionately by people who have experienced high residential mobility and who live in areas characterized by high residential mobility.*
6. *Young people who are strongly attached to their school are less likely to engage in crime.*
7. *Young people who have high educational and occupational aspirations are less likely to engage in crime.*
8. *Young people who do poorly in school are more likely to engage in crime.*
9. *Young people who are strongly attached to their parents are less likely to engage in crime.*
10. *Young people who have friendships with criminals are more likely to engage in crime themselves.*
11. *People who believe strongly in the importance of complying with the law are less likely to violate the law.*
12. *For both women and men, being at the bottom of the class structure, whether measured by socio-economic status, socio-economic status of the area in which the person lives, being unemployed, being a member of an oppressed racial minority (e.g., blacks in the US), increases rates of offending for all types of crime apart from those for which opportunities are systematically less available to the poor ( e.g., white collar crime).*
13. *Crime rates have been increasing since World War II in most countries, developed and developing. The only case of a country which has been clearly shown to have had a falling crime rate in this period is Japan.* [emphasis in the original]

As already noted, Braithwaite voiced an appreciative view of existing lines of theorizing and refrained from "trashing them" before articulating his own position. Accordingly, his perspective involved elements drawn from control theory, labeling viewpoints, subcultural and learning arguments, and opportunity theory. The unique ingredient which he added was *reintegrative shaming*, by which he meant (p. 55) "expressions of community disapproval, which may range from mild rebuke to degradation ceremonies, which are followed by gestures of reacceptance into the community of law-abiding citizens." In his view, stigmatizing forms of social disapproval frequently drive lawbreakers into further acts of misbehavior, while reintegrative shaming often works to bring deviants back into line.

A large part of Braithwaite's analysis centered on the personal characteristics and societal conditions that encourage or discourage reintegrative shaming. In particular, persons who are cut off from intensive social ties with others are least likely to be influenced by shaming, while conversely, socially bonded persons are amenable to the positive influences of shaming. Societies which are low on "communitarianism" are not likely to be highly successful at reintegrative shaming; rather, it is most effective in communitarian societies, of which Japan is a notable example.

This argument was similar to much other criminological theorizing, in that much of it was discursive in form, in which concepts were introduced, mixed in with illustrative material intended to illuminate the conceptual notions. However, one chapter was given over to a relatively formal summary of the theory. Figure 10–1 is reproduced from that chapter.

Braithwaite provided a brief summary of this theory, outlined in Figure 10–1, along these lines (pp. 100–4): First, persons who are under 15 or over 25 years of age, married, employed, and female are most likely to be tied to others in interdependency, while young, unmarried, and unemployed males are least likely to exhibit interdependency. What is the causal role of interdependency? Braithwaite (p. 100) asserted: "Interdependency is approximately equivalent to the social bonding, attachment and commitment of control theory." Interdependent persons are most susceptible to shaming, while persons who are unattached and unbonded are least amenable to it.

Societies in which interdependencies are extensive are also likely to be communitarian ones, in which interdependencies have the special qualities of trust and mutual help. Japan was invoked as an example of a modernized, highly industrialized, but at the same time, communitarian society. The contrast between Japan and the United States in this regard is fairly stark.

As Figure 10–1 indicates, Braithwaite also argued that communitarian societies are more likely to practice reintegrative shaming, while societies in which individualism runs rampant are more likely to shun and isolate deviants, including criminals; hence they endeavor to control crime through stigmatization. Figure 10–1 also indicates that stigmatizing is likely to push lawbreakers into interdependencies with other violators, thus exacerbating the criminogenic features of a social organization. Finally, Braithwaite also drew attention to systematic blockages of legitimate opportunities (economic discrimination, widespread unemployment, etc.) which contribute to the alienation of individuals and their recruitment into deviant or criminal subcultures which further encourage them to participate in lawbreaking.

Although Braithwaite's small book was provocative, he experienced

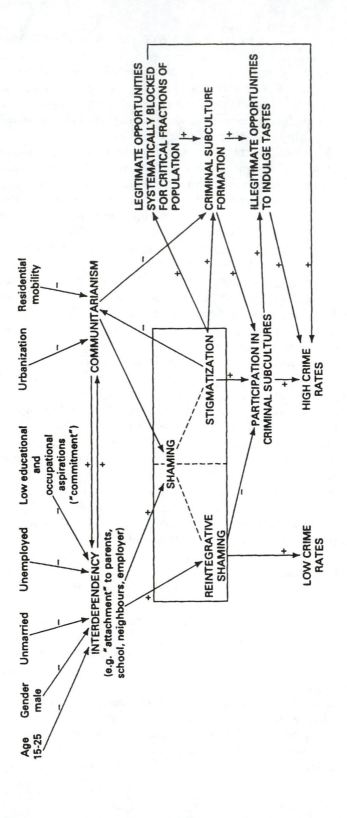

10–1  Summary of the Theory of Reintegrative Shaming (Braithwaite, 1989b: 99)

some of the same difficulties as the rest of us who tackle the task of committing our thoughts to paper; that is, there are soft spots and unclear passages in his narrative. Early in the book, he asserted that (p. 1) the key to crime *control* is reintegrative shaming, but on the same page, he also indicated that the theory seeks to specify the types of shaming which *cause* rather than prevent crime. Finally, on this same page he contended that "individuals who resort to crime are those insulated from shame over their wrongdoing." What is not entirely clear is whether the major focus of his argument is on influences that succeed or fail to deter "primary deviants" from further misbehavior, or instead, whether it also speaks to the question of why persons engage in flirtations with lawbreaking in the first place. Figure 10–1 does not clear this question up.

My interpretation is that Braithwaite's implicit argument is that persons who are unbonded or lacking in interdependency become involved in initial acts of lawbreaking because the bite of conscience is absent in their cases. They feel no *anticipatory shame* (my term) when they contemplate embarking upon misdeeds; thus they fail to police themselves by directing shame at themselves. Additionally, the most heavily emphasized argument in the theory is that persons who engage in initial acts of lawbreaking or flirtations with misconduct are less susceptible to *reactive shaming by others* (my term); thus they are likely to continue to engage in misbehavior.

Another unclear line of analysis, having to do with white-collar crime, received considerable attention in the book. For one thing, white-collar criminality did not appear in the inventory of basic facts about lawbreaking enumerated at the outset. Also, it seems doubtful that these offenders are low on interdependency in the same way as are the unskilled street criminals who commit crude predatory offenses and who are the center of much of the argument in the book.

Kathryn Farr has pointed out (1991) that the reintegrative shaming theory may also be incomplete in that it emphasizes lack of social control or unbondedness to the exclusion of other influences that may have an important role in lawbreaking. More specifically, she argued that broad social values need to be given more attention in general theories of criminality. For example, in the United States, "soft-core" pornographic magazines such as *Playboy* lend legitimacy to cultural themes which give approval to male dominance, violence against women, and other manifestations of sexism. These themes may be sufficiently powerful to draw males who are not lacking in bondedness into crimes of domination and violence against women.

Although it is possible to identify some rough spots in Braithwaite's book, it is an important recent contribution to criminological theory. One reviewer (Scheff, 1990) likened Braithwaite to a "new Durkheim," and also concluded that "it will, I believe, generate new ideas and research into the forseeable future." However, that forecast may be overly optimistic.

## Gottfredson and Hirschi's General Theory

I have already commented upon Gottfredson and Hirschi's (1990) venture into general theory, which would be more accurately titled *A General Theory of Some Instances of Some Forms of Crime.*

A number of things might be said about this relatively small book. For one, much of it was drawn from various already-published articles by the authors, dealing with crime and age relationships, social control, and other matters. The book reprised a number of the pithy observations that they had made earlier. For example, they criticized those criminologists who have oversold longitudinal research studies as the way to criminological salvation, as well as those who have contributed to criminological confusion with the notion of "criminal careers."[10] Then, too, their remarks about biological positivism, and in particular, the shortcomings of twin studies, were revealing. However, the book will ultimately be judged on the basis of whether the authors made a persuasive case for the general theory which they have put forth.

Gottfredson and Hirschi's central claim was straightforward, to wit, criminal offenders and other deviants are characterized by low self-control. Most of the other causal influences that loom large in the thinking of other criminologists were dismissed as secondary or unimportant influences, at best, or as wrongheaded, at worst.

Another key claim in the book was that most lawbreaking is "ordinary crime" which consists of trivial and mundane criminal acts (p. 16). This theme was repeated a number of times in their descriptions of "the typical or standard burglary," "the typical or standard robbery," "the typical or standard homicide," and the like. Their description of "the standard or ordinary embezzlement" (p. 39), which they treat as a major form of white-collar crime, asserted that "in the ordinary embezzlement a young man recently hired steals money from his employer's cash register or goods from his store." According to the authors, embezzlement of large amounts of money by older employees in positions of trust is a "rarity."

Many criminologists are likely to be troubled by these claims and will ponder such questions as "how trivial, how typical, or how rare?" Then, too, the assertion that most offenders who engage in repeated offenses tend to carry out a wide range of crimes is not clearly supported by the evidence. Much of the available data indicates that although repeat offenders do not usually specialize in a single form of crime, neither are their offending careers entirely unpatterned.

Polk (1991) has taken issue with Gottfredson and Hirschi's contentions about "the typical homicide," arguing that few of the Australian homicide episodes he studied fit their characterization. Other critics have suggested that Gottfredson and Hirschi drew a distorted picture of white-collar crime. For one thing, embezzlements frequently depart markedly from their description, being carried out by older persons and involving relatively large amounts of embezzled funds. Even more to the point, the evidence on which they based their claims about white-collar crime did not include any of the savings and loan plunderers or other corporate miscreants.

Although a number of criticisms can be made of this theory of low self-control, one of the most serious is that of Akers (1991: 203–4), having to do with the tautological nature of the argument. As he indicated, "Gottfredson and Hirschi do not define self-control separately from the propensity to commit crimes. G & H use 'low self-control' and 'high self-control' simply as labels for this differential propensity to commit crime. . . . Thus it would appear to be tautological to explain the propensity to commit crime by low self-control. These are one and the same, and such assertions about them are true by definition."

Gottfredson and Hirschi constructed a general theory of crime that involved a stunningly simple basic thesis, namely that low self-control, which takes shape relatively early in the lives of persons who exhibit it, leads to a variety of forms of deviant behavior: criminality, drunkenness, absenteeism, philandering, reckless driving, and so on. Moreover, individuals who engage in one or another of these kinds of behavior are likely to be involved in others of them as well. Low self-control arises out of family settings in which parents fail to observe deviant tendencies on the part of their children, and in addition, in which they fail to administer punishment to their misbehaving offspring.

What shall we conclude about these claims which comprise Gottfredson and Hirschi's general theory? On the one hand, there is considerable evidence that a substantial number of "garden-variety" offenders do exhibit short-term goals, lack of planning and foresight, and other characteristics that are consistent with the notion of low self-control. Also, while Akers's criticism regarding the tautological features of the Gottfredson and Hirschi argument is warranted, there is no readily apparent basis for concluding that this is a fatal flaw of their theory; rather, it should be possible to measure low self-control, the independent variable, separate from indicators of deviance and criminality, the dependent variable(s).

In my opinion, the major flaw in this general theory is that its authors have tried to stretch it so as to encompass a sizable quantity of criminal conduct to which it does not apply. More correctly, they constructed a conception of what they termed "ordinary crime" (pp. 15–44) which emphasized spontaneity, lack of planning, low rewards from lawbreaking, lack of specialization in offending, and the like said to be common to persons who engage in "ordinary crimes." Additionally, the ordinary crimes which they discussed in detail were burglary, robbery, homicide, automobile theft, rape, white-collar crime and embezzlement, and drug and alcohol use. But many kinds of criminality are not included in this list, and a large number of burglaries, homicides, embezzlements, or other offenses probably do not fit their descriptions of "the standard or ordinary embezzlement" or the "standard or ordinary homicide." Gottfredson and Hirschi have expounded an ambiguous general theory of crime, both because they failed to spell out the boundary conditions of the argument, that is, the forms of behavior to which it applies, and also because they have not been sufficiently attentive to the exceptions to their claims about "ordinary" crimes that must be explained.

## CONCLUDING REMARKS

This chapter has endeavored to sort out the various meanings of the notions of general theory and theoretical integration. Additionally, it examined efforts that have been made to articulate general and/or integrated theoretical arguments. Two concluding observations about these efforts are in order. First, there is a good deal of variability among these products; thus some are broader and more general than are others and some endeavor to merge more factors or variables than do others. In short, the ideas of general and integrated theory admit of several meanings. A second observation is that all of the formulations considered in this chapter were relatively discursive in form. A number of them are less than clear about the dependent variable that they endeavor to explain, while others contain unclear concepts, fuzzy propositions, and the like.

Some critics have argued that general or integrated theory efforts have not succeeded and that further ventures will inevitably fail. This pessimistic viewpoint often rests on observations about the presumed heterogeneity of criminality. According to the pessimists, this heterogeneity means that specific theories are required for the various forms of lawbreaking.

Although this heterogeneity contention is plausible, it is not logically compelling. Gottfredson and Hirschi (1990) and others may be correct in their claims that certain common threads run throughout a host of seemingly unlike forms of criminal conduct and that all of them can be dealt with within a general theory.

However, my own suspicion is that the pessimists are right. As a quick perusal of any contemporary criminology textbook quickly indicates (Gibbons, 1992a), the compass of criminal law in contemporary societies is extremely wide, covering myriad acts which appear to have little in common with each other, save for the fact that they have been prescribed or proscribed by some legislative body. While criminologists have made relatively little progress toward the development of an agreed-upon taxonomic system for sorting forms of crime into meaningful sociological groupings (Farr and Gibbons, 1990), my guess is that progress toward more powerful etiological formulations lies in the direction of theories tied to or focused upon specific forms of lawbreaking. If we take seriously the claim that criminology deals with lawbreaking in all of its forms, we may well discover that the more modest goal of developing a "family of theories" makes the greatest sense for the criminological enterprise.

## NOTES

[1] I have refrained from speaking of general theories of *crime* in this chapter even though some of the major theoretical works that are discussed here have been identified by their authors as general theories of crime (Gottfredson and Hirschi, 1990; Braithwaite, 1989b). Instead, I have identified the arguments discussed in this chapter as theories dealing with criminality, criminal behavior, delinquency, and delinquent behavior. It seems preferable to reserve the term; *theories of crime* for those efforts that have been made to account for the creation, by legislatures and other lawmaking bodies, of criminal statutes, delinquency codes, and the like. Put another way, the general theories discussed in this chapter center on attempts to account for the law-violating behavior of persons, rather than the social forces that have led to the creation of legal norms.

[2] On the other hand, sound etiological theory ought to have important policy implications and ought to inform efforts to deal with crime and its control. For one example of a work of general theory which contains a number of implications for public policy, see Braithwaite, 1989b.

[3] For some relatively detailed comments about the flaws in anomie theory, see Gibbons and Jones, 1975: 88–97. For a discussion regarding the development of differential association theory, see Gibbons, 1979: 48–61. The nature of containment theory and its strengths and weaknesses are discussed in Gibbons and Krohn, 1991: 107–9.

[4] Two examples of theories that have attended to both of these causal issues are Johnson, 1979 and Colvin and Pauly, 1983.

[5] Braithwaite (1989a: 130) has spoken at some length about the possibility of general theory in criminology. He argued that "it is nonsense to suggest that because the behaviour subsumed under the crime rubric is so disparate, with such complexly different causal histories, general theories of crime are impossible. A theory of any topic X will be an implausible idea unless there is a prior assumption that X is an explanandary kind. To be an explanandary kind X need not be fully homogeneous, only sufficiently homogeneous for it to be likely that every or most types of X will come under one or more of the same causal influences. There is no way of knowing that a class of actions is of an explanandary kind short of a plausible theory of the class being developed. In advance, giraffes, clover and newts might seem a hopelessly heterogeneous class, yet the theory of evolution shows how the proof of the pudding is in the eating."

[6] A large part of this commentary on theoretical integration has been cannibalized from an earlier essay by Gibbons and Farr, 1990.

[7] The end product of this part of Pearson and Weiner's (1985: 128) efforts is a figure labeled "Dynamic Model of the Probability of Criminal Behavior," involving a flow diagram which looks vaguely like a path diagram and to which a variety of pseudomathematical notations are attached. But it is difficult to see how this presentation represents an advance over a more discursive version of the same argument, for it has only the appearance and not the substance of precision.

[8] These remarks about quarrels over the meaning and significance of empirical findings assume that the disputants are all devotees of scientific method and practitioners of scientific inquiry. Although they apply the same scientific standards to the data, they disagree because of flaws in those data. However, there is reason to suspect that some of these quarrels are between criminologists who play fast and loose with the evidence and others who play by the rules of proper inference and the like. In particular, a number of the conclusions of Wilson and Herrnstein (1985) appear to constitute stretching of the data beyond what can reasonably be concluded from those data.

[9] See footnote 1. Technically speaking, Braithwaite presented a general theory of criminality (behavior) rather than of crime (the nature and origins of legal rules). In my discussion of

Braithwaite's book, I follow him in speaking of "crime," but readers should interpret these comments as having to do with "criminal behavior."

[10]When either sociologists or laypersons speak of careers, they usually have in mind a long-term sequence of steps or stages through which individuals proceed, with each step being a prerequisite to movement to the next career position. A military career is a clear example in that persons who are appointed as officers, particularly after having gone through one of the military academies, expect to move, over time, from being an ensign or second lieutenant to an appointment as an admiral or general. Similarly, academic careers involve the movement of persons from instructorships or an assistant professorship to higher steps, ultimately ending with a professorship, or in some cases, appointment as a dean or other upper-level academic administrator.

Persons who speak of careers in crime or of career offenders often slur over the fact that many so-called criminal careers start and end when persons are still in their teens, and also that many so-called careerists in lawbreaking are involved in only a small number of offenses while criminally active. Additionally, there is considerable variability over time in the criminal acts that are committed by those lawbreakers who engage in large numbers of offenses; hence it is misleading to identify them as career offenders.

# CHAPTER 11

# The Future of Criminological Theory

## INTRODUCTION

I have utilized a good bit of my own criminological "stuff" in the pages of this book; that is, I have drawn upon papers and books that I have produced.[1] My publications date back to the 1950s, with my first published article, on sex differences in juvenile court referrals, appearing in 1953. I have been involved in criminological work for about four decades. I completed my undergraduate education in sociology and criminology in 1950, the year that Edwin H. Sutherland died, and received a Ph.D. in 1956. I have been a witness, over these four decades, to the expansion of the criminological enterprise in the United States and elsewhere that I described in Chapter 3. Also, I have known many of the leading figures in the development of criminology since the 1950s. In this concluding chapter, I want to draw upon this background to comment upon the future of criminological theory. Let me begin by reprising the major themes in the preceding chapters.

## CRIMINOLOGY: PAST DEVELOPMENTS AND CURRENT ISSUES

Chapter 1 dealt with the disciplinary status of criminology and of its newer relative, criminal justice. I argued that criminology is not a separate discipline; rather, it has been for the most part, an area of specialization within sociology. I also contended that criminal justice is not a distinct discipline; instead, it draws upon a number of disciplines for its sustenance.

Although quarreling about the disciplinary status of criminology and criminal justice has occupied the time of a number of persons, in my view, that sort of academic "navel gazing" is much less significant than is the job of spelling out the major tasks that characterize criminology and criminal justice as scholarly enterprises.[2] I argued that the central business of criminology is *causal* analysis, while criminal justice is much more concerned with principles and tactics of crime *control.* Also, Chapter 1 identified "the rates question" and the "Why do they do it?" query as the two related but separate etiological or causal questions on which criminological inquiry is centered.

Chapter 1 also introduced another theme which runs throughout this book, namely, that inquiry in criminology (and in other social science fields) ought to be an activity in which theorizing and research are intimately linked parts. Although many persons in criminology or sociology view themselves either as "theorists" or as "methodologists," this division of labor is counterproductive. If we are to make progress in the direction of greater understanding of the mainsprings of conforming and lawbreaking conduct, we will need theoretical statements that are sufficiently clear and precise that they lend themselves to research examination. Theories ought to compete in the marketplace of ideas, and the winner(s) in this competition should be those that pass the test of evidence.

Chapters 2 and 3 presented an abridged version of *The Criminological Enterprise* (Gibbons, 1979), which traced the development of sociological criminology from about 1900 to the late 1970s. That book used a relaxed definition of "theory," in the same way that many criminologists continue to identify, as theories, accounts of "how things work" that vary markedly in terms of conceptual and logical rigor. That book indicated that criminological theory, defined in this broad way, grew in scope and sophistication from the 1930s to the 1970s.

Even though some contemporary criminologists have argued that criminological theorizing has fallen out of fashion in recent years, I have argued otherwise (Gibbons, 1992b). In a comment on Braithwaite's (1989a) pessimistic remarks on the current state of theory, in which he declared that criminologists have nothing to say to policy makers because they have failed to develop general and verified causal theories, I noted that he was born in 1951, the year I entered graduate school. Further, I remarked:

> From my longer time perspective, our situation seems less dismal than described by Braithwaite. There is currently a good deal of interest in criminology in "theory work," that is, construction of causal arguments and research scrutiny of them. Our stockpile of theoretical claims and research evidence has grown markedly since the 1950s when Sutherland's theory of differential asso-

ciation was about the only game in town and in which criminology textbooks were long on opinions and short on facts. We had no routine activities theorizing or research in the 1950s, no evidence on income inequality and crime, no substantial body of data on unemployment and crime, no sophisticated theories to account for state-by-state variations in forcible rape rates, very few detailed analyses of white-collar crime, and no large literature on homicide. This list could be expanded considerably. In short, when compared with the 1950s, we enjoy a surfeit of theoretical arguments and research evidence on which further work might proceed.

Unfortunately, the other side of this coin is that even though we now have a much larger supply of explanatory arguments and a much increased supply of research evidence, there is little agreement among criminologists regarding their evaluations of these theoretical statements or their judgments with respect to the significance of many of the research findings. There are a variety of explanations for this state of affairs, one of which is that while the research output has increased, we still often find ourselves limited to a few investigations of one or another topic. These studies have often employed different measures and data relative to the concepts being explored, differing samples, and the like. However, I have emphasized that one of the major problems of criminology centers on theoretical issues. As I indicated in detail in Chapter 5, much of what passes for theory consists of highly discursive arguments, sometimes complicated by odd conceptual language that has been employed by the theorist.

Chapter 4 dealt with the unresolved problem of "the dependent variable" or what might also be termed the heterogeneity issue. Some criminologists have contended that the differences that can be observed among offenders do not make a difference as far as theorizing is concerned. For example, Gottfredson and Hirschi (1990) have argued that most lawbreakers, along with many other kinds of deviants, share a number of characteristics in common, a central one of which is low self-control. Accordingly, while it may be useful to examine how low social control is implicated in legally different kinds of lawbreaking, special theories for these varieties of misconduct are not required. On this same point, Braithwaite (1989a) has asserted that even though the behavior subsumed by the crime rubric is disparate, it does not necessarily follow that separate theories are required for the different forms that can be observed. According to Braithwaite (1989a: 130), "giraffes, clover and news might seem to be a hopelessly heterogeneous class" but the evidence from genetics indicates otherwise.

Logic is on the side of those who contend that commonalities may be identified among seemingly disparate phenomena and that a single explanation for all of them may exist. Even so, the accumulated evidence is on the side of those who contend that criminality is so heterogeneous that it cannot be accounted for by a single etiological account, however complex. Chapter 4 made the case for classificatory or taxonomic systems that sort crime or criminals into groupings that make theoretical sense. Regrettably, there is little indication that criminologists are about to embrace a *shared* scheme for sorting criminal patterns or offenders into types or patterns.

Chapter 5 involved some more detailed comments about the two central questions posed by criminologists, namely "the rates question" and "the Why do they do it?" query. Regarding the latter, two basic "models" or portrayals of etiological processes have been employed by theorists and researchers: the historical-developmental view and a situational-mechanistic approach. Also, the mysteries of causation have been approached from biological and sociobiological directions, from psychological and psychiatric orientations, and from sociological viewpoints which assume that criminality is most often carried on by normal persons who find themselves in abnormal situations. Chapter 5 also took note of recursive and nonrecursive formulations. The first of these is made up of one-way causal arguments, while the latter refers to more complex explanatory accounts which entertain the possibility that etiological factors may have two-way effects; that is, such matters as poor parent-child relations or school failure may be both a cause of law-breaking and, at a later point in a causal sequence, a consequence of involvement in misbehavior. One thing that we have learned over a half century of inquiry is that causal processes are considerably more complex than portrayed in premodern criminology.

Chapter 5 also returned to the matter of criminological theorizing, and in particular, the conceptual and logical structure of theories. Criminological formulations can be arrayed along a scale in terms of conceptual and logical rigor, with broad, sensitizing, but essentially untestable perspectives on one end and formal theories on the other. Few if any formal theories currently exist in criminology; instead we have a few semiformal theories and a host of what might be termed "ruminations" and "conjectures," along with some "embryo theories" (Schrag, 1967: 244). Schrag has described embryo theories and the processes by which they are constructed in the following way:

> The construction of embryo theories, of course, is guided by the same general objectives and procedures outlined above for more formal theories. Researchers work alternatively from an *a priori* base by deductive analysis and from an empirical base by inductive methods. They try as best they can to define their concepts meaningfully, to formulate their assumptions with some precision, and to trace the development of their arguments logically from assumptions to conclusions. But the absence of an established foundation of information and technology forces them to stay close to the observed data and to utilize mainly the language of everyday discourse. Technical concepts and specialized methods tend to focus on the development of conceptual systems that are rich in descriptive content but deficient in predictive and explanatory power. The refinements that produce empirical competence are achieved by successive revisions and formalizations which result from the practical test of a theory.

In the discussion that followed this characterization of embryo theories, Schrag (1967: 245–53) singled out the formulations by Cohen (1955) and Cloward and Ohlin (1960), having to do with the social influences that are related to the origin and persistence of gang or subcultural delinquency, in order to illustrate the processes through which discursive arguments can be made more explicit, or in other words, how they might be converted into embryo theories. These involve the identification of the basic assumptions and logical structure of the arguments, along with linkage of key concepts to empirical indicators, and from these, identification of researchable hypotheses or what Schrag termed theorems. Finally, the embryo theory would undergo revision and/or amplification as research findings relative to it are produced, and in turn, that revised theory would be "fine-tuned" further by empirical investigations that would be undertaken to examine it.

My remarks in Chapters 1 and 5 and elsewhere in this book indicated that my views of inquiry and the theory-research process parallel the recommendations by Schrag. I argued for strategies of "sneaking up on reality by successive approximations" involving repeated efforts to refine or formalize our explanatory formulations, both by making conceptual refinements to them and by putting them to empirical test. I want to return to this argument later in this chapter.

Chapter 6 dealt with social-structural theories directed at explanation of crime patterns and crime rates. Criminologists have acquired a substantial body of evidence dealing with various correlates of lawbreaking: age relationships, sex variations, racial and class patterns, and economic correlates such as unemployment and income inequality. Most of the research on these demographic and social-structural correlates of criminality has been centered on relatively crudely defined patterns or types of lawbreaking, and in particular, Part I felonies in the FBI Uniform Crime Reports system of classification. No one has been audacious enough to attempt the construction of a "grand theory" dealing with crime in all of its forms and with all of the social, economic, and demographic influences that are involved in it. Furthermore, the likelihood of success for such a venture is slight.

Chapters 7 and 8 turned attention to the "Why do they do it?" question and to the various answers that have been offered to it. Many of these answers by sociologists and economists have been psychological in nature in that they have identified phenomena located "inside the heads" of actors as major causal influences. The list of causal arguments by sociologists includes differential association and social learning theories, social control formulations, labeling and "risk-taking" views, and situational hypotheses. These formulations all share one thing in common—they are discursive and plagued with fuzzy concepts and the like. Even so, the existing evidence suggests that all of them have something important to say about lawbreaking.

Less enthusiasm was expressed for the rational choice theorizing that has been produced by economists and some other scholars in recent years. I agree with Akers (1990) that as far as this work is concerned, there is less there than meets the eye. While rational choice notions have stimulated researchers to produce some valuable data on the decision-making activities of real-life offenders, the theory itself is unexceptional.

Two basic points were made in Chapter 8. The first was that the accumulated evidence on biological and sociobiological factors in lawbreaking must be taken seriously. Among other things, this means that criminologists are going to have to become more literate about biology so that they can evaluate the claims of sociobiological investigators.

The second major point was that we need to "bring psyches back in" to criminology. For one thing, we need to acknowledge the existence of "monsters" or "socialization failures" within the offender population. But even more important, criminologists must give considerably more attention to the part played by individual differences in psychological characteristics between those who violate the law and those who do not. Chapter 8 argued that there probably are observable relationships between particular types of offenders and particular psychological characteristics. Andrews and Wormith (1989), Katz (1988), Pallone and Hennessey (1992) and a few others have begun to explore the linkages between criminality and individual characteristics, but much more work remains to be done.

Chapter 9 commented on postmodernism and on some new versions of criminological thought that are linked, at least tenuously, to postmodernist thinking. Several things can be said about postmodernism and the "new criminologies." For one, Denzin (1986) has argued that postmodernist theorists have been on solid ground when they have identified massive changes in the world social order that have occurred after World War II. According to Denzin, these changes have undermined mainstream social theories which have described nation-states as functionally integrated and relatively self-contained "societies."[3] And, as we saw in Chapter 9, he also contended that the empirical situation of the postmodern world demands that traditional thoughtways in criminology and other fields of sociology be revised.

A second observation is that the future of critical and constitutive versions of criminology is less clear. On the one hand, many criminologists would probably concede that there are some provocative claims and ideas that have been put forth by criminologists of these persuasions. On the other hand, much of this theorizing is discursive and plagued as well by terms and expressions that are peculiar to it. For that reason alone, many mainstream criminologists are likely to dismiss this form of "new criminology."

The prospects for feminist criminology are considerably brighter. While there is much more work to be done on feminist perspectives, these viewpoints have already had an important impact upon mainstream criminology.

Chapter 10 examined the recent interest in integrated and general theories. That chapter indicated that while the idea of theoretical integration is straightforward, that is, it will lead to greater explanatory power, the integration of theories is more difficult than first appearances suggest. Critics of theoretical integration have argued that these efforts often result in products which make a "hash" of the constituent arguments which they endeavor to blend together. Put another way, it is often difficult if not impossible to integrate two or more theories that are based on different basic assumptions without doing violence to those postulates.

Chapter 10 also asked whether general theories are possible. There is no single answer to that question, for much depends upon what is meant by general theory. On the one hand, efforts to construct theoretical arguments that span virtually the entire spectrum of lawbreaking, (e.g., Gottfredson and Hirschi, 1990) have not been markedly successful. On the other hand, some theorists such as Braithwaite (1989b) have pursued a more modest goal of creating a general theory which applies to one identifiable segment of the lawbreaker population. Critics have been more generous in their evaluation of those efforts. For my part, I am skeptical of formulations that are intended to account for crime in most or all of its forms. However, even though I have voiced reservations about some parts of Braithwaite's argument (Gibbons, 1991), I believe that efforts of that kind may eventually pay off.

## CRIMINOLOGICAL THEORY IN THE TWENTY-FIRST CENTURY

Sociologists have been notoriously poor prognosticators regarding either the future of their discipline or the anticipated developments in the social world that they are trying to understand. Accordingly, in criminology, one would be well advised to refrain from predictions, and certainly from forecasts about the shape of the field several decades down the road. Or, if any forecast is to be offered, it probably should be that criminological theorizing will continue to move in a variety of directions, as it has in the past. Many of the problems of past and current criminological theorizing that have been identified in this book will probably continue to plague the field.[4] In particular, we are likely to be presented with more discursive theories in the decades ahead and also with such lines of argument as constitutive and critical criminology, as well as the continuation of mainstream viewpoints. However, it is conceivable that increasing numbers of criminologists will be persuaded of the need to improve their "crime talk" and to develop theoretical arguments that are more precise and formalized than many of the formulations that are now called theories.

How might criminologists go about sharpening their arguments? Let me address this question by directing attention to a recent contribution by Braithwaite (1991). By now, readers should be quick to recognize his name for it has appeared repeatedly in these pages. He has been one of the most prolific contributors to the theoretical literature of criminology over the past two decades; indeed, it would be difficult to identify any other criminologist who has outshone him in theorizing during this period.

Braithwaite's 1991 essay on inequality and its relationship to both common crime and white-collar offending nicely illustrates the growing sophistication of criminological arguments; thus it is possible to point to a number of its positive features. At the same time, it provides a good example of the problems of theory construction and exposition which need to be addressed by criminologists. It is for these two reasons that I have singled it out.

Braithwaite (1991) attempted to identify and integrate a number of separate criminological themes, which taken together, might provide at least a partial explanation both of "common crimes" and of white-collar lawbreaking. By common crimes, he meant crude property offenses such as burglary and larceny and crimes of violence such as assault and homicide.

Braithwaite (1991: 40) provided a capsule summary of this theory, in which he asserted:

> A general theory of both white-collar and common crime can be pursued by focusing on inequality as an explanatory variable. Powerlessness and poverty increase the chances that needs are so little satisfied that crime is an irresistible temptation to actors who have nothing to lose. . . . When needs are satisfied, further power and wealth enables crime motivated by greed. New types of criminal opportunities and new paths to immunity from accountability are constituted by concentrations of wealth and power. Inequality thus worsens both crimes of poverty motivated by *need* for goods for *use* and crimes of wealth motivated by *greed* enabled by goods for *exchange*. Furthermore, much crime, particularly violent crime, is motivated by the humilation of the offender and the offender's perceived right to humiliate the victim. Inegalitarian societies, it is argued, are more structurally humiliating. Dimensions of inequality relevant to the explanation of both white-collar and common crime are economic inequality, inequality in political power (slavery, totalitarianism), racism, ageism, and patriarchy. [emphasis in the original]

Although the narrative that elaborated upon it was rich in details, the general thrust of the argument is clear. Inequality, and in particular, economic inequality, is importantly implicated both in common crime and in white-collar lawbreaking. Street criminals such as unskilled predators are frequently responding to the economic precariousness that is their lot, while white-collar offenders employ their positions of economic advantage in illegal ways so as to accumulate further wealth. In short, common criminals are driven into lawbreaking by economic *need*, while higher-status persons are motivated by economic *greed*. The second, related part of this formulation centered on humiliation perceived by persons, which sometimes leads to violent acts on their part as they strike back at those who they view as responsible for their humiliation. Humiliating experiences are often relate to economic disadvantage and/or lack of political power, racism, ageism, and sexism.

Braithwaite acknowledged that this formulation was derived in considerable part from his earlier work, presented in *Inequality, Crime and Public Policy* (1979) and more recently, in *Crime, Shame, and Reintegration* (1989b). Also, he indicated that his ideas were importantly shaped by Katz's (1988) theorizing in *Seductions of Crime*. He avoided the strategy that has often been employed by theorists in the past, in which the formulations of others are first trashed, and instead, he explicitly endeavored to build on work that preceded his own.[5]

There are a number of positive features to this inequality argument. For one, although it was essentially discursive, Braithwaite did make an effort to identify some of the basic assumptions on which it was built and also to isolate the empirical claims that the theory generates. He identified a number of relatively explicit hypotheses which might be subjected to research scrutiny.

Another virtue of the argument is that it is a multifactor formulation which makes a place for explanatory variables at several levels. Braithwaite (1991: 54) listed these as (a) the reasoning individual, (b) the somatic (emotions such as rage, humiliation, and the like), (c) the micro interaction level (experiences such as public humiliation, public condemnation as an offender, etc.), and (d) the macro level (age structure, relations of production, and patriarchal social relationships). I have argued in this book for causal formulations that deal jointly with social-structural factors in lawbreaking, with interactional experiences, and with characteristics of individuals that play a part in their behavior.

However, there are also parts of this perspective with which one might cavil. For one, Braithwaite (1991: 40) began by taking issue with Sutherland's (1983: 7) claim in *White Collar Crime* that "a general theory that crime is due to poverty and its related pathologies is shown to be invalid" (if it can be shown that white-collar crimes are widespread). Braithwaite (1991: 40) declared: "I want to reject Sutherland's view that the widespread reality of white-collar crime means that poverty and inequality cannot be important variables in a general theory of crime."

What Braithwaite failed to indicate is that these words by Sutherland first appeared in the 1949 edition (p. 10) of his book. The first chapter contained a relatively detailed discussion of "poverty and its related pathologies," in which Sutherland made it abundantly clear that these terms referred to *absolute* poverty, along with such "pathologies" as lack of adequate housing, inadequate education, and alleged biological and intellectual inferiority. In the 1940s, when sociologists spoke of poverty, they meant these kinds of things, rather than feelings of relative deprivation, income inequality, and the like. The idea of income inequality is an invention of the 1970s.

On this same point, Braithwaite (1991: 40) followed the remarks above with the contention that "inequality is relevant to the explanation of both crime in the streets and crime in the suites." What he failed to acknowledge is that in the 1949 edition of *White Collar Crime* (pp. 7–8), Sutherland concluded: "The answer is that the causal factor is not poverty in the sense of economic need, but the social and interpersonal relations which are associated sometimes with poverty and sometimes with wealth"!

Although Sutherland's views regarding poverty and crime seem to have anticipated some of Braithwaite's contentions, it is clear that the latter's explication of crime-inequality relationships has taken us considerably further than did the former's relatively terse remarks. In this sense, it is probably of no great consequence that Braithwaite seemingly erred in his interpretation of Sutherland's views.

But there are some other difficulties that are encountered with this theoretical argument. As I have indicated, "need" and "greed" figure prominently in it. At one point, Braithwaite (1991: 42) indicated: "I am not interested in a positivist definition of need. I am interested in the phenomenon of need being socially constructed in culturally contingent ways that motivate crime."[6] Although need and greed were not explicitly defined, these terms were used in much the same way as they are employed by laypersons. Also, while Braithwaite alluded in one place to organizations, the notions of need and greed were employed as they are by lay citizens, namely as characteristics of *individuals*. A critic of the argument might point to the evidence on white-collar crime (Gibbons, 1992a: 284–317) which indicates that these violations are sometimes carried out by persons who appear not to be personally greedy but who feel driven to lawbreaking by pressures from higher-ups in the organization. For example, Smith's (1961) study of the electrical conspiracy case involving the major manufacturers of large electrical machinery such as turbines indicated that a number of the involved lawbreakers were reluctant participants who felt under great pressure to behave contrary to their own personal preferences.

Braithwaite (1991: 44) also muddied the waters with the following assertion: "Crime can be motivated by: (a) a desire for goods for use; (b) a fear of losing goods for use; (c) a desire for goods for exchange, or (d) a fear of losing goods for exchange." Although it may be that all four of these exist in the empirical world, (d) in particular would strike some as a peculiar notion of "greed."

In that part of his essay where inequality and humiliation were discussed, Braithwaite (1991: 50) endeavored to account for the low rates of violence and other kinds of protest actions on the part of women, who are subjected to discrimination and humiliation in patriarchal societies. He invoked the concept of hegemony, arguing that women are subject to such pervasive domination under patriarchal arrangements that many of them come to accept male definitions of women's place in the scheme of things.

In other words, women have been induced to accept the ideology of male superiority because men enjoy unchallenged hegemony over women. So far, so good. But Braithwaite then raised the question of how he would operationalize "the infamously vague concept of hegemony" and responded that he would do it "through measuring the things to which the theory proposes that hegemony leads—shame and guilt when it is present, humiliation and anger when it is not." At least at first glance, this strategy appears to be similar to the psychiatric use of the notion of sociopathy, in which criminality is attributed to sociopathy on the basis of observations that the putative "sociopath" is engaged in lawbreaking and deviance.

These "soft spots" in this formulation are probably not fatal flaws; rather, it would be possible for Braithwaite or someone else to revise the argument so as to clarify these fuzzy portions. Further, it might also be possible to integrate it with all or part of Coleman's (1987) somewhat parallel theorizing about the factors and conditions that account for white-collar crime. Much depends upon criminologists heeding the advice offered by Braithwaite (1989a) in another essay, where he argued that criminologists must "abandon the theoretical nihilism that unites us against anyone who scans the horizon beyond their entrenched niches of expertise, nurture bold and general theory, and work cooperatively to build upon it rather than kill it in the womb."

I have no quarrel with this broad recommendation, and I agree with Braithwaite that criminologists have too often adopted a "search and destroy" posture toward the work of others. At the same time, I want to emphasize, one last time, that in nurturing theory and building cooperatively upon the contributions of others, it is imperative that we produce increasingly more rigorous theories as well as ones that are pregnant with new ideas. Talking about crime and criminals is too important to be left to those who are unable to "talk straight."

## NOTES

[1]My preference, as well as that of some of my criminological colleagues such as Ken Polk, is to speak of "my stuff" rather than "my work," "the corpus of my work," or in some similar way. As Andy Warhol once put it, "we will all be famous in the future, but only for fifteen minutes." For most of us, fame is fleeting if we manage to achieve it at all! Put another way, insights, ideas, and theories in criminology often arise, enjoy a short period in the limelight, and fade away; thus a degree of modesty about the value of one's ideas is in order.

[2]By "academic navel gazing," I mean such activities as the production of rankings of academic departments in terms of prestige, rankings of journals in terms of "importance" or other criteria, and the production of essays in which the authors agonize about the personal problems that are often encountered when one is a sociologist or criminologist. In my view, there is altogether too much of this sort of commentary in our journals and not enough attention to the real or substantive problems which the discipline is supposed to be attacking. Also, I agree with Cressey's (Laub, 1983: 163) observation that "being a sociology professor beats the hell out of working in a bakery. It even beats being an undertaker, an auto mechanic, or a shoe salesman." From my own

experiences, I would add that it also beats the hell out of picking oysters, pulling 2 by 4s off the green chain, and working as a busboy.

[3]Nike International, headquartered in a suburb of Portland, Oregon (Beaverton) nicely illustrates some of the changes that have occurred in the international marketplace. Nike has grown in the period of two or three decades from a small regional company manufacturing athletic shoes into an international giant. It merchandises a large variety of athletic shoes, including a popular running shoe, the Nike Pegasus. That shoe is manufactured in Indonesia by an independent company under contract to Nike, at a cost of about $15 per pair. In turn, the shoes sell in the American market for about $65. Nike also merchandises a large variety of clothing and other athletic and leisure accessories. The company has no manufacturing facilities of its own; instead, it chases low-cost labor throughout the Far East, contracting with various companies to produce shoes and other products. Nike's advertising budget far exceeds its investment in product development. Among its paid spokespersons are professional basketball stars Michael Jordan and Charles Barkley. Nike is currently involved in aggressive advertising campaigns, designed not only to capture a large share of the American market for athletic shoes, apparel, and sundry products, but also to persuade persons around the world that their lives will be deficient if they are not dressed in Nike apparel or shod in Nike shoes.

[4]Kathryn Farr and I (1989) have drawn upon our experiences as Assistant Editor and Editor respectively of *Crime and Delinquency* to address a major problem in criminological theorizing that has not been mentioned here, namely the lack of basic writing skills on the part of many of the persons who have submitted papers to that journal, as well as to the general sloppiness, inattention to style requirements, etc., that plague many of the submissions we receive. I have assembled a large collection of "howlers" from these submissions and from other writings of criminologists. For example, one author wrote of Einstein and asserted that the practical utility of certain of his ideas was not recognized until his death from adventures in space! In another case, an author contended that we need more interview data from rapists like Scully (Diane) and Marolla (Joseph). Scully and Marolla are researchers who interviewed a group of convicted rapists! Finally, another criminologist asserted that delinquency is caused by Travis Hirschi, who wrote about lack of social bond! Less humorous but equally serious are the innumerable instances of fractured syntax, misspellings, mangled names of other authors, etc., that fill the pages of many of the papers submitted to the journal.

These problems encountered in the production of *Crime and Delinquency* are not peculiar to that journal. For example, Michael Tonry (personal communication) has indicated that a considerable share of the commissioned pieces in the *Crime and Justice* series have required extensive editorial work on his part and that in a number of instances, the final products probably should have listed Tonry as a coauthor.

Farr and I argued that this problem of bad writing is a *systemic*, rather than an *individual* one. For one thing, there are entirely too many persons who are deficient in writing skills to view this solely as an individual shortcoming. Also, my guess is that few if any doctoral programs in criminology or criminal justice make systematic efforts to teach students to write. Instead, a few students who have somehow or other learned to write well do turn up in our programs, but we do little to add to their skills. A few students manage to link up with a faculty member who can write reasonably well and they receive a fair amount of training in writing during the production of their dissertation. But many students who enter our programs come to us with limited writing skills. In turn, in the fashion of "the blind leading the blind," they are guided through their program and the dissertation by professors who write poorly, so that they come out the other end of the graduate program pretty much in the same condition as when they entered.

[5]Another argument upon which Braithwaite drew was Cohen and Machalek's (1988) "evolutionary biological" theory of expropriative crime. Cohen and Machalek endeavored to deal with the question of how forms of "deviant" behavior come to be engaged in by normal persons. They began their exposition by reviewing theoretical and research contributions of contemporary behavioral ecology and evolutionary biology, taking note of a number of key concepts from those fields that might be applicable to criminology: "behavioral strategies," "strategy evolution," "resource holding potential," "adaptation," and "advantage." Resource holding potential, for example, refers to characteristics of individuals or groups which either provide them advantages in the competitive struggle for resources or which put them at competitive disadvantage. To illustrate, the resource holding potential of females, young persons, or blacks or

other minority group members is less than that of other, more socially favored groups. Cohen and Machalek (1988: 465) provided this summary statement regarding their argument: "We interpret criminal behaviors by which offenders expropriate goods or services from others as expressions of *diverse behavioral strategies* that derive from normal patterns of population-level social organization and interaction."

The Cohen-Machalek argument was a relatively rich one, dealing with sociocultural factors that contribute to criminality, constitutional factors that may affect the likelihood of lawbreaking, developmental experiences, inequalities or asymmetries in the values placed upon resources by different individuals or groups, variations in resource holding potentials, variations in opportunities to engage in criminality, and certain other factors. Adjectives such as "imaginative" or "provocative" come to mind as descriptive of it.

At the same time, the argument was another case of relatively discursive theorizing. Much of the supportive argumentation for it is derived from plant or animal ecology. In all likelihood, some criminologists are likely to view this "theory" as an important new contribution, as did Braithwaite. Other criminologists may be less positive in their judgments, holding that at least some share of the Cohen-Machalek argument is another case of "old wine in new bottles." For example, consider the following assertion (Cohen and Machalek, 1988: 495): "As we have seen, a RHP deficiency may increase the probability that a person will adopt an expropriative strategy in a particular opportunity structure because he is forced to 'make the best of a bad job.'" The thrust of this statement is fairly clear, namely that persons who are marginalized, unemployed, and the like may get involved in activities such as strong-armed robbery, not because they positively value such activities or strategies, but rather, because these are the only behavioral possibilities that they perceive as open to them.

There are some important insights in the Cohen and Machalek perspective, such as their comments on the ways in which *shared*, illegitimate (criminal) adaptations may arise among persons who are not psychologically distinguishable from persons who are more favorably situated in social and economic terms. The "bottom line" is that time will tell whether this viewpoint will become seized upon by others as the focus of new lines of criminological investigation or instead, if it will become still another theoretical contribution which makes no impact upon the field.

[6]Braithwaite did not identify the nature of a positivist definition of need. My suspicion is that many neopositivists actually define need as socially constructed in culturally contingent ways.

# References

ADAMS, WILLIAM P., PAUL M. CHANDLER, and M. G. NEITHERCUTT, "The San Francisco Project: A Critique," *Federal Probation* (December 1971): 45–53.

ADLER, FREDA, *Sisters in Crime* (New York: McGraw-Hill, 1975).

AGNEW, ROBERT, "Foundation for a General Strain Theory of Crime and Delinquency," *Criminology* (February 1992): 47–87.

AKERS, RONALD L, "Linking Sociology and Its Specialties: The Case of Criminology," *Social Forces* (September 1992): 1–16.

AKERS, RONALD L, "Self-Control as a General Theory of Crime," *Journal of Quantitative Criminology* (No. 2, 1991): 201–11.

AKERS, RONALD L, "Rational Choice, Deterrence, and Social Learning Theory in Criminology: The Path Not Taken," *Journal of Criminal Law and Criminology* (Fall 1990): 653–76.

AKERS, RONALD L. *Deviant Behavior: A Social Learning Approach*, 3rd ed. (Belmont, Calif.: Wadsworth, 1985).

AKERS, RONALD L., MARVIN D. KROHN, LONN LANZA-KADUCE, and MARCIA RADOSEVICH, "Social Learning and Deviant Behavior: A Specific Test of the General Theory," *American Sociological Review* (March 1979): 636–55.

ÅKERSTRÖM, MALIN, *Crooks and Squares* (New Brunswick, N.J.: Transaction Books, 1988).

ANDREWS, D. A. and J. STEPHEN WORMITH, "Personality and Crime: Knowledge Destruction and Construction in Criminology," *Justice Quarterly* (September 1989): 289–308.

ARBUTHNOT, JACK, DONALD A. GORDON, and GREGORY JURKOVIC, "Personality." Pp. 139–83 in Herbert C. Quay, ed., *Handbook of Juvenile Delinquency* (New York: Wiley, 1987).

ARON, RAYMOND, *Main Currents in Sociological Thought*, 2 vols. (New York: Basic Books, 1965, 1967).

BACKSTRAND, JOHN A., DON C. GIBBONS, and JOSEPH F. JONES, "Who Is in Jail? An Examination of the Rabble Hypothesis," *Crime and Delinquency* (April 1992): 219–29.

BANFIELD, EDWARD C., *The Unheavenly City Revisited* (Boston: Little, Brown, 1974).

BANNISTER, ROBERT C., *Sociology and Scientism* (Chapel Hill: University of North Carolina Press, 1987).

BARNES, HARRY ELMER, ed., *An Introduction to the History of Sociology* (Chicago: University of Chicago Press, 1948).

BARNES, HARRY ELMER and NEGLEY K. TEETERS, *New Horizons in Criminology*, 2nd ed. (Englewood Cliffs, N.J.: Prentice-Hall, 1951).

BARON, LARRY and MURRAY A. STRAUS, *Four Theories of Rape in American Society* (New Haven: Yale University Press, 1990).

BARTH, PAULINE, "Review," *Contemporary Sociology* (March 1991): 268–70.

BARTOL, CURT R. and ANNE M. BARTOL, *Criminal Behavior: A Psychosocial Approach*, 2nd ed. (Englewood Cliffs, N.J.: Prentice-Hall, 1986).

BECKER, GARY S, "Crime and Punishment: An Economic Approach," *Journal of Political Economy* (April 1968): 169–217.

BEIRNE, PIERS and JAMES W. MESSERSCHMIDT, *Criminology* (New York: Harcourt Brace Jovanovich, 1991).

BELLAH, ROBERT N., RICHARD MADSEN, WILLIAM H. SULLIVAN, ANN SWIDLER, and STEVEN M. TIPTON, *Habits of the Heart* (New York: Harper and Row, 1985).

BEST, STEVEN and DOUGLAS KELLNER, *Postmodern Theory* (New York: Guilford Press, 1991).

BLACKBURN, RONALD, *The Psychology of Criminal Conduct* (New York: Wiley, 1993).

BLAU, J. R. and PETER BLAU, "The Cost of Inequality: Metropolitan Structure and Violent Crime," *American Sociological Review* (February 1982): 114–29.

BLAUNER, ROBERT, "Internal Colonialism and Ghetto Revolt," *Social Problems* (Spring 1969): 393–408.

BLUMSTEIN, ALFRED, JACQUELINE COHEN, and DAVID P. FARRINGTON, "Criminal Career Research: Its Value for Criminology," *Criminology* (February 1988): 1–74.

BLUMSTEIN, ALFRED, DAVID P. FARRINGTON, and SOUMYA D. MOITRA, "Delinquency Careers: Innocents, Desisters, and Persisters." Pp. 187–219 in Michael Tonry and Norval Morris, eds., *Crime and Justice*, Vol. 6 (Chicago: University of Chicago Press, 1985).

BORITCH, HELEN, "Gender and Criminal Court Outcomes: An Historical Analysis," *Criminology* (August 1992): 293–325.

BRAITHWAITE, JOHN. "Poverty, Power, White-Collar Crime and the Paradoxes of Criminological Theory," *Australian and New Zealand Journal of Criminology* (January 1991): 40–58.

BRAITHWAITE, JOHN, "The State of Criminology: Theoretical Decay or Renaissance," *Australian and New Zealand Journal of Criminology* (September 1989a): 129–35.

BRAITHWAITE, JOHN, *Crime, Shame, and Reintegration* (Cambridge: Cambridge University Press, 1989b).

BRAITHWAITE, JOHN, *Inequality, Crime and Public Policy* (London: Routledge and Kegan Paul, 1979).

BRALY, MALCOLM, *False Starts* (Boston: Little, Brown, 1976).

BRANNIGAN, AUGUSTINE, "Postmodernism." Pp. 1522–24 in Edgar F. Borgatta and Marie L. Borgatta, eds., *Encyclopedia of Sociology* (New York: Macmillan, 1992).

BRODSKY, STANLEY L., MARTHA L. BERNATZ, and WILLIAM B. BEIDELMAN, "The Perfect Crime: An Investigation of the Gasoline Station Drive-Away," *British Journal of Criminology* (October 1981): 350–56.

CALAVITA, KITTY and HENRY D. PONTELL, "Heads I Win, Tails You Lose: Deregulation, Crime, and Crisis in the Savings and Loan Industry," *Crime and Delinquency* (July 1990): 309–41.

CARR , LOWELL J., *Delinquency Control* (New York: Harper & Row, 1950).

CARROLL, LEO and PAMELA IRVING JACKSON, "Inequality, Opportunity, and Crime Rates in Central Cities," *Criminology* (May 1983): 178–94.

CAVAN, RUTH SHONLE, *Criminology*, 3rd ed. (New York: Crowell, 1962).

CHAIKEN, JAN and MARCIA B. CHAIKEN, *Varieties of Criminal Behavior* (Santa Monica, Calif.: Rand, 1982).

CHAMBLISS, WILLIAM, "Toward a Political Economy of Crime," *Theory and Society* (Summer 1975): 152–53.

CHAMBLISS, WILLIAM and ROBERT B. SEIDMAN, *Law, Order, and Power* (Reading, Mass.: Addison-Wesley, 1971).

CHIRICOS, THEODORE G., "Rates of Crime and Unemployment: An Analysis of Aggregate Research Evidence," *Social Problems* (April 1987): 187–212.

CICOUREL, AARON V. , *The Social Organization of Juvenile Justice* (New York: Wiley, 1968).

CLARKE, RONALD V., ed., *Situational Crime Prevention* (New York: Harrow and Heston, 1992).

CLINARD, MARSHALL B. and RICHARD QUINNEY, *Criminal Behavior Systems*, 2nd ed. (New York: Holt, Rinehart & Winston, 1973).

CLOWARD, RICHARD A. and LLOYD E. OHLIN, *Delinquency and Opportunity* (New York: Free Press, 1960).

COHEN, ALBERT K., "The Assumption That Crime Is a Product of Environments: Sociological Approaches." Pp. 223–43 in Robert F. Meier, ed., *Theoretical Methods in Criminology* (Beverly Hills: Sage, 1985).

COHEN, ALBERT K., *Deviance and Control* (Englewood Cliffs, N.J.: Prentice-Hall, 1966).

COHEN, ALBERT K., "The Study of Social Disorganization and Deviant Behavior." Pp. 461–84 in Robert K. Merton, Leonard Broom, and Leonard S. Cottrell, Jr., eds., *Sociology Today* (New York: Basic Books, 1959).

COHEN, ALBERT K., *Delinquent Boys* (New York: Free Press, 1955).

COHEN, ALBERT K., ALFRED LINDESMITH, and KARL F. SCHUESSLER, eds., *The Sutherland Papers* (Bloomington: Indiana University Press, 1956).

COHEN, BERNARD P., *Developing Sociological Knowledge*, 2nd ed. (Chicago: Nelson Hall, 1989).

COHEN, LAWRENCE E., "Review: Throwing Down the Gauntlet: A Challenge to the Relevance of Sociology for the Etiology of Criminal Behavior," *Contemporary Sociology* (March 1987): 202– 5.

COHEN, LAWRENCE E. and RICHARD MACHALEK, "A General Theory of Expropriative Crime: An Evolutionary Ecological Approach," *American Journal of Sociology* (November 1988): 465–501.

COHEN, LAWRENCE E., MARCUS FELSON, and KENNETH C. LAND, "Property Crime Rates in the United States: A Macrodynamic Analysis 1947–1977; with *ex Ante* Forecasts for the Mid-1980s," *American Journal of Sociology* (January 1980): 90–118.

COHEN, LAWRENCE E. and MARCUS FELSON, "Social Change and Crime Rate Trends: A Routine Activities Approach," *American Sociological Review* (August 1979): 588– 607.

COLEMAN, JAMES WILLIAM, "Toward an Integrated Theory of White-Collar Crime," *American Journal of Sociology* (September 1987): 406–39.

COLOMY, PAUL, "Donald Cressey: A Personal and Intellectual Remembrance," *Crime and Delinquency* (July 1988): 242–62.

COLVIN, MARK and JOHN PAULY, "A Critique of Criminology: Toward an Integrated Structural-Marxist Theory of Delinquency Production," *American Journal of Sociology* (November 1983): 513–51.

CONGER, JOHN JANEWAY and WILBUR C. MILLER, *Personality, Social Class, and Delinquency* (New York: Wiley, 1962).

CONKLIN, JOHN, *Robbery and the Criminal Justice System* (Philadelphia: Lippincott, 1972).

CORNISH, DEREK B. and RONALD V. CLARKE, eds., *The Reasoning Criminal: Rational Choice Perspectives on Offending* (New York: Springer-Verlag, 1986).

CRESSEY, DONALD R., *Criminal Organization: Its Elementary Forms* (New York: Harper & Row, 1972).

CRESSEY, DONALD R., "Epidemiology and Individual Conduct: A Case from Criminology," *Pacific Sociological Review* (Fall 1960): 47–58.

CRESSEY, DONALD R., "The Differential Association Theory and Compulsive Crimes," *Journal of Criminal Law, Criminology and Police Science* (May–June 1954): 49–64.

CRESSEY, DONALD R., *Other People's Money* (New York: Free Press, 1953).

CROMWELL, PAUL F., JAMES N. OLSON, and D'AUNN W. AVARY, *Breaking and Entering* (Newbury Park, Calif.: Sage, 1990).

CULLEN, FRANCIS E., *Rethinking Crime and Deviance Theory* (Totowa, N.J.: Rowman and Allenheld, 1984).

CURRIE, ELLIOTT, *Confronting Crime* (New York: Pantheon, 1985).

DALY, KATHLEEN and MEDA CHESNEY-LIND, "Feminism and Criminology," *Justice Quarterly* (December 1988): 497–583.

DANZIGER, SHELDON, "Explaining Urban Crime Rates," *Criminology* (August 1976): 291–95.

DAVIS, NANETTE J., *Sociological Constructions of Deviance* (Dubuque, Iowa: Brown, 1975).

DEFLEUR, MELVIN and RICHARD QUINNEY, "A Reformulation of Sutherland's Differential Association Theory and a Strategy for Empirical Verification," *Journal of Research in Crime and Delinquency* (January 1966): 1–22.

DEKESEREDY, WALTER S. and MARTIN D. SCHWARTZ, "British Left Realism on the Abuse of Women: A Critical Appraisal." Pp. 154–71 in Harold E. Pepinsky and Richard Quinney, eds., *Criminology as Peacemaking* (Bloomington: Indiana University Press, 1991).

DENZIN, NORMAN K., "Postmodern Social Theory," *Sociological Theory* (No. 4, 1986): 194–204.

DODD, STUART CARTER, *Dimensions of Society* (New York: Macmillan, 1940).

DRAPKIN, ISRAEL, "Criminology: Intellectual History." Pp. 546–56 in Sanford E. Kadish, ed., *Encyclopedia of Crime and Justice*, Vol. 2 (New York: Free Press, 1983).

EDITORIAL, *Crime and Social Justice* (Spring-Summer 1974).

ELLIOTT, DELBERT S., "The Assumption that Theories Can Be Combined with Increased Explanatory Power: Theoretical Integrations." Pp. 123–49 in Robert F. Meier, ed., *Theoretical Methods in Criminology* (Beverly Hills: Sage, 1985).

ELLIOTT, DELBERT S., DAVID HUIZINGA, and SUZANNE S. AGETON, *Explaining Delinquency and Drug Use* (Beverly Hills: Sage, 1985).

ELLIOTT, DELBERT S., SUZANNE S. AGETON, and RACHELLE J. CANTER, "An Integrated Theoretical Perspective on Delinquent Behavior," *Journal of Research in Crime and Delinquency* (January 1979): 3–27.

ELLIOTT, MABEL A., *Crime in Modern Society* (New York: Harper, 1952).

ELLIS, LEE, *Theories of Rape* (New York: Hemisphere Publishing Co., 1989).

ELLIS, LEE and DONALD M. BURKE, "Sex, Sex Orientation and Criminal and Violent Behavior," *Personality and Individual Differences* (No. 12, 1990): 1207–12.

ELLIS, LEE and HARRY HOFFMAN, eds., *Crime in Biological, Social and Moral Contexts* (New York: Praeger, 1990).

EMPEY, LAMAR, *American Delinquency*, rev. ed. (Homewood, Ill.: Dorsey, 1982).

ERLANGER, HOWARD S., "The Empirical Status of the Subculture of Violence Thesis," *Social Problems* (December 1974): 280–92.

EYSENCK, SYBIL B. and H. J. EYSENCK, "Crime and Personality: An Empirical Study of the Three-Factor Theory," *British Journal of Criminology* (July 1970): 225–39.

FARIS, ROBERT E. L., *Chicago Sociology—1920–1932* (San Francisco: Chandler, 1967).

FARIS, ROBERT E. L., *Social Disorganization*, 2nd ed. (New York: Ronald, 1955).

FARR, KATHRYN ANN, personal communication, 1991.

FARR, KATHRYN ANN and DON C. GIBBONS, "Observations on the Development of Crime Categories," *International Journal of Offender Therapy and Comparative Criminology* (December 1990): 223–37.

FARR, KATHRYN ANN and DON C. GIBBONS, "Why Can't Johnny and Jane Write? More Observations from the Editors' Desks," *Crime and Delinquency* (April 1989): 309–15.

FARRINGTON, DAVID F., "Age and Crime." Pp. 189–250 in Michael Tonry and Norval Morris, eds., *Crime and Justice*, Vol. 7 (Chicago: University of Chicago Press, 1986).

FIALA, ROBERT, "Postindustrial Society." Pp. 1512–22 in Edgar F. Borgatta and Marie L. Borgatta, eds., *Encyclopedia of Sociology* (New York: Macmillan, 1992).

FINESTONE, HAROLD, *Victims of Change* (Westport, Conn.: Greenwood, 1976a).

FINESTONE, HAROLD, "The Delinquent and Society: The Shaw and McKay Tradition." Pp. 23–49 in James F. Short, Jr., ed., *Delinquency, Crime, and Society* (Chicago: University of Chicago Press, 1976b).

FISH, VIRGINIA KEMP, "Review," *Deviant Behavior* (January-February 1990): 99–102.

FISHBEIN, DIANA H., "Biological Perspectives in Criminology," *Criminology* (February 1990): 27–72.

GAGNON, JOHN H. and WILLIAM SIMON, *Sexual Conduct* (Chicago: Aldine, 1973).

GARABEDIAN, PETER G., "Social Roles in a Correctional Community," *Journal of Criminal Law, Criminology and Police Science* (September 1964): 338–47.

GEIS, GILBERT, "Editorial: Revisiting Sutherland's *Criminology*," *Criminology* (November 1976): 303–6.

GELSTHORPE, LORAINE and ALISON MORRIS, "Feminism and Criminology in Britain," *British Journal of Criminology* (Spring 1988): 93–110.

GIBBONS, DON C., *Society, Crime, and Criminal Behavior*, 6th ed. (Englewood Cliffs, N.J.: Prentice-Hall, 1992a).

GIBBONS, DON C., "Talking About Crime: Observations on the Prospects for Causal Theory in Criminology," *Criminal Justice Bulletin*, Sam Houston State University, 1992b.

GIBBONS, DON C., "Review," *Crime and Delinquency* (October 1991): 579–81.

GIBBONS, DON C., "Comment—Personality and Crime: Non-Issues, Real Issues, and a Theory and Research Agenda," *Justice Quarterly* (September 1989): 311–23.

GIBBONS, DON C., "Review," *Society* (May-June 1987): 92–93.

GIBBONS, DON C., "The Assumption of the Efficacy of Middle-Range Explanation: Typologies." Pp. 151–74 in Robert F. Meier, ed., *Theoretical Methods in Criminology* (Beverly Hills: Sage, 1985).

GIBBONS, DON C., "Mundane Crime," *Crime and Delinquency* (April 1983): 213–27.

GIBBONS, DON C., *The Criminological Enterprise* (Englewood Cliffs, N.J.: Prentice-Hall, 1979).

GIBBONS, DON C., "Offender Typologies: Two Decades Later," *British Journal of Criminology* (April 1975): 140–56.

GIBBONS, DON C., "Say, Whatever Became of Maurice Parmelee, Anyway?" *Sociological Quarterly* (Summer 1974): 405–16.

GIBBONS, DON C., "Observations on the Study of Crime Causation," *American Journal of Sociology* (September 1971): 262–78.

GIBBONS, DON C., "Problems of Causal Analysis in Criminology: A Case Illustration," *Journal of Research in Crime and Delinquency* (January 1966): 47–56.

GIBBONS, DON C., *Changing the Lawbreaker* (Englewood Cliffs, N.J.: Prentice-Hall, 1965a).

GIBBONS, DON C., "The Asexual Image of Man in Sociology," unpublished, 1965b.

GIBBONS, DON C., and KATHRYN ANN FARR, "Theoretical Development and Integration in Criminology," unpublished, 1990.

GIBBONS, DON C., and JOSEPH F. JONES, *The Study of Deviance* (Englewood Cliffs, N.J.: Prentice-Hall, 1975).

GIBBONS, DON C., and MARVIN D. KROHN, *Delinquent Behavior*, 5th ed. (Englewood Cliffs, N.J.: Prentice-Hall, 1991).

GIBBS, JACK P., *Control: Sociology's Central Notion* (Urbana: University of Illinois Press, 1989).

GIBBS, JACK P., "The State of Criminological Theory," *Criminology* (November 1987): 821–40.

GIBBS, JACK P., "The Methodology of Theory Construction in Criminology." Pp. 23–50 in Robert F. Meier, ed., *Theoretical Methods in Criminology* (Beverly Hills: Sage, 1985a).

GIBBS, JACK P., "Review Essay," *Criminology* (May 1985b): 381–88.

GIBBS, JACK P., *Sociological Theory Construction* (Hinsdale, Ill.: Dryden, 1972).

GILLIN, JOHN L., *Criminology and Penology* (New York: Century, 1926).

GLASER, DANIEL, "Reconceiving Some Confounding Domains in Criminology: Issues of Terminology, Theory, and Practice." Pp. 23–46 in Joan McCord, ed., *Facts, Frameworks, and Forecasts, Vol. 3, Advances in Criminological Theory* (New Brunswick, N.J.: Transaction Publishers, 1992).

GLASER, DANIEL, "Crime Causation." Pp. 307–8 in Sanford H. Kadish, ed., *Encyclopedia of Crime and Justice* (New York: Free Press, 1983).

GLASER, DANIEL, *Crime and Social Policy* (Englewood Cliffs, N.J.: Prentice-Hall, 1972).

GLASER, DANIEL, "Criminality Theories and Behavioral Images," *American Journal of Sociology* (March 1956): 433–44.

GLAZER, BARNEY and ANSELM L. STRAUSS, *The Discovery of Grounded Theory* (Chicago: Aldine, 1967).

GLUECK, SHELDON and ELEANOR GLUECK, *Unraveling Juvenile Delinquency* (Cambridge: Harvard University Press, 1951).

GORDON, DAVID M., "Capitalism, Class, and Crime in America," *Crime and Delinquency* (April 1973): 163–86.

GOTTFREDSON, MICHAEL R. and TRAVIS HIRSCHI, *A General Theory of Crime* (Stanford: Stanford University Press, 1990).

GOTTFREDSON, MICHAEL R. and TRAVIS HIRSCHI, "The True Value of Lambda Would Appear to Be Zero: An Essay on Career Criminals, Criminal Careers, Selective Incapacitation, Cohort Studies, and Related Topics," *Criminology* (May 1986): 213–24.

GREENBERG, DAVID F., "Age, Crime, and Social Explanation," *American Journal of Sociology* (July 1985): 1–21.

GREENBERG, DAVID F., "Delinquency and the Age Structure of Society," *Contemporary Crises* (April 1977): 189–224.

GOUGH, HARRISON G., "Theory and Measurement of Socialization," *Journal of Consulting Psychology* (February 1960): 23–30.

GOUGH, HARRISON G., "A Sociological Theory of Psychopathy," *American Journal of Sociology* (March 1948): 359–66.

GOUGH, HARRISON G. and DONALD E. PETERSON, "The Identification and Measurement of Predispositional Factors in Crime and Delinquency," *Journal of Consulting Psychology* (June 1952): 207–12.

HAGAN, JOHN, "The Poverty of a Classless Criminology," *Criminology* (February 1992): 1– 19.

HAGAN, JOHN, "The Assumption of Natural Science Methods: Criminological Positivism." Pp. 75–92 in Robert F. Meier, ed., *Theoretical Methods in Criminology* (Beverly Hills: Sage, 1985).

HAGAN, JOHN, in collaboration with CELESTE ALBONETTI, DUANE ALWIN, A. R. GILLIS, JOHN HEWITT, ALBERTO PALLONI, PATRICIA PARKER, RUTH PETERSON, and JOHN SIMPSON, *Structural Criminology* (New Brunswick, N.J.: Rutgers University Press, 1989).

HAGAN, JOHN, JOHN SIMPSON, and A. R. GILLIS, "The Class Structure of Gender and Delinquency: Toward a Power-Control Theory of Gender and Delinquency," *American Journal of Sociology* (May 1985): 1151–78.

HAGEDORN, JOHN, *People and Folks: Gangs, Crime, and Underclass in a Rustbelt City* (Chicago: Lakeview Press, 1988).

HARRIES, KEITH D., *The Geography of Crime and Justice* (New York: McGraw-Hill, 1974).

HARRIS, ANTHONY R., "Sex and Theories of Deviance: Toward a Functional Theory of Deviant Type-Scripts," *American Sociological Review* (February 1977): 3–16.

HATHAWAY, STARKE and ELIO D. MONACHESI, "The Minnesota Multiphasic Personality Inventory in the Study of Juvenile Delinquents," *American Sociological Review* (December 1952): 704– 10.

HARTJEN, CLAYTON A. and DON C. GIBBONS, "An Empirical Investigation of a Criminal Typology," *Sociology and Social Research* (October 1969): 56–62.

HAY, DOUGLAS, PETER LINEBAUGH, JOHN G. RULE, E. P. THOMPSON, and CAL WINSLOW, *Albion's Fatal Tree* (New York: Pantheon, 1975).

HAYAKAWA, S. I., *Language in Action* (New York: Harcourt, Brace, 1949).

HEALY, WILLIAM and AUGUSTA F. BRONNER, *New Light on Delinquency and Its Treatment* (New Haven: Yale University Press, 1936).

HEMPEL, CARL G., *Fundamentals of Concept Formation in Empirical Sciences* (Chicago: University of Chicago Press, 1952).

HENRY , STUART and DRAGAN MILOVANOVIC, "Constitutive Criminology: The Maturation of Critical Theory," *Criminology* (May 1991): 293–315.

HEPBURN, JOHN R., "Social Control and the Legal Order: Legitimate Repression in a Capitalist State," *Contemporary Crises* (January 1977): 77–90.

HERITAGE, JOHN, "Ethnomethodology." Pp. 588–94 in Edgar F. Borgatta and Marie L. Borgatta, eds., *Encyclopedia of Sociology* (New York: Macmillan, 1992).

HINKLE, ROSCOE C. and GISELA HINKLE, *The Development of Modern Sociology* (New York: Random House, 1954).

HIRSCHI, TRAVIS, "Review," *Criminology* (February 1987): 193–201.

HIRSCHI, TRAVIS, "Separate and Equal Is Better," *Journal of Research in Crime and Delinquency* (January 1979): 34–38.

HIRSCHI, TRAVIS, *Causes of Delinquency* (Berkeley: University of California Press, 1969).

HIRSCHI, TRAVIS and MICHAEL R. GOTTFREDSON, "Age and the Explanation of Crime," *American Journal of Sociology* (November 1983): 552–84.

HIRST, PAUL Q., "Marx and Engels on Law, Crime, and Morality," *Economy and Society* (February 1972): 28–56.

HOFFMAN-BUSTAMENTE, DALE, "The Nature of Female Criminality," *Issues in Criminology* (Fall 1973): 117–36.

IRWIN , JOHN, *The Jail* (Berkeley: University of California Press, 1985).

IRWIN, JOHN, *The Felon* (Englewood Cliffs, N.J.: Prentice-Hall, 1970).

JACKSON, BRUCE, *A Thief's Primer* (New York: Macmillan, 1969).

JANKOWSKI, MARTIN SANCHEZ, *Islands in the Street* (Berkeley: University of California Press, 1991).

JEFFERY, C. R., "Criminal Behavior and Learning Theory," *Journal of Criminal Law, Criminology and Police Science* (September 1965): 294–300.

JENSEN, GARY F., "Review: The Lingering Promise of a Structural Criminology," *Contemporary Sociology* (January 1990): 12–16.

JESNESS, CARL F., *The Jesness Inventory: Development and Validation* (Sacramento: California Youth Authority, 1962).

JOHNSON, RICHARD E., *Juvenile Delinquency and Its Origins* (Cambridge: Cambridge University Press, 1979).

JONES, DAVID, *Crime, Protest, Community, and Police in Nineteenth-Century Britain* (London: Routledge and Kegan Paul, 1982).

KAMIN, LEON, "Is Crime in the Genes? The Answer May Depend on Who Chooses What Evidence," *Scientific American* (February 1986): 222–7.

KATZ, JACK, *Seductions of Crime* (New York: Basic Books, 1988).

KEMPF, KIMBERLY F., "Specialization and the Criminal Career," *Criminology* (May 1987): 399–420.

KING, HARRY, *Box Man: A Professional Thief's Journey*, as told to and edited by Bill Chambliss (New York: Harper & Row, 1972).

KINSEY, RICHARD, JOHN LEA, and JOCK YOUNG, *Losing the Fight Against Crime* (London: Basil Blackwell, 1986).

KLEIN, DORIE, "The Etiology of Female Crime: A Review of the Literature," *Issues in Criminology* (Fall 1973): 3–30.

KNIGHT, RAYMOND A., DANIEL LEE CARTER, and ROBERT ALAN PRENTKY, "A System for the Classification of Child Molesters: Reliability and Applicability," *Journal of Interpersonal Violence* (March 1989): 3–24.

KNIGHT, RAYMOND A. and ROBERT ALAN PRENTKY, "Classification of Sex Offenders: The Development and Corroboration of Taxonomic Models." Pp. 23–54 in W. L. Marshall, D. R. Laws, and H. E. Barbee, eds., *Handbook of Sexual Assault* (New York: Plenum, 1990).

KNOBLICH, GUENTHER and ROY KING, "Biological Correlates of Crime." Pp. 1–21 in Joan McCord, ed., *Facts, Frameworks, and Forecasts, Vol. 3, Advances in Criminological Theory* (New Brunswick, N.J.: Transaction Publishers, 1992).

KOHFELD, CAROL W. and JOHN SPRAGUE, "Urban Unemployment Drives Urban Crime Rate," *Urban Affairs Quarterly* (December 1988): 215–44.

LASTRUCCI, CARLO L., *The Scientific Approach* (New York: Schenkman, 1963).

LAUB, JOHN H., *Criminology in the Making* (Boston: Northeastern University Press, 1983).

LEGER, ROBERT G., "Research Findings and Theory as a Function of Operationalization of Variables: A Comparison of Four Techniques for the Construct, 'Inmate Type,' " *Sociology and Social Research* (January 1979): 346–65.

LEMERT, EDWIN M., *Human Deviance, Social Problems, and Social Control*, 2nd ed. (Englewood Cliffs, N.J.: Prentice-Hall, 1972).

LEMERT, EDWIN M., "Paranoia and the Dynamics of Exclusion," *Sociometry* (March 1962): 2–20.

LEMERT, EDWIN M. "Dependency in Married Alcoholics," *Quarterly Journal of Studies on Alcohol* (December 1962): 590–609.

LEMERT, EDWIN M., "The Behavior of the Systematic Check Forger," *Social Problems* (Fall 1958): 141–49.

LEMERT, EDWIN M., "An Isolation and Closure Theory of Naïve Check Forgery," *Journal of Criminal Law, Criminology and Police Science* (September-October 1953): 296–307.

LEMERT, EDWIN M., *Social Pathology* (New York: McGraw-Hill, 1951).

LEONARD, EILEEN B., *Women, Crime, and Society* (New York: Longman, 1982).

LIEBERSON, STANLEY, "Einstein, Renoir, and Greeley: Evidence in Sociology," *American Sociological Review* (February 1992): 1–15.

LILLY, J. ROBERT, FRANCIS T. CULLEN, and RICHARD A. BALL, *Criminological Theory* (Newbury Park, Calif.: Sage, 1989).

LOFTIN, COLIN and ROBERT H. HILL, "Regional Subculture and Homicide: An Examination of the Gastil-Hackney Hypothesis," *American Sociological Review* (October 1974): 714–24.

LOW, DONALD A., *Thieves' Kitchen* (London: J. M. Dent, 1982).

LOWMAN, JOHN and BRIAN D. MACLEAN, eds., *Realist Criminology* (Toronto: University of Toronto Press, 1992).

LUNDBERG, GEORGE A., *Foundations of Sociology* (New York: Macmillan, 1939).

MCCAGHY, CHARLES H. "Child Molesters: A Study of Their Careers as Deviants." Pp. 75–88 in Marshall B. Clinard and Richard Quinney, eds., *Criminal Behavior Systems* (New York: Holt, Rinehart & Winston, 1967).

MCCARTHY, BILL and JOHN HAGAN, "Homelessness: A Criminogenic Situation?" *British Journal of Criminology* (Autumn 1991): 393–410.

MCKENNA, JAMES J., *An Empirical Testing of a Typology of Adult Criminal Behavior* (Ph.D. dissertation, University of Notre Dame, 1972).

MATTHEWS, ROGER and JOCK YOUNG, eds., *Issues in Realist Criminology* (Newbury Park, Calif.: Sage, 1992).

MATTHEWS, ROGER and JOCK YOUNG, *Confronting Crime* (Beverly Hills: Sage, 1986).

MATZA, DAVID, *Delinquency and Drift* (New York: Wiley, 1964).

MEIER, ROBERT F., ed., *Theoretical Methods in Criminology* (Beverly Hills: Sage, 1985).

MEIER, ROBERT F., "Review Essay: The Arrested Development of Criminological Theory," *Contemporary Sociology* (May 1980): 374–6.

MEIER, ROBERT F., "The New Criminology: Continuity in Criminological Theory," *Journal of Criminal Law and Criminology* (December 1976): 461–69.

MENNINGER, KARL, *The Crime of Punishment* (New York: Viking, 1968).

MERTON, ROBERT K., "Social Structure and Anomie," *American Sociological Review* (October 1938): 672–82.

MERTON, ROBERT K. *Social Theory and Social Structure* (New York: Free Press, 1949).

MESSERSCHMIDT, JAMES, *Capitalism, Patriarchy, and Crime* (Totowa, N.J.: Rowman and Littlefield, 1986).

MESSNER, STEVEN F. "Income Inequality and Murder Rates: Some Cross-National Findings," *Comparative Social Research* (No. 3: 1980): 185–98.

MESSNER, STEVEN F. and MARVIN D. KROHN, "Class, Compliance Structures, and Delinquency: Assessing Integrated Structural-Marxist Theory," *American Journal of Sociology* (September 1990): 300–28.

MESSNER, STEVEN F. and KENNETH TARDIFF, "The Social Ecology of Urban Homicide: An Application of the 'Routine Activities Approach,' " *Criminology* (May 1985): 241–67.

MICHALOWSKI, RAYMOND J. and EDWARD W. BOHLANDER, "Repression and Criminal Justice in Capitalist America," *Sociological Inquiry* (No. 2: 1976): 95–106.

MILLER, WALTER B., "Implications of Lower Class Culture for Social Work," *Social Service Review* (September 1959): 219–36.

MILLER, WALTER B., "Lower Class Culture as a Generating Milieu of Gang Delinquency," *Journal of Social Issues* (No. 8, 1958): 5–19.

MUGFORD, STEPHEN K., "Marxism and Criminology: A Comment on the Symposium on 'The New Criminology,' " *Sociological Quarterly* (Autumn 1974): 591–96.

NYE, IVAN F., *Family Relationships and Delinquent Behavior* (New York: Wiley, 1958).

OBERSCHALL, ANTHONY, "The Institutionalization of American Sociology." Pp. 187–251 in Oberschall, ed., *The Establishment of Empirical Sociology* (New York: Harper and Row, 1972).

ODUM, HOWARD W., *American Sociology: The History of Sociology in the U.S. Through 1950* (New York: Longmans, Green, 1951).

PALLONE, NATHANIEL J. and JAMES J. HENNESSEY, *Criminal Behavior: A Process Psychological Approach* (New Brunswick, N.J.: Transaction Publishers, 1992).

PARSONS, PHILIP A., *Crime and the Criminal* (New York: Knopf, 1926).

PARSONS, TALCOTT, *The Social System* (New York: Free Press, 1951).

PEARSON, FRANK and NEIL ALAN WEINER, "Toward an Integration of Criminological Theories," *Journal of Criminal Law and Criminology* (Spring 1985): 116–50.

PEPINSKY, HAROLD E., "Peacemaking in Criminology and Criminal Justice." Pp. 299–327 in Harold E. Pepinsky and Richard Quinney, eds., *Criminology as Peacemaking* (Bloomington: Indiana University Press, 1991).

PEPINSKY, HAROLD E., "Crime Causation: Political Theories." Pp. 323–30 in Sanford E. Kadish, ed., *Encyclopedia of Crime and Justice* (New York: Free Press, 1983).

PEPINSKY, HAROLD E., and RICHARD QUINNEY, eds., *Criminology as Peacemaking* (Bloomington: Indiana University Press, 1991.)

PETERSILIA, JOAN, PETER W. GREENWOOD, and MARVIN LAVIN, *Criminals Careers of Habitual Felons* (Santa Monica: Rand, 1977).

PETERSON, MARK A., HARRIET B. BRAKER, and SUZANNE M. POLICH, *Doing Crime* (Santa Monica, Calif.: Rand, 1980).

POLK, KENNETH, "Review," *Crime and Delinquency* (October 1991): 575–79.

QUAY, HERBERT C., ed., *Handbook of Juvenile Delinquency* (New York: Wiley, 1987).

QUINNEY, RICHARD, "The Way of Peace: On Crime, Suffering, and Service." Pp. 3–13 in Harold E. Pepinsky and Richard Quinney, *Criminology as Peacemaking* (Bloomington: Indiana University Press, 1991).

QUINNEY, RICHARD, *Class, State, and Crime* (New York: D. McKay, 1977).

QUINNEY, RICHARD, *Criminology* (Boston: Little, Brown, 1975).

QUINNEY, RICHARD, *Critique of Legal Order* (Boston: Little, Brown, 1974).

QUINNEY, RICHARD, *The Social Reality of Crime* (Boston: Little, Brown, 1970).

RECKLESS, WALTER C., *The Crime Problem*, 5th ed. (Santa Monica, Calif.: Goodyear, 1973).

RECKLESS, WALTER C., *The Crime Problem*, 3rd ed. (New York: Appleton-Century-Crofts, 1955).

REID, SUE TITUS, *Crime and Criminology* (Hinsdale, Ill.: Dryden, 1976).

REISS, ALBERT J., JR. and MICHAEL TONRY, eds., *Communities and Crime* (Chicago: University of Chicago Press, 1986).

RENGERT, G. and J. WASILCHICK, *Suburban Burglary* (Springfield, Ill.: C. C. Thomas, 1985).

ROBINS, LEE, *Deviant Children Grown Up* (Baltimore: Williams and Wilkins, 1966).

ROEBUCK, JULIAN B., *Criminal Typology* (Springfield, Ill.: C. C. Thomas, 1966).

ROSS, H. LAURENCE, "Folk Crime Revisited," *Criminology* (May 1973): 41–85.

ROSS, H. LAURENCE, "Traffic Law Violation: A Folk Crime," *Social Problems* (Winter 1960–61): 231–41.

SAH, RAAJ, "Social Osmosis and Patterns of Crime," *Journal of Political Economy* (December 1991): 1272–95.

SAMENOW, STANTON E., *Inside the Criminal Mind* (New York: Times Books, 1984).

SAMPSON, ROBERT J. and JOHN H. LAUB, "Crime and Deviance Over the Life Course," *American Sociological Review* (October 1990): 609–27.

SARRI, ROSEMARY, "Review," *Social Work* (May/June 1987): 259.

SCHAFER, STEPHEN, *Theories in Criminology* (New York: Random House, 1969).

SCHEFF, THOMAS J., "Review Essay: A New Durkeim," *American Journal of Sociology* (November 1990): 741–46.

SCHMID, CALVIN F. "Urban Crime Areas, Part I and II," *American Sociological Review* (August, October, 1960): 527–72; 655–78.

SCHRAG, CLARENCE C., "Review," *Crime and Delinquency* (January 1987): 155–60.

SCHRAG, CLARENCE C., *Crime and Justice: American Style* (Rockville, Md.: National Institute of Mental Health, 1971).

SCHRAG, CLARENCE C., "Elements of Theoretical Analysis in Sociology." Pp. 220–53 in Llewellyn Gross, ed., *Sociological Theory* (New York: Harper and Row, 1967).

SCHRAG, CLARENCE C., "A Preliminary Criminal Typology," *Pacific Sociological Review* (Spring 1961): 11–16.

SCHRAGER, LAURA SHILL and JAMES F. SHORT, JR., "Toward a Sociology of Organizational Crime," *Social Problems* (April 1978): 407–19.

SCHUESSLER, KARL F., and DONALD R. CRESSEY, "Personality Characteristics of Criminals," *American Journal of Sociology* (March 1950): 476–84.

SELLIN, THORSTEN, *Culture Conflict and Crime* (New York: Social Science Research Council, 1938).

SHANNON, LYLE W., *Changing Patterns of Delinquency and Crime* (Boulder, Colo.: Westview Press, 1991).

SHAPIRO, SUSAN. "Survey Review," *Contemporary Sociology* (May 1983): 304–7.

SHAW, CLIFFORD R., *The Natural History of a Delinquent Career* (Chicago: University of Chicago Press, 1931).

SHAW, CLIFFORD R., *The Jack Roller* (Chicago: University of Chicago Press, 1930).

SHAW, CLIFFORD R. and HENRY D. MCKAY, *Juvenile Delinquency in Urban Areas* (Chicago: University of Chicago Press, 1932).

SHAW, CLIFFORD R., HENRY D. MCKAY, and JAMES F. MCDONALD, *Brothers in Crime* (Chicago: University of Chicago Press, 1938).

SHAW, CLIFFORD R. and HENRY D. MCKAY, *Social Factors in Juvenile Delinquency*, Vol. II, National Commission on Law Observance and Enforcement, Report on the Causes of Crime (Washington, D.C.: U.S. Government Printing Office, 1931).

SHOEMAKER, DONALD J., *Theories of Delinquency* (New York: Oxford University Press, 1984).

SHOVER, NEAL, "Burglary." Pp. 71–113 in Michael Tonry, ed., *Crime and Justice* (Chicago: University of Chicago Press, 1991).

SIMON, RITA JAMES, *Women and Crime* (Lexington, Mass.: Heath, 1975).

SIMPSON, SALLY, "Feminist Theory, Crime, and Justice," *Criminology* (November 1989): 605–31.

SMITH, RICHARD AUSTIN, "The Incredible Electrical Conspiracy: Parts I and II," *Fortune* (April, May 1961): 132–218; 161–224.

SPITZER, STEVEN, "Toward a Marxian Theory of Deviance," *Social Problems* (No. 5, 1975): 636–51.

STEFFENSMEIER, DARRELL J., "Crime and Contemporary Woman: An Analysis of Changing Levels of Property Crime, 1960–75," *Social Forces* (December 1978): 566–84.

STEFFENSMEIER, DARRELL J., EMILIE ALLAN, MILES HARRAR, and CATHY STREIFEL, "Age and the Distribution of Crime," *American Journal of Sociology* (July 1989): 803–31.

STEWART, JAMES B., *Den of Thieves* (New York: Simon and Schuster, 1991).

SUTHERLAND, EDWIN H., "Crime of Corporations." Pp. 78–96 in Albert K. Cohen, Alfred Lindesmith, and Karl F. Schuessler, eds., *The Sutherland Papers* (Bloomington: Indiana University Press, 1956).

SUTHERLAND, EDWIN H., *White Collar Crime: The Uncut Version* (New Haven: Yale University Press, 1983).

SUTHERLAND, EDWIN H., "Development of the Theory." Pp. 13–29 in Albert K. Cohen, Alfred Lindesmith, and Karl F. Schuessler, eds., *The Sutherland Papers* (Bloomington: Indiana University Press, 1956).

SUTHERLAND, EDWIN H., *White Collar Crime* (New York: Dryden, 1949a).

SUTHERLAND, EDWIN H., "The White Collar Criminal." Pp. 511–15 in Vernon C. Branham and Samuel B. Kutash, eds., *Encyclopedia of Criminology* (New York: Philosophical Library, 1949b).

SUTHERLAND, EDWIN H. *Principles of Criminology*, 4th ed. (Philadelphia: Lippincott, 1947).

SUTHERLAND, EDWIN H., "Is 'White-Collar Crime' Crime?" *American Sociological Review* (April 1945): 132–39.

SUTHERLAND, EDWIN H. "Crime and Business," *Annals of the American Academy of Political and Social Science* (September 1941): 112–18.

SUTHERLAND, EDWIN H., "White Collar Criminality," *American Sociological Review* (February 1940): 1–12.

SUTHERLAND, EDWIN H., *Principles of Criminology*, 3rd ed. (Philadelphia: Lippincott, 1939).

SUTHERLAND, EDWIN H., *The Professional Thief* (Chicago: University of Chicago Press, 1937).

SUTHERLAND, EDWIN H., *Criminology* (Philadelphia: Lippincott, 1924).

SUTHERLAND, EDWIN H., and DONALD R. CRESSEY, *Criminology*, 10th ed. (Philadelphia: Lippincott, 1978).

SUTHERLAND, EDWIN H. and DONALD R. CRESSEY, *Principles of Criminology*, 5th ed. (Philadelphia: Lippincott, 1955).

SUTHERLAND, EDWIN H., DONALD R. CRESSEY, and DAVID F. LUCKENBILL, *Principles of Criminology*, 11th ed. (Dix Hills, N.Y.: General Hall, 1992).

SYKES, GRESHAM M., *Society of Captives* (Princeton, N.J.: Princeton University Press, 1958).

TANNENBAUM, FRANK, *Crime and the Community* (New York: Ginn, 1938).

TENNENBAUM, D. J., "Research Studies of Personality and Criminality: A Summary and Implications of the Literature," *Journal of Criminal Justice* (No. 3, 1977): 1–19.

THOMPSON, E. P., *Whigs and Hunters* (New York: Pantheon, 1975).

THORNBERRY, TERENCE P., "Toward an Integrated Theory of Delinquency," *Criminology* (November 1978): 863–91.

THORNBERRY, TERENCE P. and R. L. CHRISTENSON, "Unemployment and Criminal Involvement: An Investigation of Reciprocal Causal Processes," *American Sociological Review* (June 1984): 398–411.

TITTLE, CHARLES R., "The Assumption that General Theories Are Not Possible." Pp. 93–121 in Robert F. Meier, ed., *Theoretical Methods in Criminology* (Beverly Hills: Sage, 1985).

TOBIAS, J. J., *Crime and Industrial Society in the 19th Century* (London: B. T. Batsford, 1967).

TRASLER, GORDON, "Biogenetic Factors in Crime." Pp. 184–215 in Herbert C. Quay, ed., *Handbook of Juvenile Delinquency* (New York: Wiley, 1987).

TUCHMAN, GAYE, "Feminist Theory." Pp. 695–704 in Edgar F. Borgatta and Marie L. Borgatta, eds., *Encyclopedia of Sociology* (New York: Macmillan, 1992).

TUCK, MARY and DAVID RILEY, "The Theory of Reasoned Action: A Decision Theory of Crime." Pp. 156–69 in D. B. Cornish and R. Clarke, eds., *The Reasoning Criminal* (New York: Springer-Verlag, 1986).

TUNNELL, KENNETH, *Choosing Crime* (Chicago: Nelson Hall, 1992).

TURK, AUSTIN T., "Review Essay: Seductions of Criminology: Katz on Magical Meanness and Other Distractions," *Law and Social Inquiry* (Winter 1991): 183–94.

TURK, AUSTIN T., *Political Criminality* (Beverly Hills: Sage, 1982).

TURK, AUSTIN T., *Criminality and the Legal Order* (Chicago: Rand McNally, 1969).

TURNER, JONATHAN H., "Positivism." Pp. 1509–12 in Edgar F. Borgatta and Marie L. Borgatta, eds., *Encyclopedia of Sociology* (New York: Macmillan, 1992).

VAN MAANEN, JOHN, *Policing: A View from the Street* (Santa Monica, Calif.: Goodyear, 1978).

VOLD, GEORGE B. and THOMAS J. BERNARD, *Theoretical Criminology*, 3rd ed. (New York: Oxford University Press, 1986).

WALDO, GORDON P. and SIMON DINITZ, "Personality Attributes of the Criminal: An Analysis of Research Studies, 1950–1965," *Journal of Research in Crime and Delinquency* (July 1967): 185–202.

WEINBERG, S. KIRSON, "Personality and Method in the Differential Association Theory: Comments on 'A Reformulation of Sutherland's Differential Association Theory and a Strategy for Empirical Verification,' " *Journal of Research in Crime and Delinquency* (July 1966): 165–72.

WELLFORD, CHARLES, "Labelling Theory and Criminology: An Assessment," *Social Problems* (February 1975): 332–45.

WEISBURD, DAVID, STANTON WHEELER, ELIN WARING, and NANCY BODE, *Crimes of the Middle-Class* (New Haven: Yale University Press, 1991).

WILLIAMS, FRANK P., III and MARILYN D. MCSHANE, *Criminological Theory* (Englewood Cliffs, N.J.: Prentice-Hall, 1988).

WILLIAMS, ROBIN, *American Society* (New York: Knopf, 1950).

WILSON, JAMES Q. and RICHARD J. HERRNSTEIN, *Crime and Human Nature* (New York: Simon & Schuster, 1985).

WILSON, WILLIAM JULIUS, *The Truly Disadvantaged* (Chicago: University of Chicago Press, 1987).

WOLFGANG, MARVIN E., ROBERT M. FIGLIO, and THORSTEN SELLIN, *Delinquency in a Birth Cohort* (Chicago: University of Chicago Press, 1972).

YOUNG, JOCK and ROGER MATTHEWS, eds., *Rethinking Crime: The Realist Debate* (Newbury Park, Calif.: Sage, 1992).

YOUNG, JOCK, "Realist Research as a Basis for Local Criminal Justice Policy." Pp. 33–72 in John Lowman and Brian D. MacLean, eds., *Realist Criminology* (Toronto: University of Toronto Press, 1992).

ZETTERBERG, HANS, *On Theory and Verification in Sociology* (Totowa, N.J.: Bedminster Press, 1965).

# Index